SOUTHERN
WAGONS
PICTORIAL

The most numerous Southern Railway wagon design — eight plank open No 31491 from Diagram 1379, completed by Gloucester Railway Carriage & Wagon Company in August 1927 — part of a batch of 125 ordered in March of that year. A textbook paint finish — or is it? The corner plates alone appear to be black — if so it is the only wagon noted to be so painted. There were no less than 7,950 wagons to this diagram but in fact the SR eight plank wagon family numbered 11,650 vehicles with almost identical bodywork, if underframe and other minor variations were ignored. *SR Official*

SOUTHERN
WAGONS
PICTORIAL

Compiled by
Mike King

An imprint of
Ian Allan Publishing

Title Page: The original wartime caption reads, 'The Southern Railway has just completed the thousandth goods wagon to carry supplies to Russia. In peacetime the same output would have been scheduled for 12 months but by working night and day, men and women in the company's employ have completed the job in ten weeks'.

Whatever the publicity staff may have said, the view is taken looking west across the main gate to Ashford Works, with the sidings of 'The Klondike' visible immediately behind the clock tower. Beyond this is the Hastings line and, just visible to the left, the footbridge leading to 'The Kimberley'. Fifty kits of Diagram 1375 open wagons are ready to leave the yard; their underframes loaded five each into 20-ton mineral wagons to Diagram 1386. The smaller components are loaded into packing cases within five plank open wagons — that nearest the camera clearly being of LBSCR origin. Note also on the right a number of corrugated steel ends for LNER covered goods wagons, also being built at Ashford. Not surprisingly for wartime, the picture is undated but from the visible evidence was taken around November 1941. *SR Official*

First published 2008

ISBN 978 0 86093 597 1

All rights reserved. No part of this book may be reproduced or transmitted in any form or by any means, electronic or mechanical, including photocopying, recording or by any information storage and retrieval system, without permission from the Publisher in writing.

© Ian Allan Publishing 2008

Published by Oxford Publishing Co

an imprint of Ian Allan Publishing Ltd, Hersham, Surrey KT12 4RG
Printed in England by Ian Allan Printing Hersham, Surrey KT12 4RG

Code: 0810/A3

Visit the Ian Allan Publishing website at www.ianallanpublishing.com

visit the Ian Allan Publishing website at: www.ianallanpublishing.com

Bibliography

Bixley, G., Blackburn, A., Chorley, R., & King, M.,	*An Illustrated History of Southern Wagons Volume One — LSWR & SDJR*	OPC 1984 and 2002
Bixley, G., Blackburn, A., Chorley, R., & King, M.,	*An Illustrated History of Southern Wagons Volume Two — LBSCR & Minor Companies*	OPC 1985 and 2003
Bixley, G., Blackburn, A., Chorley, R., & King, M.,	*An Illustrated History of Southern Wagons Volume Three — SECR*	OPC 2000 and 2004
Bixley, G., Blackburn, A., Chorley, R., & King, M.,	*An Illustrated History of Southern Wagons Volume Four — SR*	OPC 2002 and 2004
Weddell, G.,	*LSWR Carriages Volume Four — Goods, Departmental Stock & Miscellany*	Kestrel Books 2006
Turner, S.,	*The History of the Goods Rolling Stock of the LBSCR 1870-1889* (Series of articles)	*Brighton Circular*, Volumes 31 and 32, 2005/6
Maycock, R., & Silsbury, R.,	*The Isle of Wight Railway*	Oakwood Press 1999
Maycock, R., & Silsbury, R.,	*The Isle of Wight Central Railway*	Oakwood Press 2001
Maycock, R., & Silsbury, R.,	*The Freshwater, Yarmouth & Newport Railway*	Oakwood Press 2003
Maycock, R., & Silsbury, R.,	*The Isle of Wight Railways from 1923 onwards*	Oakwood Press 2006
Garner, R.,	*The Somerset & Dorset Joint Railway Locomotive & Rolling Stock Register*	S&DJR Trust 2000
Rowland, D.,	*British Railways Wagons*	David & Charles 1985
Bartholomew, D., & Barnsley, M.,	*The Midland & South Western Junction Railway Volume Three*	Wild Swan 1988
Kidner, R.,	*Service Stock of the Southern Railway*	Oakwood Press 1993
Tavender, L.,	*HMRS Livery Register No 3 LSWR & Southern*	HMRS 1970 (& Addendum 1990)
Essery, R., Rowland, D., & Steel, W.,	*British Goods Wagons*	David & Charles, 1970
Warner, S., et al	*Modern Railway Working* (Reprinted as *Railway Mechanical Engineering* in 1923)	Gresham Press 1912

Various official documents formerly part of British Transport Historical Records and now housed as part of the National Archive at the Public Record Office, Kew. These are now filed under references RAIL 411, 414, 626, 633, 635, 645, 648 and 649 categories.

Contents

Bibliography   **Page 4**
Author's Notes and Acknowledgements   **Page 5**

Chapter 1. - LSWR Wagons   **Page 6**
Chapter 2. - SDJR Wagons   **Page 68**
Chapter 3. - LBSCR Wagons   **Page 85**
Chapter 4. - Minor Companies' Wagons   **Page 116**
Chapter 5. - SECR Wagons   **Page 128**
Chapter 6. - Southern Railway Wagons   **Page 150**

Appendix — Southern Railway Goods Rolling Stock Orders   **Page 186**

Author's Notes and Acknowledgements

It is now almost 25 years since Volumes One and Two of *An Illustrated History of Southern Wagons* were published — and more than five years since the final volume in the series was completed. Inevitably, over such a long period of time, a number of new photographs and, to a lesser extent, additional information has come to the surface. This is undoubtedly true for the LSWR, SDJR and LBSCR; due partly to the elapse of time since original publication, but also due to the fact that, back in the early 1980s, the market for wagon books was somewhat uncertain and the then owners of OPC prudently limited each volume to a maximum of 112 pages. The amount of information to hand for Volume One in particular, even in 1984, exceeded the space available and some exclusions had to be made. This same limitation was not imposed on Volumes Three and Four, so these covered their respective subject areas very much more comprehensively — but even here there is no shortage of additional material now available.

In view of the continuing high levels of interest in wagons, particularly amongst modellers, it was felt that one further book might be a useful addition to the original series - hence *Southern Wagons Pictorial*. In a follow-up publication of this nature, it is perhaps inevitable that coverage of each subject area will vary in scope and detail and this time will concentrate more on photographs of the wagons in traffic rather than on drawings and official views — since the majority of these appeared in the original series. Frequent reference to the original volumes will be made and it will be assumed that the reader has access to them — to avoid unnecessary repetition. There will also be occasions when the information presented here — particularly with regard to some drawings — will not be guaranteed as accurate as those in the original volumes, however in these cases we are now reaching the 'edge' of our certain knowledge and it is necessary to accept this or omit the information altogether. Where this has been done, it has been pointed out and if the opportunity to revise these drawings presents itself in subsequent reprints, then this will be done.

The temptation to broaden the subject area was also considered, but later rejected. Gordon Weddell has recently placed on record what little information exists about LSWR wagons pre-1880, while Simon Turner has done likewise for the LBSCR — his efforts being published in the *Brighton Circular*. Members of the South Eastern Society (SECSOC) are doing the same for the SER/LCDR and hopefully the results of their research will be published in due course, while those enthusiasts interested in the Isle of Wight have the recent series of Oakwood Press books by Messrs Maycock and Silsbury at their disposal. Details of all these publications may be found in the Bibliography. And so this book will stick to the original brief of 1981 — to deal primarily with those wagon types that became Southern Railway stock in 1923 and those built subsequently to Southern designs — even if they did not appear until after Nationalisation, filling any gaps that existed in our knowledge at the time of previous publication, wherever possible. Some gaps remain and it is probably inevitable that this will always be so, but one lives in hope of seeing photographs of, for example, the LSWR or LBSCR plate glass wagons — one never knows what might turn up in the future.

This (probably final!) offering on the subject of Southern wagons is a solo effort, unlike the original series, so responsibility for any errors will be mine alone. In conclusion, I would like to thank all the photographers for their contributions (all are individually credited, where known), and all those individuals who have provided information specifically for this present volume. In alphabetical order they are: John Arkell, Roger Carpenter, Phil Coutanche, Ted Crawforth, Richard Dagger, the late Roger Kidner, David Larkin, John Minnis, Colin Paul, Adrian Swain, Harold Tumilty, Terry Walsh and The Lens Of Sutton Association.

Finally, I would like to pay tribute to the late Ted (A. E.) West, founder member of the South Western Circle, of whose negative collection I am, at present the custodian. Ted always wished to produce a series of books on Southern wagons and took very many photographs of them in the hope that they might eventually be included in such a publication. I am pleased to include so many examples of his work in this, and in the previous series of four volumes.

Mike King
Woking
March 2008

Readers may also be interested to know that The Lens Of Sutton Association have many more photographs of Southern (and other companies) wagons in their collections. Details may be obtained from them at 46 Edenhurst Road, Birmingham B31 4PQ.

Chapter 1.

LSWR Wagons

The London & South Western Railway was easily the largest pre-Grouping constituent of the Southern Railway, so it is hardly surprising that it contributed the greatest number of wagons to the new company pool — in total more than 15,000 vehicles. This was some 26% more than the South Eastern and 42% more than the Brighton. However, when compared with the respective route mileages, a slightly different picture emerges, as follows:

| Company | Route mileage | Number of wagons owned | | Number of wagons |
		Published (1)	Actual (2)	owned per route mile
LSWR	1,020½	15,264	15,303	15
LBSCR	457	11,041	10,764	23.5
SECR	638	12,165	12,125	19
SDJR*	106	1,355	1,357	12.8

Sources: The Railway Year Book (1) and SR renumbering registers (2)
* Figures for the SDJR are given for 1914, before the goods rolling stock was divided between the LSWR and Midland Railway. Figures for the other companies are for January 1923.

This demonstrates the fact that, away from the capital, the LSWR served relatively few large areas of population and its sprawling system, particularly in the west, did not generate the same levels of traffic as the more heavily populated southeast. However, a glance at the various tables of wagon stock as at January 1923 (reproduced at the end of Chapter One in each respective volume) will show the LSWR stock to be more diverse in nature than those from the other companies and several of the more specialised vehicle types present here are almost absent from the LBSCR and SECR fleets.

Above: **Plate 1** The caption on the reverse states that this is the 5.50pm meat special about to leave Southampton Docks. The train ran at express speed to Nine Elms, arriving there at 8.17pm. It also points out, not strictly accurately, that the train is composed entirely of insulated containers. In fact, 'H15' class 4-6-0 No 524 is hauling nine ex-LSWR refrigerator vans (as the fitted head) followed by at least 16 insulated containers to Diagrams 3001 or 3002 mounted on a variety of road van trucks and three plank dropside open wagons. At this date (February 1929) no purpose-built container wagons had been completed by the Southern Railway.
Southern Railway Magazine

Dropside open wagons & stone trucks

We begin again at Diagram 1301; the first diagram in the Southern Railway wagon stock book. At some time after the Grouping (probably during 1933), this diagram was further sub-divided to separate out the various constructional and operating differences, as follows:

Diagram	Allocation	Underframe Type	SR Numbers (extant 1933)	Examples of LSWR Numbering
1301	Traffic Dept	Steel	331/45/6/75	2, 326/51,1842
1301A	Engineers Dept	Steel	Between 61767 & 61859*	ED 289-324/90-429
1301B	Traffic Dept	Timber	3, 348/52/9/66/74/6/80/8, 403/10/2/3	929, 481, 647, 1035, 2679, 7926, 8808/11

* The Engineer's Department (ED) stock may not have been so accurately recorded as the Traffic department vehicles, as it is known that wagons 61767/79 and 61817 (ex-LSWR ED numbers 108, 285 and 347, all built in 1887) were three timber-framed examples allocated to the Engineer's Department, yet each was still assigned to Diagram 1301A. Just whether this was in error, or that this sub-diagram applied to all ED wagons regardless of construction is not known, however it illustrates the difficulty that the chief rolling stock clerk, Mr. Pepper and his staff must have faced when trying to accurately maintain their records. Based at Grosvenor Road offices they could hardly expect to see individual wagons on their doorstep and so would have to rely on reports from staff out on the line. The Civil Engineer generally looked after his own wagons and this difference, particularly for vehicles mainly used to carry ballast, might have been regarded as academic. It is hardly surprising that today's enthusiasts encounter errors and inconsistencies.

By 1933 only 17 traffic and 60 ED wagons remained in capital stock (compared with the combined starting total of 183 wagons in 1923), although by this time at least 20 were in departmental service, including Nos 0572s-0583s inclusive at Southampton Docks. By 1948 the traffic total had dwindled to just seven, with 46 in Engineer's stock. What may have been the last traffic department survivor was No 374, withdrawn in 1953, although several of the ED examples managed to survive until around 1960, some being transferred to internal use at Redbridge sleeper works during the 1950s.

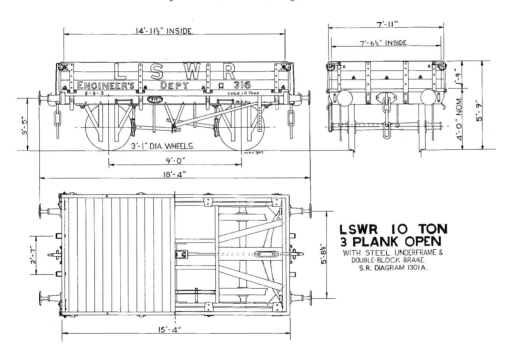

Figure 1 illustrates the steel-framed version of Diagram 1301A, 80 of which were built between 1896-9. Most of these were allocated to the Engineer's Department to replace wagons hired from Messrs J. T. Firbank and were initially intended for conveying ballast from Southampton Docks to Basingstoke — probably in connection with quadrupling and improving the main line. Their recorded cost was £65 each (of which around £15 would have been for the Fox pressed steel underframe, supplied by the Leeds Forge Company). Although Panter's cross-lever brake was in favour at this time, these wagons were equipped with double-block brake gear on one side only, as the operating lever of the Panter gear would have fouled the drop door. Any wagon still in service after January 1939 would have needed a second set of brakes to be added on the other side (the Southern's 'Freighter' brake). One earlier wagon is recorded on a steel underframe, this being LSWR No 8872 (later allocated SR No 421 but instead to departmental stock as No 0257s in 1924), built in 1891. This was part of a consecutively numbered batch otherwise on timber underframes, so must have been experimental and was the only survivor of this particular batch at the Grouping. The brake gear arrangement is thought to have been a single block on one side only.

Above:

Plate 2 A general view of Southampton Town station and yard, looking towards the docks, circa 1900. Beside the detail of the station and three B4 dock tanks at work, the two Diagram 1301A dropside wagons in the foreground are of particular interest. They are ED Nos 316/9 (later SR Nos 61807/10). Both are presumably in red oxide livery and carry the 'Engineer's Dept.' lettering across the lower plank, together with some other stencilled instruction adjacent to the 'R' of LSWR, perhaps to do with their duties between Southampton and Basingstoke, as these are part of the batch ordered to replace the Firbank wagons. They are clearly loaded with ballast — notice the canvas flaps protecting the axle boxes from the stone dust. Diagram 1309 open No 4657 accompanies them — this being to Type 3 in our original classification of four/five plank open goods wagons. No sheet rail is carried and the wagon is loaded with boxes and folded tarpaulins. This vehicle failed to become SR stock at the Grouping but LSWR Nos 4656/8 did receive their allocated SR Nos 2721/2 after 1923. Apart from several more Diagram 1309/10 opens visible on the next road, the two wagons far left also deserve mention. The farthest is a Diagram 1595 batten wagon loaded with timber poles, while the nearer wagon, on close examination, is a long two-plank bogie vehicle with a floor cut-out. It can therefore be none other than the unique Diagram 1788 bogie open wagon for the Signal Engineer, LSWR No 11813/ED 46/SR 64557. A drawing of this wagon appears in *LSWR Carriages Volume Four* (see Bibliography). *T. Chambers*

Left:

Plate 3 A view taken at Wadebridge loco shed around 1920 — the subject of the whole picture being Beattie well tank No 298. Two Diagram 1301B dropside wagons are visible — the nearest being No 08470 — its ciphered number indicating that it has been relegated to the duplicate list; due for early replacement and allowing the number to be reallocated to a new wagon. However, it also carries a 'Bodmin & Wadebridge Line' stencil so it is one of the three plank dropside wagons shipped by sea to the line in 1889/90 while still physically isolated from the rest of the LSWR system. The wagons are probably loaded with sea sand, brought in through Wadebridge quay and used to improve the agricultural soils in the upper Camel valley. Obligingly, the Bodmin & Wadebridge would unload the sand at any point along the line, although the local landowner was required to remove it within the hour or pay a hefty penalty! *H. V. Tumilty Collection*

The three plank dropside wagons shipped to the Bodmin & Wadebridge line numbered 71 examples — in three distinct batches. From limited photographic evidence and LSWR minutes of the period, their details appear to be as follows:

Date	Details	B & W Numbers	LSWR Numbers
Nov 1887	25 wagons with old wheelsets & ironwork	1-25	Random between 289 and 5910
Nov 1888	21 wagons on capital a/c	26-46	8452-72
June 1890	25 additional wagons to be supplied on capital a/c	47-71	8808-32

B & W numbers not necessarily in same order as LSWR numbers.

It is probable that the first batch were of only 7 tons capacity and those surviving in 1923 (or their replacements) may have become SR Nos 1-3/5-14. An example of the 7 tonners may be found in **Plates 101-103,** whilst in use as a crane runner. It is therefore likely that the wagon illustrated in **Plate 129** of *Volume One* is one of these, complete with self-contained buffers and canvas flaps over the axle boxes, rather than an example of Diagram 1731 as previously suggested. Both of the later batches supplied to the line had standard buffers, no canvas flaps and each batch featured a slightly different lettering layout. Besides sand, coal would have been a regular inbound load, while china clay or stone blocks would have travelled in the other direction — mostly loaded at Wenford Bridge. Once the B & W was physically connected to the rest of the LSWR in 1895, many of these wagons remained allocated to the branch — some examples continuing to be labelled 'Bodmin & Wadebridge Line' until at least the 1920s.

Some others on the main LSWR system were permanently allocated to the Locomotive Department for supplying sand between Nine Elms and the various locomotive sheds. These were stencilled 'For sand only. Loco Dept' along the bottom plank, beneath the 'L' of LSWR, with the exact routing on the crib rail below this — in the form 'Between Bournemouth & Nine Elms' or similar. Some others were actually three plank fixed sided opens, with conventional corner plates and diagonal strapping in the usual positions; but whether these were rebuilds or purpose-built as such is not known. Only three examples have so far been identified, LSWR Nos 8699, 8701/7, so perhaps this was a batch of 25 numbered between 8683 and 8707. They mostly appear in the background of locomotive photographs at Nine Elms, so again may have been used for loco sand traffic, although they would also have been suitable for the conveyance of stone blocks. None of these survived to become SR stock at the Grouping.

Below:
Plate 4 This interesting photograph dates from 1910 and was originally published in both the *South Western Magazine* during that year and again in the *Railway Magazine* for October 1911, the latter along with the caption 'A train of granite blocks from De Lank Quarry'. The *SW Magazine* gave a little more detail, telling us that the stone was loaded at Wenford Bridge and was destined for Hartlepool. The blocks are loaded onto various dropside wagons, of which the nearest eight and the last are to Diagram 1301. All except the seventh from the camera have timber underframes, although only the nearest pair (LSWR No 4573/SR No 392 and LSWR No 8652/SR No 409) may be identified. However, at least the first four carry 'Bodmin & Wadebridge Line' stencils. The seventh is on a steel underframe — identifiable by the slightly lower overall height and the presence of pressed steel doorstops. The two slightly larger dropside wagons towards the front of the train are Diagram 1317 four plank stone trucks. These are more heavily laden, as befits their 15-ton payload. Two Diagram 1410 vans and Diagram 1541 brake van No 6986 (later SR No 54685) complete the train, headed by the inevitable Beattie well tank. On the adjacent road, two more Diagram 1301s are well laden with sand or coal. Wenford Bridge might have been one of the most remote locations on the Southern, but could regularly dispatch upwards of 40,000 tons of minerals per annum — mostly stone and china clay. *LSWR Official*

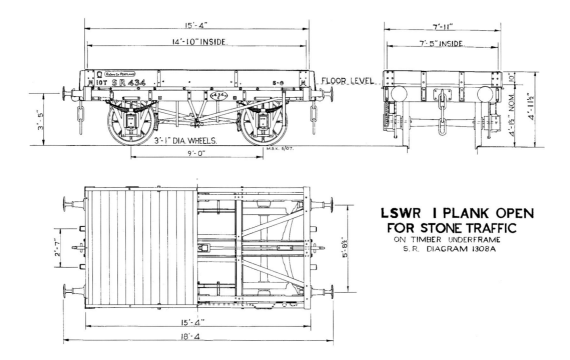

15'-4"
14'-10" INSIDE.
7'-11"
7'-5" INSIDE.
FLOOR LEVEL
N 10T SR 434
5-0
3'-5"
3'-1" DIA. WHEELS.
9'-0"
M.S.K. 5/07.
4'-1½" NOM
10"
4'-11½"
2'-7"
5'-8½"
15'-4"
18'-4"

**LSWR I PLANK OPEN
FOR STONE TRAFFIC**
ON TIMBER UNDERFRAME
S.R. DIAGRAM 1308A

Figure 2 In a similar manner to Diagram 1301, those Diagram 1308 stone trucks extant in 1933 were further sub-divided, but this time by carrying capacity rather than by constructional details — a more important consideration when dealing with the transport of stone blocks. Diagram 1308 remained applicable to the 12 tonners (all on steel underframes) while 1308A was allocated to the 10-ton vehicles (most were on timber underframes). One 15-ton wagon remained in service at the time, but was withdrawn in November 1933 before a separate diagram number (presumably 1308B) was allocated. Wagon No 434, illustrated in **Plate 42** of *Volume One* and drawn here, is thus to diagram 1308A. In earlier years the LSWR stone trucks were regularly seen at Portland but after 1895 Wenford Bridge was added to the sphere of operation although in SR days most wagons received 'Return to Portland' boards.

Details of those one plank wagons extant in 1933 are as follows:

SR No	LSWR No	1933 Diagram	U/frame type	Date w/drawn
429	1216	1308A	Steel	1954
431	5281	1308A	Timber	4/47
434	9094	1308A	Timber	1954
7575	4717	1308	Steel	9/38
7580	5275	1308	Steel	7/37
7582	5278	1308	Steel	10/34
7583	5280	1308	Steel	1950
7584	5288	1308	Steel	7/37
9129	52	(1308B?)	Timber	11/33

Left:
Plate 5 The Southern perpetuated the LSWR four plank dropside design; allocated SR Diagram 1317. This design began life as a fixed sided vehicle and all LSWR examples were rebuilt as four plank dropsides in 1907. Being strongly built, they lasted well and at least five of the LSWR examples (SR Nos 9130/2/3/5/9) were still in traffic in 1935. SR-built No 61126 is seen in British Railways unfitted/unpainted livery at Yate (near Bristol) on 20 April 1961. It has lost the 'Return to Portland' board but apart from the addition of a metal door bang is still almost in original condition. Quite why it has found its way onto the former Midland route between Gloucester and Bristol is uncertain, however there were stone quarries in the vicinity. A census dated 1 January 1961 shows 12 wagons to the diagram remaining in traffic, while an observer at Eastleigh recorded Nos 61121/2/32/5 at this location during 1962. *Colin Roberts*

Most of the other steel underframed wagons numbered between 7570 and 7586 were withdrawn between 1928 and 1932, while timber framed 10-ton wagons Nos 428/30/2/3 were all withdrawn by 1928 before receiving SR livery or numbers. Similar 15-ton wagons allocated SR numbers 9131/8 did not even survive beyond 1923, also being scrapped as LSWR Nos 8634 and 10435. Wagon 8634 is recorded in the register as having hinged dropsides instead of the one plank fixed sides on the remainder.

The LSWR operated about 35 stone trucks, but the traffic may have fluctuated, since in October 1893 the General Manager reported that an arrangement for the hire of 30 ten-ton wagons had been agreed with The Bath Stone Firms Ltd, at a rate of 13/- (65 pence) per wagon per calendar month. It is not known for how long this agreement continued, however this company had wagons based at Portland for many years and Gloucester Railway Carriage & Wagon Company photograph No 1818, dated September 1898, illustrates a wagon operated by Hard Stone Firms Ltd of Bath, lettered 'Empty to Wenford Sidings, L&SWR', so perhaps the hire continued over a fairly long period.

Left:
Plate 6 Things are not always what they seem! At first sight four plank dropside No 214sm (skillet match truck for ex-SECR crane 214s) appears to be a former LSWR stone truck, but the SR service stock register tells a different story. The wagon was formerly Diagram 1309 open No 3177 and was reconstructed into the form shown in June 1935, replacing the previous 214sm (an ex-LCDR three plank open goods wagon to Diagram 1326). A glance under the wagon would have revealed a standard LSWR timber underframe, without the additional strengthening members that characterised LSWR stone trucks. The location is Botley on 29 June 1950 and the wagon would soon be renumbered as DS3118. The whereabouts of the accompanying crane was not recorded, however this was allocated to Botley from the late 1940s until withdrawn in 1956. *D. Cullum*

Four/five plank open goods wagons

Readers may perhaps be thankful to know that the number of identified variants of this large group of wagons remains at 18 — as described on pages 13/14 of *Volume One*. However, one more SR diagram variant has been found — 1309A — although the exact differences between this and the standard Diagram 1309 have yet to be discovered. Only three such wagons are listed in SR registers: numbers 697, 4768 and 4993 (formerly LSWR Nos 316, 8996 and 10392 respectively). All three come from widely different batches and no dimensional differences are shown in the register to indicate why they vary from the others.

Before proceeding to new illustrations, a few additional points of clarification from matters illustrated in *Volume One* may be in order. **Plate 19** showed type 3 wagon No 7348 at Plymouth in the 1890s. It is now known that 200 such wagons were completed at Nine Elms during 1884/5, taking LSWR Nos 7273-7472, although by the Grouping many of these would have been replaced by new construction — not necessarily of the same type as it was not at all unusual, for example, to replace opens with covered goods wagons as requirements changed.

In **Plate 20** a Diagram 1311 open wagon to type 4 was illustrated, lettered 'Coal Only'. What is not visible from the photograph is that the lettering 'Loco Dept' appeared on the left hand side of the wagon, again on the fourth plank down, to the left of the drop door. Sixty of these square-ended wagons were so allocated in June 1897, specifically for the supply of loco coal to the various sheds in the West Country — from Exmouth Junction westwards. Apart from No 8970 illustrated, only No 8969 (later SR No 4754) has so far been positively identified. It is therefore possible that the whole batch were consecutively numbered, as up to 150 identical wagons to Diagram 1311 were completed in 1891/2, numbered between 8886 and 9035 — those surviving after 1923 being allocated SR numbers between 4702 and 4787. By this time some of the wagons had been scrapped and replaced by round-ended opens to Diagrams 1309/10. The coal was landed at Fremington Quay (between Barnstaple Junction and Torrington) and the wagons were labelled 'Return Empty to Fremington' beneath the 'Loco Dept' insignia. Most other locomotive coal was delivered in private owner wagons; by far the greatest share of this traffic being in the hands of Messrs Stephenson Clarke, although Guest, Keen & Company, Barber Walker and Bestwood each received a small share of the traffic from time to time. From 1923 almost the entire Southern Railway locomotive coal supply contract was awarded to Stephenson Clarke Ltd.

The location of the accident visible in **Plate 21** of *Volume One* is Easton, Isle of Portland, on 26 September 1903. This proves that the '100 extra wagons for Southampton Docks', type 10 in our survey on page 14, were not confined there nor was it likely that they were finished in red oxide livery. Clearly the order process reflected a need but almost certainly these wagons to Diagram 1303 entered the general pool and this allowed 100 much older wagons to be transferred to docks use. Perhaps because they re-used old components, they were early casualties and only SR Nos 4, 74/8/9, 80/4/6, 115/7 survived beyond 1930 and all were withdrawn less than five years later. Similarly, few Diagram 1302 wagons to type 11 survived after 1935 — only Nos 15/8/9, 35/7, 45/8 and ex-duplicate wagons 19265-7/9-71 being listed at that time.

The unusual tarpaulin sheet rails carried by wagon No 203 in **Plate 23** were evidently a trial fitting, as in May 1895 William Panter reported on these (and probably others) and, after consultation with the Goods Manager, recommended the use of Williams Patent sheet supports in future. This therefore confirms the date of the picture.

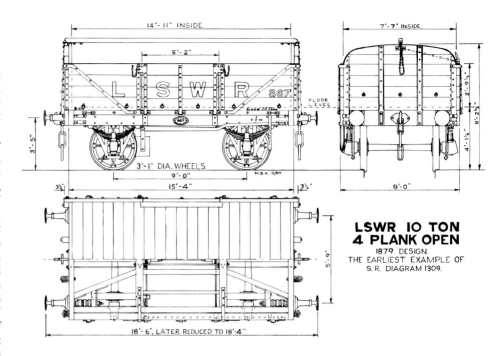

LSWR 10 TON
4 PLANK OPEN
1879 DESIGN.
THE EARLIEST EXAMPLE OF
S. R. DIAGRAM 1309.

Figure 3 Identifiable Adams open goods wagons to type 1 do not often appear in photographs and this drawing is based on one taken at Wimborne prior to 1905. The picture is not suitable for reproduction, but shows LSWR No 867 still in 1881 condition save for a replacement door and removal of safety chains. Between 1879 and 1883 more than 500 such wagons entered traffic, many built by either Midland RCW Co or Birmingham RCW Co, as well as in the company's workshops at Nine Elms. As far as can be ascertained, 300 of those built on capital account were numbered somewhere in the range between LSWR Nos 6540 and 6977, with further batches taking Nos 6998-7197 and 7223-72 inclusive. Very few of these survived the Grouping — most being replaced by more modern vehicles from 1900 onwards. LSWR No 867 was withdrawn in 1905 and replaced by a similar Diagram 1309 vehicle that was renumbered as SR No 989 in March 1929. This became service vehicle No 01254s in May 1944, part of an ARP train based at Purley. The appearance of this later wagon can only be guessed at — Type 14 or 15 being the most likely. If the former, then it would have resembled the Adams original very closely, save for updated brakes and axle boxes.

Below:
Plate 7 This Diagram 1309 wagon is listed on page 23 of *Volume One* as a type 15 vehicle — a typographical error — as it should read type 5. Photographed somewhere in North Wales in 1923, LSWR No 5158 became SR No 3011 in July 1928 and was withdrawn three years later, still in the condition shown with double block brakes on one side only. It was built in 1899 and the bodywork style, with five planks and conventional steel corner plates on a timber underframe, is one of the most common Diagram 1309 variants. Large numbers of these were built on renewal account and so took the widely scattered numbers of the wagons they replaced. *J. P. Richards*

Between 1900 and 1902 a total of 60 almost identical five plank round-ended open wagons were constructed by the Midland Railway Carriage & Wagon Company for the Midland & South Western Junction Railway. The LSWR appears to have played no obvious part in this process, other than to perhaps supply the drawings, although this is not recorded either. However, the wagons were too similar for this to have come about purely by chance. The MSWJR would have been familiar with LSWR wagons at Andover Junction — and LSWR wagons would have regularly traversed its line so it appears likely that the close working relationship between the two companies would have extended to this facility. These were MSWJR Nos 279-98 and 359-98 and most became GWR property in 1923.

Above:

Plate 8 The first Fox pressed steel underframe kits were ordered from the Leeds Forge Company in May 1892, 100 sets initially being provided at a cost of £17 per set. Diagram 1309 vehicle No 9129 is typical of the first batch of wagons to utilise these underframes and was outshopped from the new Eastleigh Carriage & Wagon Works in July 1893. This was an early example of type 6, being equipped with double block brakes on one side only, from the series numbered 9095-9194. It was not long before many others followed, including LSWR Nos 9642-9841, 10012-81, 10187-10432 and 10561-10635, plus many more with random lower numbers charged to renewal, instead of capital account. LSWR No 9129 failed to survive the Grouping, but similar wagons were allocated SR numbers between 4821-61, 4916-5008/43-71 after 1923. In 1896 the design was superceded by type 8, on a revised Fox underframe and these withstood the ravages of time rather better, as relatively few type 6 wagons became SR capital stock in 1923, although several hundred had become service vehicles from 1919 onwards. Many other railways, both at home and abroad, used the products of the Leeds Forge Company at the time and an article about the company appeared in *Engineering* for 6 April 1894. *LSWR Official*

Above:

Plate 9 The author makes no apology for including this print again (it was originally reproduced as **Plate 24** in *Volume One*), however this is a much clearer copy and greater detail may be seen. Type 6 wagon No 010323 of 1896 vintage appears at Southampton Docks around 1928 having been transferred to internal use at the docks in 1921; one of exactly 200 such transfers from 1919 onwards (SR service stock numbers 0285s-0484s). Allocated SR No 0463s, it was never repainted and was scrapped in June 1930 still in the livery as photographed, to be replaced by another Diagram 1309 wagon which did carry that number. Panter's cross-lever brake is fitted; a characteristic of the last type 6 opens built in 1896. The square-ended open behind, to type 7, is also mounted on an 1892-Fox pressed steel underframe — one of relatively few Diagram 1311 wagons of this type dating from 1893/4 and equipped with double block brake gear on one side only. Another type 7 wagon may be seen in **Plate 104**. *J.G. Coltas*

Right:

Plate 10 Type 8 five plank opens were by far the most consistent in terms of bodywork design, with more than 3,500 examples being completed between 1896 until 1911. All utilised the later Fox pressed steel underframe, identifiable by the angled (instead of vertical) ends to the headstock — compare with **Plates 8 and 9**. Whilst bodywork variations were few, the type of brake gear varied considerably. Being 2½ inches deeper internally than their predecessors, these wagons were allocated SR Diagram 1310. SR No 6295 was photographed at Swindon soon after being repainted in SR livery in January 1929 and still retains Panter brake gear. It was built in 1899 as LSWR No 12084, remaining in traffic until June 1930. The complete batch of 399 identical

wagons was numbered LSWR 11814-12212, later SR 6025-6423. The additional odd wagon on this order, LSWR No 12213, was the unique experimental 25 ton bogie open, type 12 in our classification, that later became SR No 9140. For a drawing of this wagon in its original form, the reader is referred to Gordon Weddell's *LSWR Carriages Volume Four* (see Bibliography). *R. S. Carpenter Photos*

Left:

Plate 11 Originally reproduced in the *South Western Gazette* for 1 May 1907 and unfortunately not the clearest of images, this view of Diagram 1310 wagon No 8686 (later SR No 4642, renumbered in June 1929) is the only known picture of the eight LSWR wagons equipped with Frampton's patent brake gear. There were two versions of this, known to the LSWR as types A and B. The former dates from 1903, the latter from the autumn of 1904. Presumably type B incorporated modifications following experience with the original version and it is the later style that was fitted to wagon 8686 in December 1904. The photograph was taken in March or April 1907 and shows that the wagon is lettered 'To work only between Nine Elms & Southampton Docks' — as were all the Frampton-braked wagons — presumably to allow the operation to be monitored more easily. Also visible on the crib rail, above the brake handle are the words 'To apply brake press handle down'. A round tie bar is also fitted between the axle boxes — perhaps to offset the 23:1 theoretical leverage applied by the mechanism, which might otherwise distort the underframe by spreading the axle boxes apart. *LSWR Official*

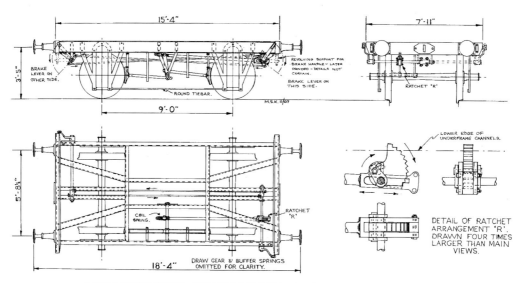

ARRANGEMENT OF FRAMPTON'S PATENT BRAKE ON LSWR DIAGRAM 1310 OPEN WAGONS.

Figure 4 A drawing of Frampton's patent brake type B, as fitted to six LSWR wagons during 1904. This is redrawn from *Modern Railway Working*; published in 1912 by the Gresham Press and supplemented by the drawings provided to the Patent Office by Mr H. S. Frampton, who was a builder's merchant living in Winchester. Between 1902 and 1906 he registered no less than nine patents, of which seven refer to either-side brake gear. That fitted to LSWR wagons appears to draw on a combination of three of them. Subsequent to the initial fitting, the South Western added a revolving support for the brake lever, however exact details of this are lacking. One must conclude that the gear was not entirely successful in normal use, as the cost of fitting was borne by Mr Frampton himself and no other wagons were so equipped.

Type A brake probably only varied in detail concerning the ratchet arrangement and may not initially have been capable of operating as a 'right-handed cross-cornered' brake using the twin pull rods running the full length of the wagon. Details of the two wagons fitted with this earlier version in May 1903 are:

LSWR No	SR No	SR Diagram	Withdrawal date
542	744	1310	March 1933
12028	6239	1310	April 1934

Apart from wagon 8686, two other Diagram 1310 wagons were fitted with type B in 1904, along with three Diagram 1316 eight plank opens. Numbering details of these are not known.

Following submission of a report on either-side wagon brakes by the Carriage & Wagon Superintendent in March 1906 (presumably by Surrey Warner, immediately following his appointment); the

General Manager recommended that 100 wagons built on renewal account be fitted with Dean/Churchward brake gear. Having come from Swindon, Warner would, of course, know all about this as it had been fitted to GWR wagons for a number of years previously. The cost was estimated to be about £4-10-0d (£4.50) per wagon.

Because they were renewals, their numbers were widely scattered and only the two examples given on page 23 of *Volume One* are known. A wagon so equipped could still be seen at Eastleigh Works in the late 1950s, but no trace of its former identity could be discovered.

Right:
Plate 12 Another Diagram 1310 five plank open, LSWR No 13931 (later SR No 7254) dating from 1910. Apart from being one of the last wagons built to this diagram, it also has McCord's patent frictional bearing springs — one of 60 such sets purchased by the LSWR at a cost of £4 per set in June 1910. One could therefore logically describe this wagon as Type 8A in our survey — all other details being as for a standard type 8 open on the 1896 Fox underframe. Just whether all 60 sets were mounted beneath this particular batch of wagons is uncertain — the order for 100 open wagons placed in May 1910 actually being fulfilled as follows:

LSWR Nos	SR Nos	Underframe	SR Diagram	Total
13857-76/9-98	7180-99, 7202-21	Timber	1309	40
13877/8/99-13856	7200/1/22-78	Steel	1310	60

Just why Nos 13877/8 (SR 7200/1) fall out of sequence is not known, however it is tempting to suggest (but not confirmed) that the McCord spiral springs were fitted to these 60 steel-underframed wagons to Diagram 1310. The LSWR purchased more of these fittings in 1918 and an eight plank open is illustrated in **Plate 38** of *Volume One*. The brake gear on wagon 13931 is of the Morton clutch pattern — this and the two brake blocks being on the side away from the camera. The only clue to the location comes from the chalked destination — Llantrisant in South Wales, between about 1920 and July 1928, when the wagon received SR livery.
R. S. Carpenter Photos

Right:
Plate 13 One of the timber underframed vehicles to Diagram 1309 from the same order as wagon 13931, SR No 7184 (ex-LSWR No 13861), was photographed at Cardington (Bedford) on 26 November 1938. The fact that this has conventional leaf springs lends some weight to the theory that just the steel-framed examples were equipped with spiral springs, however no other photographs of the batch are known to prove this theory any further. Wagon No 7184 was recorded by the photographer as being extremely weathered and that the lettering had been recently (and rather crudely)
over painted — note the somewhat untidy appearance of the company initials. This view shows the Morton brake gear while **Plate 35** in *Volume One* is a close-up of the dog-clutch mechanism itself. This wagon dates from 1911 and ran until April 1946. *A. E. West*

Left & centre left:
Plates 14 and 15 Two views of type 15 Diagram 1309 open No 4342 (ex-LSWR No 7817 of 1900 vintage), exhibiting post-1936 SR lettering and an overhaul date of July 1937, at which time the original double block brake gear was duplicated on the other side. This wagon uses ironwork taken from a type 2 or 3 wagon of the mid-1880s and was transferred to departmental stock as No 0645s in May 1948 — the third wagon to carry this service stock number. The date and location were not recorded, but to judge from the loading gauge and signal in the background of **Plate 15**, might be somewhere on the LNWR, *circa 1939. Both G. H. Platt*

Bottom left:
Plate 16 By 1948 very few LSWR four/five plank opens remained in ordinary traffic. Diagram 1309 type 16 wagon No 2251 was one, transferred to departmental stock in February 1953 by the simple expedient of adding the letters 'DS' in front of the existing running number. The Railway Executive Committee advocated this numbering process soon after Nationalisation — perhaps to preserve the former identity of goods wagons and so assist with maintenance of them. The Southern Region was opposed to this idea on the grounds that it might lead to confusion and from 1950-54 utilised a series of numbers in the DS3XXX range for many of its departmental conversions. Some 1949/50 transfers kept their old numbers, while from about 1953 onwards most SR wagon transfers did finally adhere to the REC ruling. Wagon No 2251 was built in 1913 as LSWR No 3676; one of the last examples of Diagram 1309 to be completed and was equipped with Morton brakes. When photographed in the mid-1950s it was remarkable in retaining its round ends, although there is ample evidence of replanking. The pre-Grouping company initials are beginning to reappear through the degraded SR brown paint finish.
T. A. Barry collection

By 1948 just 76 wagons to Diagram 1309, two wagons to Diagram 1310, 56 wagons to Diagram 1311, two wagons to Diagram 1312 and four wagons to Diagram 1313 remained in ordinary traffic — compared with the starting total of 7,205 four/five plank LSWR open wagons in 1923. Some 1951-7 withdrawal details are as follows:

Year	Diagram 1309	Diagram 1311	Diagram 1313
1951	1383, 4255/6, 7204	874, 4084, 7403/13/6/26	4706
1952	850, 1645, 7209, 7305	1301, 2042, 2148, 4178, 4281, 4630	None listed
1953	2251, 3686, 4152, 7280*	2718, 2944, 4698/9, 4780, 7419	2855
1954	2582	1254, 3359, 4130*	None listed
1955	None listed	1439, 2804, 3414, 7415	None listed
1956	None listed	None listed	None listed
1957	None listed	None listed	None listed

*Illustrated in *Volume One*, **Plates 34 and 36** respectively.
No Diagram 1310 or 1312 withdrawals listed during these years.

Most of the wagons listed above then entered internal use, renumbered in the BR (Southern Region) 08XXXX number series. Apart from Nos 4130 and 7280, the appearance of the others may only be guessed at, but it is most likely that the Diagram 1309 wagons were to type 16 while Diagram 1311 would be to type 17. The January 1961 census states that just one wagon to each of Diagrams 1309/11/12 remained in ordinary service, although the accuracy of this must surely be doubtful.

Eight plank open goods wagons

Right:
Plate 17 One of the earlier Diagram 1316 wagons with double block brakes on one side only, SR No 8548 (ex-LSWR No 5332, renumbered in October 1928 and withdrawn in September 1937) was still so equipped when photographed in pre-1936 SR livery — date and location not recorded. Note also the ten-spoke wheelsets — probably another indication that this wagon was built as a 15 tonner and downrated after June 1913. Freighter brakes would have had to be provided by January 1939, to satisfy Board of Trade regulations, although as noted earlier, three of these 1904 vintage wagons were equipped with Frampton's patent brake when new. Most of these wagons were charged to renewal account and their LSWR numbers span from 17 (lowest) to 15083 (highest). One batch did nominally replace some SDJR vehicles in 1920 and these wagons were numbered 14701-14/29-48. *Edwards Bros*

Construction of these began in 1904, following the example of the LNWR, Midland and GNR — all of which had recently introduced larger 15-ton capacity wagons in an attempt to increase payload by up to 50% without a similar increase in tare weight. However, not all traders were ready to accept the larger wagons and production of smaller 10 and 12-ton vehicles would continue for many years to come. Indeed, all except one batch of 50 LSWR 15 tonners were downrated to 12 tons from June 1913 onwards. Two LSWR designs concern us here; allocated SR Diagrams 1314 and 1316, while two subsequent rebuilds added Diagrams 1315 and 1320, but as we have already seen, different constructional techniques would later add two more sub-diagrams from about 1933.

Right:
Plate 18 Post-1936 SR livery is carried by Diagram 1316 open No 9178, photographed at Clacton in 1948. This was built in December 1924; part of SR order E9 for 100 wagons placed in May 1923 (SR Nos 9141-9240). Note the different style of top door hinge, as used on both SR-built batches, lift-link brakes, Shepherd's patent axle boxes and ribbed buffer casings. The right-hand wheels are also disc — relatively unusual on LSWR wagons. The metal plate visible above the brake rack is a recent repair job to defective planking and typical of World War Two onwards. Withdrawal was recorded in 1952. *G. J. Clark*

Left:

Plate 19 One hundred further eight plank opens were ordered by the Southern Railway in March 1924, initially on order E30, but this order number was swiftly reallocated elsewhere and replaced by E77 in January 1925; again for 100 open wagons of LSWR design. The reason for the change of plan is not clear, but E77 were unusual in that these were on timber underframes — all previous Diagram 1316 opens were on Fox pressed steel frames and for this reason alone were allocated Diagram 1316A after 1933. Quite why these had timber underframes is not recorded, but perhaps the stock of Fox underframe kits had been exhausted and as the Leeds Forge Company was about to be swallowed up in the Metropolitan consortium, maybe it was unable to supply any more at what was considered a reasonable price. SR No 9271 was photographed at Exeter in 1955, wearing the remains of BR unfitted stock light grey livery, with black number patches — probably the livery that many of these wagons carried in their final days. The January 1961 census records just 10 remaining in ordinary traffic at that time, although quite a number could be found in departmental or internal-user service. *P. Coutanche*

Centre left:

Plate 20 In 1935, 20 wagons to Diagram 1316 were converted to carry grain by the simple expedient of through-planking the doors, sealing the gaps in the planks with pitch and the provision of nothing more sophisticated than a hole in the floor, controlled by a valve, for unloading purposes. These replaced 20 purpose-built LSWR hoppers that had previously been used since 1898 for grain traffic landed at Southampton Docks. Just whether the rebuilt Diagram 1316 wagons ever served this location is not known, but by 1936, when this photograph was taken, all were operating between Whitstable Harbour and flourmills near Ashford, Kent. No less than six are visible at the Harbour — Nos 8660, 8926 and 9237 being identifiable. Diagram 1320 was allocated and all retain sheet rails, the grain being protected by tarpaulin sheets. All are stencilled 'When empty return to Whitstable Harbour', but note that no 'Grain' branding is carried (unlike on the 1952 livery, visible in **Plate 41** of *Volume One*). Instead all carry the non-common-user 'N' stencil on the corner plates. They remained on this duty until the branch closed in December 1952 and all 16 survivors were condemned during 1953, confirming that they were not redeployed elsewhere after closure of the line. *J.W. Sparrowe*

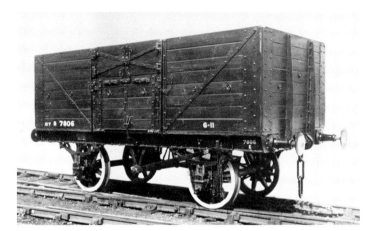

Above:

Plate 21 The final eight plank design incorporated Railway Clearing House (RCH) standards and dates from 1920/1. Diagram 1314 was Surrey Warner's first (and only) essay into this field. In December 1919 the General Manager had recommended that an outstanding order for 250 open goods wagons be placed with external contractors, as Eastleigh Works was suffering from post-war labour shortages and there had been some delay in production. By May 1920 the situation was no better, so the order was increased to 400 wagons, resulting in two versions of the design. The original 250 were ordered from Metropolitan Railway Carriage & Wagon Company (although some records state that construction was actually undertaken by Birmingham RCW Co) and were on steel underframes, later allocated to SR diagram 1314A. SR No 7806 was photographed as part of the Ashford 1948 series of views. It began life as LSWR No 6380, not being renumbered or repainted into SR livery until February 1931 — a relatively late renumbering. The original cost is recorded as £366 and the wagon ran until 1951. Note the general similarity with the contemporary Maunsell/Lynes product for the SECR (Diagram 1355). As with Diagram 1316, all wagons were charged to renewal account and the only consecutive batch of LSWR numbers were 14715-28, later SR Nos 7958-71. *BR Official*

Right:

Plate 22 The 150 further wagons were ordered in May 1920 from Messrs Harrison & Camm and these were on timber underframes, costing £335 each. Photographs of Diagram 1314 wagons in traffic seem almost absent, so this batch is again illustrated using the Ashford 1948 official series. SR No 7633 (ex-LSWR No 1661) ran from 1921 until 1958. A total of 303 (of both versions) were still in traffic at Nationalisation and just two are recorded by the 1961 census. Most withdrawals occurred between 1947 and 1955. The exact reason for taking this 1948/9 series of wagon photographs is unknown, however they may have been provided for the newly formed British Railways 'Ideal Stocks Committee' to ponder over while considering the form that new wagon construction would take after 1949. Whatever the reason, they provide an excellent snapshot of the wagon fleet and most extant SR diagrams managed to be included. *BR Official*

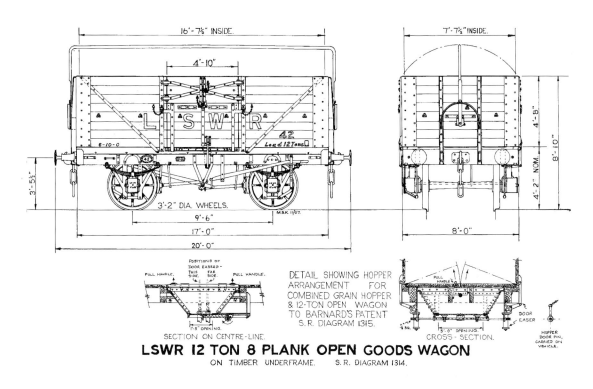

LSWR 12 TON 8 PLANK OPEN GOODS WAGON
ON TIMBER UNDERFRAME.   S.R. DIAGRAM 1314.

Figure 5 A drawing of the timber-underframed version of Diagram 1314, including the modification for the solitary Diagram 1315 convertible grain hopper rebuild, SR No 7986. Whether this wagon ran to or from Whitstable Harbour or had another specific duty allocated is not known, nor have any photographs been found.

Covered goods wagons

Unlike the open goods wagons, which came in a number of different lengths and designs, almost all LSWR covered goods wagons built from 1885 onwards exhibited a family likeness; being 18ft long over headstocks and characterised by external timber cross-framing. Indeed, the late Frank Foote used to refer to them as 'XXX' or 'XWX'-framed vans and a glance at the photographs will immediately reveal his logic in applying these descriptions. Construction ceased in 1926, by which time almost 3,000 vehicles had been turned out by either Nine Elms or Eastleigh Carriage & Wagon Works — and it seems that none were ever built by outside contractors during this period. Piecemeal replacement of the oldest vans began around 1901, often resulting in consecutively numbered vans of widely varying ages or different diagrams and these differences were never really sorted out by the SR renumbering scheme of 1923. Despite their age, some vans of 1885-vintage did become SR stock at the Grouping, although most of these had been withdrawn or transferred to departmental stock by 1930, often without receiving their allocated SR numbers or livery. Many more were transferred in later years and could still be seen in sheds and yards until the late 1960s. Others were grounded both on and off the railway as storage huts and some of these have only recently disappeared from the scene. The last few to remain in capital stock were withdrawn in 1964 — examples of Diagrams 1406/8/9 lasting until then.

In *Volume One* the vans were separated into two groups by usage (largely dictated by the amount of ventilation provided) but this time around they will be separated into low-roof and high-roof designs. With but one exception in the first group the former date from 1885-1912, the latter from 1912 until 1924. The exception is the final type of low-roof meat van, constructed in 1915/7/26 and therefore the final design to appear — and also the last to be built.

Low-roof designs

The earliest design was also the most numerous variant — later allocated to SR Diagram 1410 and over 1,200 were completed between 1885 and 1912. This diagram included both timber and steel underframes — probably because the Southern's rolling stock staff decided that it would be too complicated to try to separate them out — despite doing so for nearly all the other diagrams. Timber underframes were used throughout the period; while steel made single appearances in 1889 and 1895 (LSWR No 8486/SR No 43277 and LSWR No 6505/SR No 43148 respectively) — presumably both experimental — before general use of Fox pressed steel components began in 1899.

Figure 6 This shows the 1885 design on a timber underframe with a single block brake on one side only — the earliest variant to Diagram 1410. This would be typical of construction up to 1892, after which double block brakes would be used, but still on one side only. No ventilation was provided originally — at least not for the general stock — although a few (possibly rebuilds) were provided with side and end ventilators, as well as through vacuum pipes, at various times and these were allocated to SR Diagram 1402; six randomly numbered examples on timber underframes so far being noted. Apart from the use of steel underframes, 20 identical ventilated vans were built new in 1905/6 and these are illustrated in **Plate 30,** also being allocated to Diagram 1402. Provision of a single ventilator at high level at each end commenced in 1899 on new construction and from 1902, following a request from the General Manager, similar provision was made on existing vans as they passed through shops, at a cost of 10/- (50 pence) per van. It is not known how long this took to implement, but a five/eight year period between overhauls may be considered reasonable, to judge from the time taken to renumber and repaint the stock into SR livery after the Grouping. **Figure 6** also illustrates the small LSWR lettering in use prior to around 1891/2.

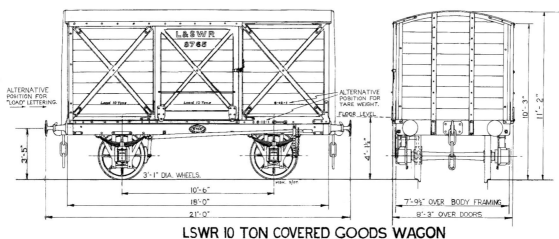

LSWR 10 TON COVERED GOODS WAGON
WITH TIMBER UNDERFRAME
1885 DESIGN — 1892 DESIGN WITH DOUBLE-BLOCK BRAKE GEAR.

Some LSWR number blocks for Diagram 1410-type vehicles are as follows:

Date Built	LSWR Nos	Total	Remarks
1889	8473-8582	110	Nos. 8553-72 were later meat vans. Timber u/f.
1889/90	8708-8807	100	A few were later ventilated vans. Timber u/f.
1892	9195-9274	80	A few were later ventilated vans. Timber u/f.
1893/4	9442-9641	200	A few were later ventilated vans. Timber u/f.
1899/1900	12214-12388	175	Steel underframe and Panter's brake gear.
1910	14057-76	20	Timber underframe.
1911/12	14407-81	75	Timber underframe.

It should be noted that by no means all of the early examples survived to receive SR numbers after 1923 and in many instances replacement vans (not necessarily to Diagram 1410) carried the same LSWR numbers after 1901. Many LSWR numbers in the ranges 5626-75, 6075-6174 and 6473-6522 were also allocated to Diagram 1410 vans, but as most were replacements for much earlier vehicles, not every number was re-used, nor were consecutively-numbered vehicles always identical.

Left:
Plate 23 An early timber-underframed van to Diagram 1410, LSWR No 1922, dating from 1888. This was renumbered as SR 42554 in August 1924 and was withdrawn in July 1930. By this time it was recorded as having double block brake gear — clearly on one side only — although when built only a single block would have been provided. Planking is 8½in on the sides and sliding doors (these usually, but not always matched) and 6½in on the ends — a very common combination, however just whether this was the case in 1888 cannot be confirmed. As a general rule, older vans received wider planking all round but this often changed, particularly during and after World War One. Note also the end ventilator — added post-1902. The photograph was taken at an unknown location on the Midland Railway, *circa* 1920. *HMRS Collection*

Right:
Plate 24 One of the last Diagram 1410 vans to be built, LSWR No 14411 (later SR No 44158, renumbered as late as January 1930) is seen standing in an up goods train awaiting the road at Addlestone Junction in April 1924. The west-north side of the Weybridge/Byfleet/Addlestone triangle was often used to hold goods trains awaiting a path westwards onto the main line or eastwards towards Feltham yard, as in this case, fitted in between the frequent passenger services. Wagon No 14411 was part of a batch of 75 vans completed in 1911/12 (LSWR Nos 14407-81, later SR Nos 44154-228), but apart from the provision of Morton brake gear is almost identical to the 1888 van seen in the previous picture. The photographer would have described this as an 'XXX' van. *F. Foote*

Left:
Plate 25 Apart from the two earlier steel-framed vans already noted, Fox 18ft pressed steel underframes made their appearance in 1899, at the same time as end ventilators and, for Diagram 1410 at least, Panter's cross-lever brake gear. Van No 43943 (formerly LSWR No 12223) was part of the initial batch of 175 vehicles, LSWR Nos 12214-388 (SR Nos 43934-44106 and 44272/3 — the last two being renumbered out-of-sequence) completed in 1899/1900 and was photographed at Huntingdon North on 29 November 1953, carrying rather worn British Railways grey livery, but without black number patches, so was presumably an early repaint in this livery. The Panter brake gear did not survive the rough and tumble of goods working and its replacement commenced in 1918 — in this instance by two sets of independent brakes. To a Southern man, this would be described as a 'Freighter' brake. Note the various destinations chalked on — including Stoke, Hockley, Tipton, Lincoln, Newcastle and Ladbroke. Not one on the Southern, but it gives some idea of the wanderings of goods vehicles under common-user policy. Withdrawal was recorded in 1955. *A. E. West*

Right:
Plate 26 A good view of the end detail on van 43943, showing the 8½in planking all round. Older vans and those with timber underframes usually had rectangular coupling plates instead of the hexagonal fitting seen here. *A. E. West*

Below:
Plate 27 A superb official portrait of steel-underframed van 44030 (ex-LSWR No 12312 of 1900 vintage); part of the Ashford 1948 series of views. The livery is SR brown with a small 'S' prefix instead of the company initials above the number. Indeed, the repainted patch over the former position may be seen, clearly indicating that this wagon was not fully repainted for the photograph. Planking is 8½in on sides and doors, 6½in on the ends. Panter's cross-lever brake was originally provided, changed to Freighter at an unrecorded date — which could be any time between 1918 and 1939. Note also the odd buffer casings and wheelsets — the nearer set being closed 10-spoke pattern, the farther set open 8-spoke. Mix and match were the order of the day by the 1940s. Withdrawal was recorded in 1953. Out of a starting total for this diagram of 1010 vans at Grouping (plus two for Messrs Pooley's weighing machines), 254 remained in general service in 1948, reducing to just two by the January 1961 census. *BR Official*

Right:

Plate 28 In 1902, 20 vans were built at Eastleigh for the Somerset & Dorset Joint line. Ten were ordinary covered goods vehicles to the usual LSWR specification, and these were the last ones built without end ventilators. The vans re-entered LSWR stock in 1914 and were by then certainly unique in being unventilated — a distinction they retained until after the Grouping, as the Southern allocated the eight remaining joint line vans to Diagram 1412, to distinguish them from other Diagram 1410 vehicles. Their SR numbers were 44261-8. The two missing vans had by this time been rebuilt as meat vans, and feature in the next photograph. Departmental No 598s was one of the SDJR vans and was photographed at Dinton in June 1948. It was previously SR No 44261 and LSWR No 15191, however the exact SDJR number cannot be quoted other than being within the range 1202-21. It entered CME service in February 1948; the new departmental number has caused confusion, since the van has both an 'S' prefix and suffix letter, in two different sizes! The Southern fitted end ventilators after 1923, to bring the vans into line with Diagram 1410, however the diagram number was never amended from 1412. Replanking of the ends with 6½in timbers has taken place — as the originals had 8½ in all round. Double block brakes were originally provided on one side, duplicated at some time prior to 1939. Similar ex-SDJR van No 44262 also survived to BR days and was included in the Ashford 1948 series of photographs. *J. H. Aston*

Centre right:

Plate 29 Ten of the vans built for the SDJR in 1902 were for fresh meat traffic, as illustrated in **Plate 69** of *Volume One*, having four side and five end vents. However, by 1924 there were 12 such vans in existence to be allocated to SR Diagram 1485, so it is almost certain that two of the ordinary covered goods wagons were converted for this traffic *circa* 1922. SR No 51159 was photographed as part of the Ashford 1948 series but differs from the van illustrated in *Volume one* by having just one end vent. It is therefore suggested (but not confirmed) that this is one of the two rebuilds. Again, the exact SDJR number cannot be confirmed beyond the range 1202-21, however the former LSWR number was 15179. Through vacuum pipes were provided on this van in 1922, perhaps confirming the date of conversion to a meat van, but these were removed in June 1931, while the original double block brake gear on one side was duplicated in January 1930. Withdrawal came in 1954. *BR Official*

Right:

Plate 30 In addition to the half dozen converted ventilated vans noted against **Figure 6**, another 20 were built new on steel underframes in 1905/6 and these also became part of Diagram 1402 after the Grouping. The final survivor was SR No 42077 (ex-LSWR No 6077) which became departmental van No 1936s in March 1944 and lasted long enough to be transferred to the Western Region in 1963, as part of the former SR network west of Salisbury. It was last seen marked condemned at Lydford Junction in 1966, but is seen here at Broad Clyst permanent way depot in May 1959. The number carried is incorrect — it should read DS1936, so someone made a mistake when repainting the vehicle into the BR departmental series. The livery is very pale grey (by 1966 it appeared almost white) and Freighter brakes, long springs

and 3ft 5in Mansell wheels are retained, indicating its former passenger-rated status. Even the through vacuum pipes are still carried, probably seldom needed for its departmental duties. All these fittings are typical of Diagram 1402 — the vehicles being intended primarily for fruit traffic. A few vans were dual (ie, vacuum and Westinghouse) piped originally — the Westinghouse fittings being removed during the mid-1930s. At least one van of this type was sold to the Army and survived at Longmoor Camp until the mid-1960s, as did several to Diagram 1410. *A. E. West*

Some examples of Diagram 1402 are as follows:

LSWR No	SR No	U/frame	Brake	LSWR No	SR No	U/frame	Brake
1399	42010	Timber	DP	1670	42015	Steel	VP
4750	42061	Timber	VP	8518	42101	Steel	VP
8801	42120	Timber	VP	9553*	43653	Steel	VP

*This van was rated at 10 tons capacity; all the others were 8 tons.

Right:

Plate 31 Also built primarily for fruit traffic in 1908-10 were the 150 vans later allocated to SR Diagram 1401. These had timber underframes and were fully vacuum fitted (noted as AVB — automatic vacuum brake — in the registers) with eight brake blocks, 11ft wheelbase and passenger-rated running gear with 3ft 5in Mansell wheels. The usual five side vents were provided, but no end vents at all. Instead, two roof-mounted torpedo vents were provided. By no means all were actually labelled 'Fruit', either before or after the Grouping, but LSWR No 4030 was one of 90 specifically equipped with wire shelves and had clearly been freshly stencilled for the traffic when photographed — even if it had not been otherwise repainted. This delightful period piece was taken at Bursledon (Hants) at an unrecorded date that could be at any time between 1910 and 1928, when the van was renumbered as SR 42054. Swanwick, Botley and Bursledon were typical of several stations in Hampshire that loaded large quantities of soft fruit

during the summer months for conveyance to London and the Midlands. Note the chalked destination; Barnoldswick (Lancs), on the L&Y/Midland route from Burnley to Skipton, giving some idea of how far the fruit travelled to market. The fruit specials generally left Hampshire in the late afternoon, allowing the produce to be on sale by the following morning. Other company's vans were also used, especially from the Midland and LNWR, while many LSWR passenger-rated vans and (until 1930) ancient six-wheeled converted carriages were also pressed into service — such was the traffic volume over the short soft fruit season. This van was withdrawn as early as March 1933. In later years, SR-built vans and containers were employed. *Mrs J. Philip Collection*

Below:

Plate 32 A Diagram 1401 van sold out of service to become a private-owner wagon — it is registered as such in the Southern Railway private-owner wagon register (entry No 765, dated 28 March 1939, as also recorded on the wagon plate). On this date it became the property of Horsham-based firm Chipman Chemical Company, which for many years has held a weed-killing contract with British Railways and many of their successors — and clearly did so prior to Nationalisation too. Formerly SR No 42170 and LSWR No 14101,

the van was photographed at Peterborough on 3 May 1953, carrying the owner's stock number 002 and its mid-green livery. Also visible is part of the train of similarly liveried tank wagons and (just seen in the foreground) an LNER 20-ton fitted goods brake van. Some modifications have been made to equip the wagon as a staff riding van, including two end windows (there was a single window in the centre at the other end), additional grab rails, footsteps and a stove, to judge from the presence of the chimney in the roof. LSWR numbers for most of these vans are widely scattered — the lowest being 686, the highest 10072, however one batch were charged to capital account and took LSWR Nos 14077-14106. Other sample numbers were 1116, 2007, 5662 and 9001. *A. E. West*

Right:

Plate 33 In November 1892 the LSWR took over control of Southampton Docks and soon there was a considerable increase in both fresh and refrigerated meat traffic. For a number of years the company's stock of meat vans had stood at 50 vehicles — indeed the entire stock of Adams-period small vans had been replaced between 1886 and 1889 by new 18ft examples — the survivors of which later became SR Diagrams 1483 (vacuum-fitted and passenger-rated) and 1484 (goods-rated). The former vans were quite distinctive and examples may be seen in **Plates 55** and **192**. The latter were, in effect, Diagram 1410 with side and end ventilators. From 1889 this was turned into a very similar passenger-rated design on an 11ft wheelbase — finally allocated to SR Diagram 1481 at the Grouping. A total of 150 vans were built between then and 1912 — the majority appearing between 1890 and 1895. All except the final 25 built in 1912 were equipped with AVB and power brakes — the last batch just having through vacuum pipes and lift-link brake gear. LSWR No 14591 was one of the 1912 vans and is seen at Plymouth Friary on 14 June 1926, still in pre-Grouping livery. The later SR livery of stone buff colour and the running number 51138 were not applied until January 1929, while the van remained in service until April 1946. Most of the later vans had five side vents, but as **Plate 65** in *Volume One* illustrates, the earlier vans had only four; that on the door being omitted. *H. C. Casserley*

Some examples of numbering of Diagrams 1481 and 1484 meat vans are as follows:

Date Built	LSWR Numbers	Total	Survivors to SR Numbers	Brake
1886-9	5179, 8553/5/8-60/2 5/7/8/70, 1333	12	51146-56/8 (These 12 are to SR Diagram 1484)	Hand
1892	9275-9294	20	51070-88	AVB
1893	9352-9401	50	51157, 51089-51128	AVB
1912	14582-98	17	51129-44	VP

As usual, by no means all survived to SR days and some numbers were reallocated to other diagrams before 1923.

Below right:

Plate 34 In 1898/9 a batch of 30 vans were built and specifically labelled for butter traffic. These were allocated to SR Diagram 1413 and were rarely photographed. In *Volume One*, **Plate 61** shows such a van at Southampton Docks, confirming that it had a timber underframe and was equipped with five side and five end vents, plus four torpedo vents on the roof — the maximum provision for any of these vans. Evidence that these specialised vehicles could travel far from home comes from this view, showing one in a southbound LNWR goods train of some 60 mineral wagons behind a 'Super D Goods 0-8-0', at Castlethorpe troughs (south of Rugby). The Diagram 1409 van behind confirms that the date is no earlier than the summer of 1913. The butter van is from the original batch as one van was lost in an accident and was replaced by a steel-framed version in 1906. This newer vehicle outlasted all the originals by almost 20 years and as SR No 43925 was scrapped in 1953. No photographs taken during Southern Railway days are known, so exact livery/lettering details cannot be confirmed, but as the vans were goods-rated and numbered in the ordinary covered goods wagon series, it is presumed that they were painted wagon brown rather than stone colour. *HMRS Collection*

Above:

Plate 35 The full glory of SR stone colour with Venetian red lettering and white roof is carried by ex-works Diagram 1482 meat van No 51041 at Salisbury in June 1935. It is doubtful if this colourful livery would remain pristine for very long. Note the telegraphic code of 'Mica' carried on the crib rail. This was the last design of low-roofed LSWR van and dates from 1915, having five end and six side vents (the extra one being on account of the two hinged doors instead of a single sliding door). The former LSWR number was 8140 — a direct replacement for a Diagram 1483 van of 1887 vintage and it was originally repainted into SR livery in October 1928, so probably the 1935 overhaul was its second under SR ownership. LSWR livery for these vans was the standard brown colour. Withdrawal for this van came in 1956 — one of the last ex-LSWR survivors. At least one of these vans was sold to the War Department and ended its days at RNAD Bedenham (Gosport) in 1993, subsequently being purchased for preservation by the Somerset & Dorset Railway Trust and it may now be seen at Washford, on the West Somerset Railway. *J. G. Griffiths*

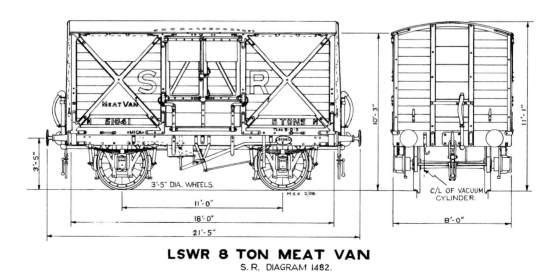

LSWR 8 TON MEAT VAN
S. R. DIAGRAM 1482.

Figure 7 The final LSWR covered goods wagon design of 1915/7/26, SR Diagram 1482. The last batch of 25 vans were completed by the Southern under order No E107, in 1926, but were almost indistinguishable from the LSWR-built vehicles. Examples of LSWR numbering are 4743, 5185, 8146, 9280 and 9370 — all being replacements for earlier meat vans of Diagrams 1481 or 1483 type. Frank Foote would have described this as an 'XWX'-framed van, the underlining denoting the drop flap door.

Above:

Plate 36 The Ashford 1948 series includes Diagram 1482 van No 51034, carrying the usual early BR lettering layout on either SR brown or possibly even BR crimson lake livery, as some ventilated meat vans were so finished shortly after Nationalisation. This was formerly LSWR No 5308 — a replacement for an earlier diagram 1481 vehicle. All 45 vans survived until 1945 but withdrawal then commenced in earnest and most of the LSWR-built examples were withdrawn by 1957. The SR-built batch (Nos. 51171-95) fared slightly better, but only one remained in traffic by August 1961, when it was reduced to ordinary covered goods wagon status. The number of this final survivor is not known, but surprisingly was one of the LSWR-built vans. *BR Official*

Table 1
Summary of low-roof van diagrams

SR Diagram	Capacity (Tons)	Under-frame	Wheel base	Pass/goods rated	Brakes	Doors	Ventilators Side	Ventilators End	Ventilators Roof	Designated traffic
1401	8	Timber	11ft	Pass	AVB	Sliding	5	none	2	Fruit/Ventilated
1402	8 or 10	Timber or steel	10ft 6in	Pass	VP or DP	Sliding	5	1	none	Ventilated
1410	10	Timber or steel	10ft 6in	Goods	Hand	Sliding	none	1	none	General goods *See note 1*
1412	10	Steel	10ft 6in	Goods	Hand	Sliding	none	none	none	SDJR Road Vans *See note 2*
1413	10	Timber or steel	10ft 6in	Goods	Hand	Sliding	5	5	4	Butter *See note 3*
1481	8 or 10	Timber	11ft	Pass	AVB or VP	Sliding	4/5	5	none	Meat
1482	8	Timber	11ft	Pass	AVB	3-part	6	5	none	Meat
1483	8	Timber	11ft	Pass	AVB	2 (hinged)	Side/end louvres			Meat *See note 4*
1484	10	Timber	10ft 6in	Goods	Hand	Sliding	4/5	5	none	Meat
1485	10	Steel	10ft 6in	Goods	Hand or VP	Sliding	5	1/ 5	none	SDJR Meat Vans *See note 5*

Note 1. No end ventilators provided before 1899. From 1902 these were added to existing vans as they were overhauled.
Note 2. No end ventilators provided until after 1924. Two vans rebuilt to Diagram 1485 around 1922.
Note 3. One steel framed replacement van built in 1906. This van alone (SR No 43925) remained in service until 1953.
Note 4. At least one van received sliding doors prior to 1923. Others had a single end ventilator fitted in place of the louvres.
Note 5. Two vans rebuilt from Diagram 1412 around 1922 —these two had only a single end ventilator.
For Diagram 1405 vans allocated to the Mechanical Engineer's Department, see the section on goods brake vans.

High-roof designs

Construction of these commenced in 1912, although one timber-underframed van to Diagram 1407 may have been an earlier prototype, as some records state that this van (LSWR no. 8573) was built in 1910 — other sources give 1912. With the exception of the banana van, all were goods-rated and unfitted, with just a single ventilator at each end. The Southern perpetuated the final covered goods design on a steel underframe and the last 200 vans were turned out from Eastleigh Works in 1923/4.

Above:

Plate 37 An interesting comparison between low and high-roof designs, photographed at Forest Hill in 1956. Both vans have been transferred to the Commercial Department for storage purposes and renumbered into the BR 08XXXX internal-user series — effectively barring the vans from leaving the yard. This was a very common use for older covered goods wagons in the 1950s and 1960s — at all sorts of locations — and very few saw any further service thereafter; most being broken up on site once the yard closed or their duties ceased. To the left is Diagram 1410 van No 44092 (ex-LSWR No 12374 of 1900), now renumbered as 080597, while to the right is Diagram 1406 van No 43523 (ex-LSWR No 9245 of 1912), now renumbered as 080261. The latter is one of 110 high-roof vans completed during 1912, but still retaining external sliding doors. Just four of these vans were completed on timber underframes (allocated SR Diagram 1407); the rest were on steel underframes, as seen here. Both vans were withdrawn in April 1960, their replacements at Forest Hill being a pair of ex-LMS vehicles, so presumably they were no longer fit for storage purposes by that time.
The Lens of Sutton Association

All of Diagrams 1406/7 were charged to renewal account, so there are no consecutive batches of either LSWR or SR numbers. A few examples are:

Diagram 1406 (on steel u/frame)

LSWR No	SR No	Date Wdn
26	42232	1953
1715	42497	1954
5531	42921	1962*
9456	43567	10/63#

* One of the last survivors in capital stock.
# Renumbered as DS43567 some time around 1960.

Diagram 1407 (on timber u/frame)

LSWR No	SR No	Date Wdn
8926	43439	9/34
9315	43547	4/33

The last survivor to Diagram 1407 was SR No 42461, withdrawn in 1956.

From December 1912 the sliding door design was replaced by one with a three-part door (i.e. two hinged doors over a drop flap — described by Frank Foote as 'X<u>W</u>X'-framed) and this became standard until production ceased in 1924, by which time just over 1,000 vans were completed — almost all on renewal account — to two SR diagrams (1408 on steel underframe, 1409 on timber underframe). For all practical purposes this was irrelevant; indeed the South Western did not bother to issue separate diagrams and it fell to the Southern's rolling stock clerks to sort them out — although several anomalies have been spotted amongst the vehicles. In real terms a timber-underframed van stood 1½in higher overall than the equivalent on a steel frame, but this would be of no concern to the traffic department, as internal cubic capacity was the same. Lift-link brake gear, with two brake blocks appear to have been standard for almost all vans while Shepherd's patent axle boxes were nigh-on universal fittings.

LSWR records show that there was just one van in stock on 31 December 1912, rising to 154 a year later. These were all on timber underframes — construction on steel did not commence until 1916 and the combined total had reached 803 vans by the Grouping. One van on a timber underframe was rebuilt as a covered grain hopper in 1920 — allocated SR Diagram 1411. No photograph is known, but the van (SR No 42473) was seen passing through Eastleigh in a Southampton Docks-bound goods train on 11 May 1933 — the observer noting that it was equipped with one sliding panel in the roof. What was not so obvious was the hopper bottom unloading facility.

Right:

Plate 38 The timber-underframed high-roof van — SR Diagram 1409 — is represented by No 42800 (ex-LSWR No 4232, built in 1913), seen at Renfrew on 8 September 1946, carrying SR post-1936 lettering. There were very few differences amongst the 606 vans to this diagram; probably the only one of note was the change from 8½in to 6½in planking during World War One. Van 42800 has, on close inspection, one door with the narrower planking (perhaps a complete replacement) but is otherwise sheeted entirely from 8½in timbers. Only one modification from the original design is evident — namely the overhanging roof at the eaves — when built this would have been flush with the side framing (compare with **Plate 39**). This van survived until 1952. *A. G. Ellis*

Centre right:

Plate 39 The steel-underframed version appeared in 1916, never being as numerous as the timber-framed vans. LSWR No 5432 illustrates the standard pre-Grouping livery as well as the original flush eaves/side framing detail. The later SR number was 42914 and the van remained in service until January 1958. From a study of photographs, it appears that all these were planked with 6½in timbers. *J. Tatchell Collection*

Below right:

Plate 40 SR pre-1936 livery is carried by Diagram 1408 van No 44366 — one of 100 ordered by the Southern Railway in 1923/4, under order E3, SR numbers being 44326-44425. Note the fabricated buffer casings, which were peculiar to this batch and the previous lot of 100, completed earlier in 1923. These may have been supplied by the Leeds Forge Company and manufactured from pressed steel components, along with the underframe. Also unusual are the disc wheels — a rare fitting on LSWR wagons. This van ran from March 1924 until 1957. As usual, a Diagram 1408 van from this batch (SR No 44377) was included in the Ashford 1948 series and, apart from the provision of 8-open spoke wheels, was identical to that illustrated. Being of more recent construction, 385 out of the original stock of 396 vans remained in traffic at Nationalisation (compared with 485 to Diagram 1409); by 1961 these totals had reduced to just 9 and 5 respectively. *Edwards Bros*

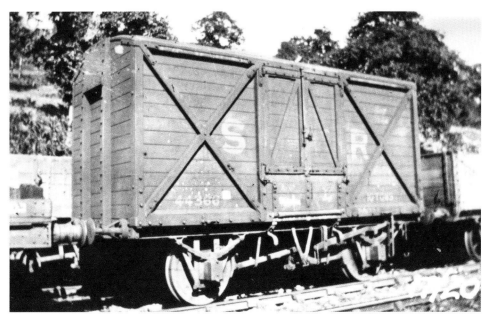

Right:

Plate 41 A Diagram 1408 van in internal use by the Operating Department — at Barnstaple Victoria Road (ex-GWR) station and clearly repainted in BR grey livery, the repaint date of 8/3/61 being legible on the solebar. The white 'X' further indicates that the van was restricted to yard use only. Number 081093 was formerly SR No 42266 and previously LSWR No 680. It was one of at least three vans at this location and served there from March 1959 until well after the station closed to passengers in the following year — quite possibly until complete closure in 1970. This view dates from August 1962. Note that a new number plate has been affixed at the left-hand end of the crib rail, although the former LSWR wagon plate still remains in place to the right of the brake rack. *A. E. West*

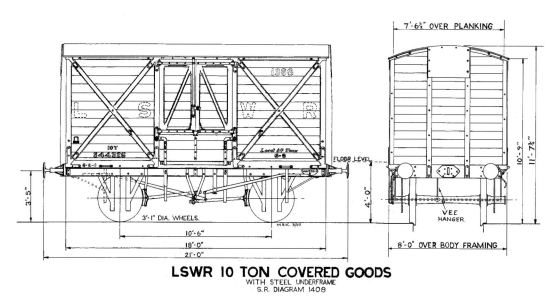

LSWR 10 TON COVERED GOODS
WITH STEEL UNDERFRAME
S.R. DIAGRAM 1408

Figure 8 A drawing of the steel underframed high-roof van to Diagram 1408. This shows details for the SR-built vans of 1923/4 and is based on a 1950s photograph of the first vehicle on SR order E3, completed in December 1923.

Some examples of numbering are as follows:

Diagram 1408 (on steel u/frame)			Diagram 1409 (on timber u/frame)		
LSWR No	**SR No**	**Date Wdn**	**LSWR No**	**SR No**	**Date Wdn**
205	42235	1957	794	42273*	1955
3511	42730	183s, 9/44	1667	42484	1953
4608	42842	081303, 7/61	6947	43176	01011s c5/47
5763	42980	c1960	10299	43848	080602, 1/56
8711	43348	081181, 1/60	15024	44243	1956

* This van was renumbered at Exmouth Junction carriage and wagon repair shops, September 1930. A small number of vehicles were renumbered here and at other outstations in the 1928-33 period, including New Cross Gate and Streatham Hill, as well as at Ashford, Lancing or Brighton Works.

Right:

Plate 42 Between 1913 and 1915 a batch of 100 insulated vans were built for banana traffic; later SR Diagram 1463. Possibly the banana traffic failed to develop under wartime conditions as 50 were sold to the War Department as soon as April 1915, when the vans were still quite new. Only 49 were returned to LSWR ownership in 1921/2 and these had lost their insulation during their war service — and this was never reinstated. All 99 vans continued to be used for either banana or meat traffic until the construction of new vans during the 1930s relegated many (particularly the non-insulated vans) to ordinary covered goods wagon status. However, it is unclear whether any distinction was made between the insulated and non-insulated vans or whether the latter were always painted standard brown instead of stone buff colour. By 1938 a number had definitely been repainted brown to reflect their ordinary status, while the loss of banana traffic during the Second World War resulted in many being withdrawn, such that only 29 remained in traffic by September 1946. The War Department acquired several yet again, as illustrated by WD 47265, seen at Arncott, at the

southern end of the Bicester Army Depot system on 3 April 1960. The former sliding shutters and end ventilators have been removed and sheeted in, the vacuum brake gear has been stripped and three-link couplings have been fitted. The livery is probably khaki green. All these vans were charged to renewal account, so LSWR numbers cannot be easily quoted. Examples are 1444, 3061, 4626, 9200, 10009 and 15147. Using Frank Foote's classification, this would be an 'XWX'-framed van. *D. J. Wigley*

Table 2
Summary of high-roof van diagrams

SR Diagram	Capacity (Tons)	Under-frame	Wheel base	Pass/goods rated	Brakes	Doors	Ventilators			Designated traffic
							Side	End	Roof	
1406	10	Steel	10ft 6in	Goods	Hand	Sliding	none	1	none	General goods
1407	10	Timber	10ft 6in	Goods	Hand	Sliding	none	1	none	General goods
1408	10	Steel	10ft 6in	Goods	Hand	3-part	none	1	none	General goods
1409	10	Timber	10ft 6in	Goods	Hand	3-part	none	1	none	General goods
1411	10	Timber	10ft 6in	Goods	Hand	3-part	none	1	none	Grain Hopper *See note 1*
1463	10	Timber	11ft	Passenger	AVB	2 (hinged)	End shutters only			Banana/Insulated

Note 1. Converted from Diagram 1409 in 1920. Sliding roof hatch and hopper bottom fitted.
One van only (SR No. 42473) which remained in service until 1949.

Refrigerator & insulated vans

All 400 of these were completed and charged to capital account between 1893 and 1912, so their numbering details could be quoted in full on page 43 of *Volume One*. Little more may be added here, save for some post-1948 withdrawal dates, which will assist BR-period modellers, as follows:

SR Diagram	No. in stock 1/1/48	Sample Numbers/Withdrawal Dates (in brackets)
1461	2	50089 (1950-see **Plate 46**), 50069 (1952).
1464 (ex-1461)	15	50044/58/85 (1951), 50069 (1952), 50066/79 (1953), 50088 (1954).
1462	151	50175 (1955), 50098, 50163, 50238 (1956), 50130/46/78, 50268, 50313/69/94 (1957).
1465 (ex-1462)	56	50166 (1955), 50344/66 (1957).

By the January 1961 census, just five refrigerator vans to Diagram 1462 and one insulated van to Diagram 1465 remained in stock, although the numbers of these late survivors are not known.

The liveries carried by these vans are perhaps their most unusual feature and worth further discussion. The earlier batches carried standard LSWR wagon brown, but from about 1907 a much paler colour was substituted. This was originally thought to be salmon pink, identical to that used on the upper panels of the carriage stock, however the late Frank Foote made a number of colour-wash drawings of LSWR stock between 1912 and 1918, these now being in the author's possession. Whilst only boyhood sketches, they are remarkable for their detail and are, of course, a contemporary source. One of these shows a refrigerator van from the 1893 batch, complete with black-painted locking bar across the doors, but finished not in coach salmon, but in a rather deeper pink colour and lettered in black — mirroring exactly the style shown on Edwards Brothers drawing No 17/17, dating from the 1930s. The LSWR Livery Register (see Bibliography) calls this colour 'shrimp pink' and this, to the author, describes Frank Foote's drawing admirably. The solebars are recorded as brown and this layout has been reproduced on **Figure 9**. Subsequently the lettering layout seems to have changed slightly (as **Plate 44**) and Venetian red was used, quite possibly with salmon or shrimp pink as the base colour. Frank goes on to record more refrigerator vans in 'pink' (no less than six being seen at Weybridge in December 1921), complete with lettering in 'dark red/brown', yet by July 1930 he records the vans in 'pink stone, lettered dark red', perhaps to indicate the change of colour to that used in SR days — described officially as light stone or buff.

In early British Railways days a small number of vans were at first painted white with black lettering, before the more practical colour of bauxite red was adopted. At least three feature in the 1948 Ashford series and two will be reproduced here. It is also now thought that the SR meat van illustrated in **Plate 90** of *Volume Four* is painted white with black lettering rather than as captioned in stone with red lettering.

Left:
Plate 43 A view taken at Southampton Docks about 1907/8, showing chilled Argentinian beef carcasses being loaded into Diagram 1461 refrigerator vans, LSWR Nos 12606/34 (later SR Nos 50054/81 part of the 1900 orders for 50 vans). These vans retain their original brown livery with white lettering. Note the display board being used to advertise the product and the thickness of the doors — necessary to provide the required levels of insulation. This photograph was originally published in the *Railway Magazine* during 1909.
H. V. Tumilty Collection

Figure 9 A drawing of the Diagram 1461 vans of 1893, LSWR Nos 9422-41, showing a variation in lettering style as portrayed by Frank Foote and by Edwards Brothers drawings, in black on pink base colour. For further explanation, see paragraph above.

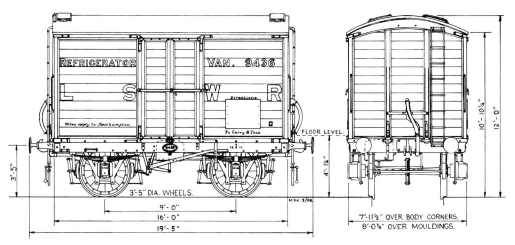

LSWR 8 TON REFRIGERATOR VAN
1893 DESIGN.   S.R. DIAGRAM 1461.
NOTE: GENERAL ARRANGEMENT DRAWING SHOWS 12 X 6½"
SIDE PLANKS & "SKEW" BRAKE RIGGING. PHOTOGRAPHS
SHOW VEHICLES WITH EITHER PLANKING BUT BRAKE GEAR
AS DRAWN.

Right:
Plate 44 One of the 1893 vans, LSWR No 9436 (later SR No 50013), dated May 1921 but at an unknown location (perhaps not even on the LSWR). This clearly carries Venetian red lettering. Apart from the three 1893 vans lost to the War Department, withdrawal of the rest of the batch commenced soon after the Grouping and all except SR Nos 50011/16 had gone by 1932. Just visible to the left is Diagram 1462 van LSWR 13636 (SR 50151) while to the right is a South Western 24ft passenger luggage van. *G. P. Keen*

Below:
Plate 45 One of a pair of rather interesting photographs in the author's possession, taken inside Eastleigh Carriage & Wagon Works in (probably) September 1918. The other view (not reproduced) was taken at 90 degrees to this and shows a blackboard that reads 'In aid of St Dunstan Hostel for blinded soldiers. This collection will be disposed of on Sat Sun, all proceeds devoted to the above need'. The fruit and vegetables have come, almost certainly, from the staff allotments and are mounted on a makeshift bench that, on closer inspection turns out to be the Fox pressed steel underframe from a type 8 open goods wagon — note that the side brackets incorporate a rebate to receive the crib rail. Behind is Diagram 1461 refrigerator van No 12615 (later SR No 50063) in pink/Venetian red livery while to the left is the veranda end of Diagram 1541 brake van 5680 (SR 54641). An interesting social comment and typical of the extra-curricular activities once commonplace throughout the railway industry. *A. R. Sedgwick Collection*

Left:
Plate 46 One of the Ashford 1948 official photographs showing Diagram 1461 van No 50089 (ex-LSWR No 12642 of 1901) — one of just two survivors to the diagram at Nationalisation, finished in white with black fittings and lettering. It would last just two more years and the final survivor (SR No 50069) would outlast it by a further two years. *BR Official*

33

Above:
Plate 47 The other refrigerator van diagram, No 1462, was represented in the Ashford 1948 series by van 50175, carrying an identical livery to No 50089, however the equivalent Diagram 1465 insulated van (with iceboxes and ladders removed) is illustrated by SR No 50234 (ex-LSWR No 13720 of 1907). Perhaps surprisingly, both types are identically lettered whereas in SR days they would have been labelled Refrigerator or Insulated van, depending on diagram. This van remained in service until 1954. *BR Official*

Above:
Plate 48 A somewhat more typical livery of dirty BR bauxite or possibly wartime red oxide with rather simpler white lettering is carried by Diagram 1465 van No 50285 (ex-LSWR No 13796), seen just prior to withdrawal at Redhill on 12 May 1951. *D. Cullum*

Livestock vehicles

Below:
Plate 49 A view taken at Ashford (Kent) on 18 September 1924, showing a Charing Cross-Dover passenger train, hauled by ex-SER 'F' class 4-4-0 No 22 passing the market sidings, where 'C' class 0-6-0 No 243 is shunting cattle wagons. All stock visible retains pre-Grouping livery. The leading cattle wagon, LSWR No 7479, was to SR Diagram 1506 and would become SR No 52145 in September 1929, running until July 1937. The second vehicle is of SECR origin, to Diagram 1518 — one of 100 completed by the Bristol Wagon & Carriage Company in 1912. *F. J. Agar*

Above:

Plate 50 The same location, but a year or two later — and from comparison of the train formation plus the position of the shadows, quite likely the same working. The first effects of the Grouping are becoming apparent as the train is hauled by ex-LSWR 'L12' 4-4-0 No 422, recently transferred to the SE Section and the train includes both SECR and LSWR stock. About 20 cattle wagons from all three SR constituent companies are visible in the market sidings, including (from right to left) LSWR Diagram 1506 wagon No 15110 (one of the SDJR batch, allocated SR No 52311 but withdrawn in October 1926 — thereby dating the picture to Summer 1925 or 1926), then an LBSCR vehicle to Diagram 1527, an LSWR example to Diagram 1503 (SR No 517XX), LSWR high-roof vehicle to Diagram 1501/2, followed by others of LSWR, LBSCR and SECR origin. As noted in *Volume Three*, the weekly Ashford Market was an important source of traffic for both the SECR and the Southern Railway. *F. J. Agar*

Above:

Plate 51 Between 1896 and 1910, a total of 150 passenger-rated 8-ton low-roof cattle wagons were put into traffic. One of the original 1896 batch, LSWR No 10450 (later SR No 51765) is seen at Eastleigh around 1910 — before the wagon number and other lettering was transferred to the end panels — although the company initials always remained on the side planking. These alone were charged to capital account and LSWR numbers for them were 10439-88, the 47 survivors taking SR numbers 51754-76/8-51801 after the Grouping, being allocated to SR Diagram 1503. However, such was the rate of withdrawal that only wagons 51773 and 51800 remained in traffic by 1935. All wagons to the diagram had an 11ft wheelbase with 3ft 5in diameter Mansell wheels; the 1896 batch being fully vacuum fitted, however 15 others had a through Westinghouse pipe in addition. The later examples were charged to renewal account and so took the widely scattered numbers of the vehicles they replaced and most of these had vacuum pipes only. These later wagons featured a slightly updated bodywork design, as depicted in **Figure 10**, while the originals had bodywork as shown in **Figure 24** of *Volume One*. *M. H. Walshaw Collection*

Above:

Plate 52 By far the most common LSWR cattle wagon design was allocated to SR Diagram 1506 — a 10-ton goods-rated vehicle with (usually) vacuum pipes only. Around 450 were built (including a handful rated at only 8 tons, with second hand wheelsets) between 1892 and 1910 and these exhibited the two bodywork variations as seen on Diagram 1503, but coupled with a 10ft 6in wheelbase and 3ft 1in diameter spoke wheels. SR No 51915, photographed from several angles in October 1934 (a ¾ view appears in *Volume One*, along with historical details) is typical of those built from 1892 until circa 1903, when the bodywork style altered. This particularly clear broadside will be of use to modellers. Originally built with hand brakes only, the wagon was equipped with a through vacuum pipe after October 1899, when it became LSWR policy to provide these on all cattle wagons. *SR Official*

Prior to the general instruction to equip all LSWR cattle wagons with vacuum pipes, a small number were fully vacuum fitted to enable them to run in passenger trains, when an urgent need to ship cattle arose and no suitable goods train service was available. LSWR instruction No 271, dated 10 December 1894, gives the following information (right):

All these wagons were of Diagram 1506 type as depicted in **Plate 80** of *Volume One*. Some had been replaced by high-roof wagons to Diagrams 1501 or 1502 before 1923. It is not known how the 'Return To' instruction was applied to the wagons, nor is it known for how long these allocations were maintained. It does give some idea of the locations used to dealing with cattle traffic in the last years of the 19th Century. Once more fully fitted cattle wagons were built, from 1895 onwards it may not have been so necessary to specifically allocate vehicles to certain locations.

Instructions to all concerned as to the use of Vacuum-Fitted Cattle Trucks.

A limited number of new cattle trucks have been fitted with the automatic vacuum brake apparatus and screw couplings, suitable for running in passenger trains. When empty, the wagons must be returned by goods train to the respective depots to which they have been allotted, according to the following list:

Station	Number Fitted	Painted Numbers of the Wagons
Reading	2	3907, 3910
Woking	2	3894, 5792
Guildford	1	3897
Eastleigh	6	1503, 2535, 2568, 2805, 3908, 5802
Southampton	2	2809, 6300
Wareham	2	1955, 2823
Dorchester	2	1959, 2815
Andover Jct	2	3876, 3909
Salisbury	2	4893, 5805
Yeovil Jct	2	2782, 2816
Exeter	4	1492, 2544, 2797, 2812
Okehampton	2	1964, 3893
Launceston	4	1521, 3883, 5798, 5812
Barnstaple	2	3886, 3889

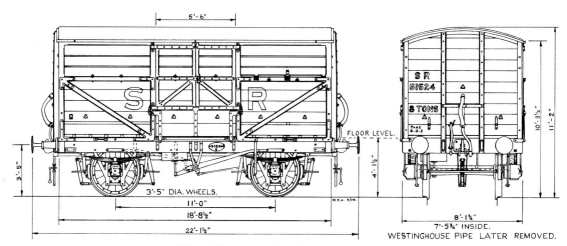

LSWR 8 TON LARGE CATTLE WAGON
S. R. DIAGRAM 1503.
BODYWORK STYLE USED FROM 1904-10.

Figure 10 A drawing showing the later style of cattle wagon bodywork to Diagram 1503 and 1506, typical of the final survivors to the diagrams. These were:

Diagram 1503	Withdrawn	Diagram 1506	Withdrawn
No 51515	1953	No 51918	1951
No 51588	1955	No 52131	1956
No 51613	1956	No 52342	1956

The only other Diagram 1506 survivor at Nationalisation was No 52163, illustrated in **Plate 84** of *Volume One*.

From 1911, Surrey Warner introduced the higher roof profile and all the subsequent 250 additions to LSWR stock were of this design, construction ceasing in mid-1923. The majority were charged to renewal account, so numbering is not consecutive. With but one exception, all had lift-link brakes and vacuum pipes, however LSWR No 5802 (later SR No 51595 to Diagram 1501) alone had full vacuum brake gear and was possibly the prototype high-roof vehicle of 1911. It should, however, be noted that this was a direct replacement for one of the Diagram 1506 vacuum-fitted wagons listed above in notice No 271 of 1894, so this could also have been the reason for the provision.

Two SR diagrams were eventually allocated — 1501 and 1502. The former were originally reserved for military horse traffic and 135 examples were built between 1911 and 1913, while the latter numbered 115 examples, dating from 1914 until 1919, with a final batch of 25 being on order at the Grouping. Apart from minor planking and underframe details, both diagrams appear identical, as do general arrangement drawings numbers E1993 and E2360 respectively. However, the SR registers state that Diagram 1502 vehicles were 2in higher at eaves level than Diagram 1501, so presumably a change of construction facilitated this improvement, although this is not apparent in photographs. After 1923 it seems that no distinction on usage was maintained and both types were used indiscriminately for all livestock traffic.

To illustrate the rapid demise of this class of vehicle, it is worth recording that, out of a total of 843 ordinary LSWR cattle wagons inherited by the Southern, 295 had been withdrawn before being renumbered or repainted in SR livery and a further 240 had been scrapped by 1931. The total had therefore reduced by some 63% inside eight years. By no means all of the withdrawals were the older stock either — some wagons to Diagrams 1501/2 had been dispatched to the breakers by this time, despite many being less than 15 years old.

Right:
Plate 53 The only LSWR cattle wagon to feature in the Ashford 1948 series was Diagram 1502 vehicle No 51745 (ex-LSWR No 9183, built in 1919). This was typical of the 28 survivors at Nationalisation; with lift-link brakes, vacuum pipe, long springs and Mansell wheels and this example ran until 1954. Perhaps predictably, many of the final batch completed in 1923 (SR Nos 51846-70) lasted until near the end, the final survivors being SR numbers 51657 and 51849, both being withdrawn in 1957. The last Diagram 1501 survivors were Nos 51682 (see *Volume One*, **Plate 86**) and 51706, withdrawn in 1955. *BR Official*

Below right:
Plate 54 Photographs of the special cattle vans remain elusive and this view of Diagram 1040 van LSWR No 12464 is the only clear one known to the author. It was taken at Exeter Queen Street around 1924 and shows the vehicle as rebuilt in 1906 with drover's compartment but still retaining Panter's cross-lever brakes — the hand lever just being visible at the left-hand end. **Figure 26** in *Volume One* shows the same vehicle as later modified with a normal lever brake handle. Once the Southern Railway had taken delivery of 50 modern special cattle vans in 1930, the earlier pre-Grouping vans were fairly quickly withdrawn and this was the final survivor to the diagram — as SR No 3651 it ran until February 1939, being outlasted by just two later LSWR vans to SR Diagram 1043 (Nos. 3676/77). Despite lasting until 1949, only one very poor photograph of this diagram is known, taken at Axminster about 1935. Drawings of the various special cattle vans, in original and rebuilt form, appear in *LSWR Carriages Volume Four*. *G. P. Keen*

Goods brake vans

LSWR goods brake vans completed from 1886 onwards are well documented, as production of the familiar vans later allocated to SR Diagram 1541 commenced at this time. However, the 10 or so years prior to the appointment of William Panter as Carriage & Wagon Superintendent are marked by either a lack, or conflicting evidence, of what was actually built. Taking the LSWR minutes of the period, the following are recorded:

Order Date	Ordered From	Possible Nos	Remarks
Nov 1875	Brown Marshalls (20 vans)*	5676-5695	As *LSWR Carriages Vol 4*, Figure 1.35
Dec 1875	Brown Marshalls (20 vans)*	5696-5715	As above
Aug 1878	Brown Marshalls (17 vans)	6320-6336	As *LSWR Carriages Vol 4*, Figure 1.36
Jan 1880	Craven Bros (20 vans)	Not known	Order possibly cancelled
Nov 1881	Metropolitan (20 vans)	6978-6997	As *LSWR Carriages Vol 4*, Figure 1.37
Nov 1884	Nine Elms (20 vans)	7769-7788	As above

*It is possible that this was only one order for 20 vans, perhaps duplicated in the minutes.

Numbering details are not confirmed by the minutes. Most of the numbers listed were re-used by newer brake vans prior to the Grouping.

Photographic evidence shows identifiable examples from the 7769-88 batch (See *Volume One*, **Plate 89**) but nothing positive from the others. However, certain other designs appear in photographs but whether these were vans built on renewal account (and not so fully recorded by the minutes) or were rebuilds/modifications of the known designs is uncertain. The January 1880 order to Cravens do not appear in later records and may have been replaced by 17 vehicles built in the same year at Nine Elms and illustrated in **Plate 56**.

Below:

Plate 55 A 'down' LSWR goods train leaves Swaythling behind Drummond 'Black Motor' No 687, *circa* 1902. The leading brake van is similar, but not identical, to No 7783 illustrated in **Plate 89** of *Volume One* — the main differences being the lack of a lantern lookout and single, instead of double diagonal body framing, although the general appearance is otherwise the same. Just whether this points to the 1881 vehicles or a rebuild is unclear, however it is known that van 7774 was damaged by fire in 1899 and repairs cost £36. At this time a new brake van cost around £150, so the rebuilding was fairly extensive. Could we be looking at this rebuild — although we will probably never know for sure? No 7774 (ciphered as 07774) became a stores van for the Chief Mechanical Engineer in 1912, renumbered as departmental No 108s. This became SR departmental No 0103s in 1923, lasting until March 1932 and included on SR Diagram 1405. We will discuss this diagram again shortly. The third vehicle in the train is a Diagram 1483 meat van — identifiable by the louvres and double diagonal ('X'-type) framing. There then follows 11 private-owner coal wagons (remember the LSWR never built any mineral wagons), while the rear brake van is to Diagram 1541. The use of a brake van at front and rear of the train was commonplace before the adoption of heavier vans from 1906 onwards. *E. Pouteau*

Right:

Plate 56 We now come to a minor mystery. The 20 vans ordered from Cravens in January 1880 cannot be traced subsequently, however 17 vehicles of an altogether different design, LSWR numbers 6523-39, are known as several became stores vans for the CME's department after 1908 and appear in the SR service stock register, where they are recorded as having been built at Nine Elms in 1880, quoted body dimensions being 18ft 6in long by 7ft 9½in wide. LSWR departmental No 94s (formerly goods brake No 06535) was one of these, seen at Eastleigh Works in April 1922. It later became SR departmental No 089s and survived until March 1932. The reader's attention is now drawn to **Plate 90** of *Volume One*, where it was suggested that the Adams van at Bodmin was LSWR No 6533. From the evidence presented here, this now seems unlikely, but the true identity of the Bodmin van remains unknown. Could it be one of the 1881 Metropolitan batch, with the lookout removed? Or was this batch built without lantern lookouts, having instead the small lozenge-shaped side window? *H. C. Casserley*

The Nine Elms 1880 vans are clearly the precursors of Diagram 1541, but here again the plot thickens, as what appears in **Plate 56** mirrors exactly SR Diagram 1405 (and its LSWR counterpart), yet the four wagon numbers listed against that diagram are from the sliding door/lantern lookout fitted vans within the 7769-88 batch. LSWR No 94s is not unique either, as the author has a sepia photograph showing SR No 090s (ex-LSWR No 95s and previously brake van 06539) and it is identical. This is in full SR livery and endorsed 'For the use of Mechanical Engineer's Department only'.

From 1886 production of the standard Panter 'road' vans, later SR Diagram 1541 began and from here onwards we are on much safer ground. Almost 500 were completed between then and 1905, making these, by a very considerable margin, the most numerous LSWR goods brake van. They were, for that matter, the most numerous SR goods brake van at the Grouping as well. Just over half were charged to capital account, therefore their running numbers are easily summarised, as follows:

Date Authorised	No	Date Built	LSWR Nos	Survivors to SR Nos
June 1887	12	1887	8170-8181	54687-54697
Nov 1887	20	1888	8382-8401	54698-54710
May 1891	20	1891/2	9036-9055	54711-54725
April 1892	12*	1892	9340-9351	54726-54736
1894	20	1894#	9942-9961	54737-54753, 55121
June 1894	50	1894/5	10082-10131	54754-54799
1897/8	50	1897/8	11061-11110	54800-54849
1898	25	1898/9	11176-11200	54850-54874
1899/1900	50**	1899/1900	12414-12463	54875-54924

* Includes two vans to Diagram 1548 (LSWR Nos 9350/1, SR Nos 54735/6) for bonded traffic to and from Southampton Docks and drawn as **Figure 28** in V*olume One*.
\# LSWR No 9944 was destroyed in an accident and a replacement was built in 1902.
** Includes six vacuum fitted vans (LSWR Nos 12424-9/SR Nos 54885-90).

In addition to these at least 220 more were charged to renewal account, the survivors being allocated SR numbers 54501-54686, duplicate 55122 and 54925-44, this last 20 being the final construction and all except one was later uprated to 15 tons tare.

Needless to say, the picture is much more complicated, construction and running numbers being extremely fragmented, so examples only are given below.

Date Built	LSWR No	SR No	Date Withdrawn	Date Built	LSWR No	SR No	Date Withdrawn
1886	4756	54602	4/25	1896	2082	54528	11/40
1887	3918	54566	10/33	1897	11	54501	8/29
1888	118	54520	7/41	1899	5692	54650	6/37
1889	3336	54557	3/30	1902	674	54925	1956
1892	18	54502	5/30	1904	6532	54939	To IOW 2/38 as No 56056

Right:

Plate 57 An early example to Diagram 1541, already in LSWR departmental service by 1910. Built in 1886 (note the very short springs, although this could be a later modification) it had become a breakdown van at Nine Elms by 1905, LSWR No 77S. Most South Western running sheds possessed one of these conversions, LSWR numbers 71s-87s being noted in the registers, although several had been replaced by other conversions before 1923. By the date of the photograph, the van had been reallocated 'For use of the Mechanical Engineer's Dept, Race Tools Only', continuing in this role until August 1935, by then specifically for Ascot race meetings and renumbered as SR 050s. Ascot station would become a hive of activity on race days, with many engines requiring turning and servicing after having arrived with the various special trains and presumably this van catered for any spares/equipment required on these days, being returned to Nine Elms after the meeting was over. The livery — at a guess, red oxide. *N. Pomfret Collection*

Below:

Plate 58 A magnificent quartet of Diagram 1541 vans outside Southampton Town station in June 1920. Thoughtfully parked in ascending numerical order, their details are, from right to left:

LSWR No	SR No	Date Built	Date Renumbered	With-drawn	Notes
4301	54600	1895	2/29	5/30	Renumbered at New Cross Gate
5193	54620	1897	12/28	10/29	
10126	54794	1895	To Isle of Wight as No 56044 in 11/25, withdrawn 1956		
11064	54803	1897	Not renumbered	3/32	One of last to retain LSWR livery

All were rated at 10 tons tare and all have 8½in side planking with LSWR fixed side lamps (painted red — confirmed by Frank Foote's boyhood colour wash drawings) as carried between 1901 and 1925. Goods brake vans tended to accumulate at certain points and in SR days many were (theoretically) allocated to specific duties to try to avoid them wandering about. However, to quote the late R. W. Kidner 'it was never long before a van labelled "To work between Hither Green and Dartford" would turn up at Exeter!'
R. K. Blencowe Collection

Right:

Plate 59 Photographed at Longmoor Downs on 3 September 1949, WD No 13140 was formerly 15-ton van SR 54936/LSWR 6524; one of the last completed in 1904. This is one of at least seven sold to the Longmoor Military Railway between 1936 and 1943, two of which were still in stock when the line closed in 1969 (one being vacuum-fitted No 54885, now preserved at Washford). WD 13140 was one of 20 uprated to 15 tons during 1922-4 and in theory allocated SR numbers between 54925-44, however No 54927 was never done, its place being taken by LSWR 12423/SR 54884 — in fact dealt with as the prototype in September 1922. The conversion work included provision of weight pockets in the underframe, filled with scrap metal, and sanding apparatus (both now removed from this van). With the exception of No 54884, all the others selected came from the newest vans completed in 1902-4 and, perhaps not surprisingly, quite a few lasted until the early 1950s. *D. Cullum*

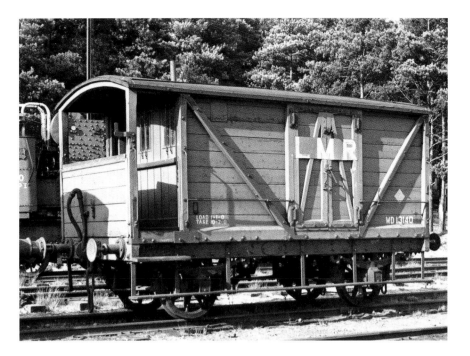

Above:

Plate 60 A 'local use' van, SR No 54535 at Petersfield on 26 May 1947, branded 'To work between Petersfield & Buriton Siding only'. This siding (actually three) was situated on the 'up' side of the line just north of Buriton Tunnel and served a chalk quarry owned in the 1930s by the Portland Cement Company. It was typical of many remote private sidings served by a local trip from the nearest yard. The van was formerly LSWR No 2189 of 1895 vintage and was allocated to this duty from November 1946 until withdrawn in 1955, although just how many trips it made during that period is questionable. Clearly this had not been its only local allocation, since the former position of another allocation board may be seen above the company initials. Note the 6½in side planking — a resheeting job that, on closer inspection, did not include the veranda end 'gate' — which retains 8½in timbers. Whether the ends have been similarly replanked cannot be stated. *The Lens of Sutton Association*

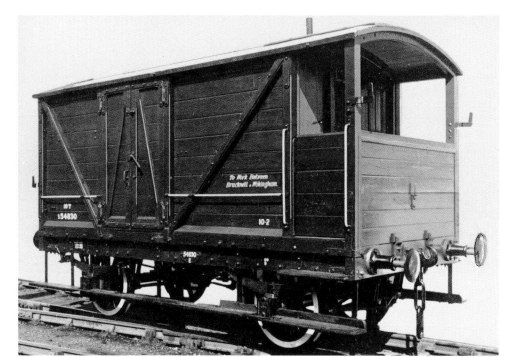

Left:
Plate 61 The Ashford 1948 series of official photographs included just one Diagram 1541 van — SR 54830/LSWR 11091, branded 'To work between Bracknell & Wokingham' — on which duty it ended its days, also in 1955. This has 8½in side planking but the veranda end has 6½in timbers and is clearly picked out in Venetian red. Note that the buffer housings are black and the fact that the van still looks brand new, despite being more than 50 years old! On page 7 of *Volume One*, it was stated that some brake vans carried buff coloured inner veranda ends in LSWR days. Photographs dated 1913 and 1920, as well as a sketch of van No 5294, completed by Frank Foote in July 1922, now confirm this.
BR Official

Above:
Plate 62 Three early transfers away from ex-LSWR lines went to the Canterbury and Whitstable branch in 1928. This was the oldest portion of the Southern Railway system, opening as an independent company as early as 1830. Clearances in Tyler Hill Tunnel, north of Canterbury, were restricted to just 11ft and this precluded many covered goods wagons from traversing the line. Six ex-SER goods brake vans were cut down for use on the branch in 1922 and were described in *Volume Three*, but these were replaced just six years later by Diagram 1541 15-ton vans 54940/1/4, similarly cut down at Eastleigh in January-March 1928 and reallocated to Diagram 1550. This diagram number also applied to one batch of SR bogie brake vans built in 1936 and was a rare example of a clerical error somewhere in the rolling stock office and almost the only occasion when the same diagram number was issued to two different vehicles at the same time. SR No 54944 is seen in the company of cut-down 'R1' class 0-6-0T No 1010 at Canterbury West on 16 March 1940. The sand pipes as fitted to all 15-ton vans may just be seen, but what is not visible is the fact that through vacuum pipes and screw couplings were provided some time during the early 1930s. The allocation board reads 'Whitstable Harbour Branch'.
V. R. Webster, Cty Kidderminster Railway Museum

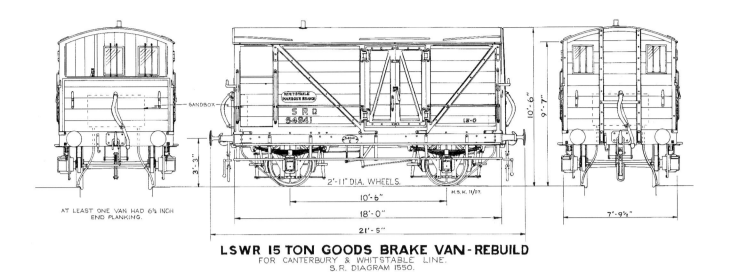

LSWR 15 TON GOODS BRAKE VAN - REBUILD
FOR CANTERBURY & WHITSTABLE LINE.
S.R. DIAGRAM 1550.

Figure 11 The Canterbury & Whitstable branch brake van conversion — SR Diagram 1550. This depicts one of the two vans to survive on the branch until 1948; number 54941. Just whether the third conversion (No. 54940) was reallocated elsewhere before scrapping in 1947 is not known.

Below:
Plate 63 A former Midland & South Western Junction Railway brake van, now GWR departmental No 1780, at Plymouth Laira in 1956 — where it had served since withdrawal from ordinary traffic in April 1936. It clearly shows its LSWR parentage, although like the open wagons described earlier the South Western appears to have played no part in the construction process. Twelve vans were built for the MSWJR in 1900/1 by outside contractors, as follows:

MSWJR Nos	Built by	GWR Nos	Planking
12-17	Oldbury, 1900	12007/20/8, 17853/938/66	8½in
18-23	Midland RCW Co, 1901	56783-8	6½in

All remained allocated to the Junction Railway section until at least 1931, when withdrawals started, so the vans would have been a regular sight at Andover Junction and possibly on through workings as far as Eastleigh or Southampton, if not elsewhere on the Southern. No 1780 was formerly MSWJR No 23 and was the last in traffic — and also by a very large margin the last in existence. Apart from the addition of a central pillar in the veranda end, they were originally almost a carbon copy of Diagram 1541. The two additional end uprights and the planking in of the side doors are both GWR modifications applied during the 1920s. Although not visible in this picture, the letters 'M&SWJR Co' are incised into the curb rail at the left-hand end. *The Lens of Sutton Association*

As the weight of goods trains increased, heavier brake vans became essential on main line services or over steeply graded lines, in order to avoid the provision of two vans and two guards per train. After 1905 all LSWR construction was of, progressively, 17, 18, 20, 24 or 25 tons tare — the first examples being, in effect, a stretched version of Diagram 1541.

Above:
Plate 64 The four vans to SR Diagram 1542 appeared in 1906 for the 'Tavy' and other principal West of England-London goods services. By the 1930s these too had been relegated to branch line or local use, in which guise SR No 54947 (ex-LSWR No 7786 — a replacement for an 1884 van) is seen at Axminster on 6 August 1955, by then lettered 'Not in common use'. Its usual sphere of operation was then the Exeter-Exmouth-Sidmouth/Seaton and Lyme Regis branches. The livery was recorded as 'dirty grey' and the van was withdrawn in the following year — the last mainland survivor to the diagram. Sister van 54946 (illustrated in **Plate 96** of *Volume One*) was withdrawn from the Lymington branch in 1954. *A. E. West*

Below:
Plate 65 Van No 54948 was sent to the Isle of Wight in October 1947, renumbered as 56058. There it was much used on ballasting work until 1966 — its larger size being useful for transporting staff and tools to the site of the work and was sometimes referred to as 'the one-ton van' on account of its load-carrying capacity, as recorded over the running number. It is seen at Cowes in August 1962 wearing faded BR grey livery with black numbering patches. *P. H. Swift*

By 1906 all that could be said of the LSWR goods brake van stock was that it was highly standardised, however there was an urgent need for something better and Surrey Warner's answer was to design a range of vans that were heavier and all had a veranda at both ends — moves that would undoubtedly be popular with the goods guards. In due course the overall length was also increased, resulting in a thoroughly modern design being produced after 1915, abandoning the traditional 'road van' concept of providing side doors to allow the carriage of small consignments and parcels to wayside stations.

Right:

Plate 66 Warner's first design appeared in 1907 and was later allocated to SR Diagram 1545. This still retained an 18ft timber underframe and side doors but the tare weight was increased to 20 tons. LSWR No 6529 became SR No 54964 in January 1924, lasting until 1946 — an early withdrawal for this diagram. This picture, although heavily retouched, shows the arrangement of LSWR lettering — a point not made clear in *Volume One*. On the other side, the company letters usually occupied the four panels across the double doors, with the number high up to the right of the lookout. On the underframe may be seen the overhaul date of 29-12-07 (in this case the original construction date), with the LSWR station code number 6 (for Eastleigh) above. Many LSWR stations were allocated a

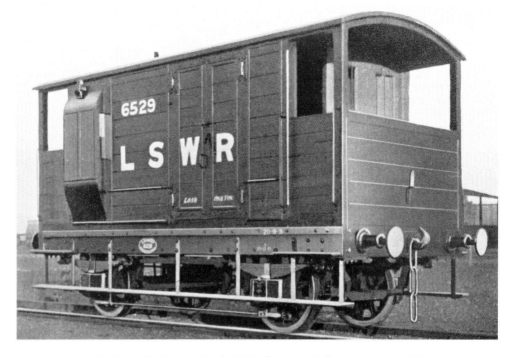

location code and these were applied to stock when examined, repaired or overhauled. The Southern Railway perpetuated the system, adding ex-LBSCR and SECR locations, while after Nationalisation all numbers were increased by 4000 (Eastleigh station therefore becoming 4006). After 1915 Eastleigh C & W Works had its own code number (15) and this would appear instead. Other known codes likely to be applied to wagons were 1 (Nine Elms), 13 (Exmouth Junction), 41 (Lancing Works), 42 (New Cross Gate), 76 (Ashford Works) and 99 (Stewarts Lane). *LSWR Official*

Below:

Plate 67 Another Diagram 1545 van, SR No 54956 (ex-LSWR No 4186) is seen at Norwood Junction on 17 April 1955, showing the opposite side and the plain appearance of the lookouts, dating from when the LSWR fixed side lamps were removed in 1925. Most of the 35 vans to the diagram survived Nationalisation, general withdrawal commencing about 1956 and none remained by the time of the 1961 survey. Goods brake vans tended not to wander far from their railway of origin, yet the author has a photograph of van 54988 taken at Cardiff General in 1955! *D. Cullum*

Above:

Plate 68 The War Department adopted the Warner design as a standard in 1917/8, albeit reduced in width by 2in, resulting in the design carrying a number of different liveries in addition to LSWR and SR. This contractor-built van (note the builders plate on the solebar) was Metropolitan Railway No 28, purchased by the company in 1921, one of at least nine such vans (Nos 26-34) and was probably photographed soon after purchase. Most later had their side doors and lookouts removed and through planked, in which condition they passed to London Transport in 1933 and to the LNER in 1937. On the original print the letters 'MET' may just be seen across the doors (this and the number are repeated on the ends), while the former WD insignia is still visible, so the van probably retains its previous ROD grey livery. *D.B. Clayton copy negative*

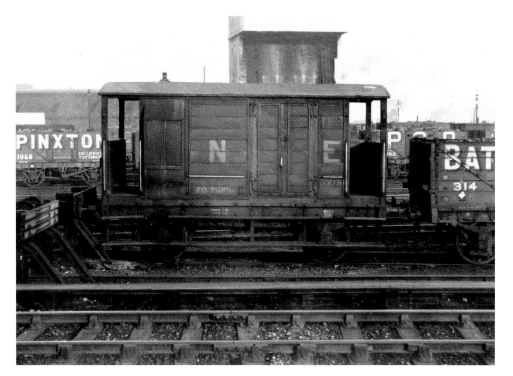

Left:

Plate 69 Some 155 vans went to the Great Eastern in 1922, to that company's Diagram 87, so came to the LNER virtually unmodified. LNER No 601770 was one of these, seen at Hornsey (GN) around 1935 and was formerly GER No 1770, built originally by Metropolitan C & W Co. Their GER numbers ran from 1750 to 1904, the LNER simply adding 600,000 to these. Most lasted well into BR days and the final survivors were condemned about 1959. *G. Hemingway*

Plate 70 The 20 vans purchased by the Southern in 1924, in lieu of 20 SECR 'dance hall' brakes are represented by No 55112, seen at Eastleigh on 6 August 1949, not long ex-works and finished in SR brown with Venetian red ends. SR Diagram 1549 was allocated to differentiate these from the genuine LSWR product, although both were barred from the Tonbridge-Hastings line by virtue of having side lookouts fitted — the narrower dimensions of the ex-WD vans making no difference to this restriction. Withdrawal of these began in 1956, with Nos 55101/2/14/6/7/9 and all had gone by the end of 1960. Most ended their days carrying BR light grey livery, No 55112 last being seen in this livery doing duty as a buffer stop at Beddington Lane engineer's yard, while 55109 ended its days as internal user No 080633 at Hythe, Hants, a rare departmental use for a goods brake van. *A. E. West*

Plate 71 Just 15 vans were built to Diagram 1544 in 1911, using 20ft long steel channel underframes and this was the last design to retain side doors for loading of small consignments. The same van as illustrated in **Plate 103** of *Volume One*, now SR No 54976, is seen at Blackwater (on the ex-SECR line from Redhill to Reading), showing the opposite side and BR unfitted grey livery. All ran until at least 1956, but again none remained in service by the January 1961 survey.
M. Rhodes

Left:
Plate 72 The same underframe was used for Warner's final LSWR brake van design, 75 of which were turned out between 1915 and 1921, all charged to renewal account and so carrying LSWR numbers scattered between 387 and 15208. Twenty-five more very similar vans were built on the underframes of the former china clay container wagons in 1922/3, bringing the total of Warner's 'new' vans to exactly 100. SR Diagrams 1543 and 1547 were allocated respectively. The former were first rated at 20 tons tare but almost all were later brought up to 24 or 25 tons with the aid of scrap metal loaded into pockets cast into the underframes. Latterly, as more modern SR 25 ton vans took over the heavier duties some, including SR No 55032, seen here at Brockenhurst in very pale grey livery in May 1953, reverted towards 20 tons. Withdrawal of these commenced in 1957 and such was the rate of withdrawal that only two (Nos. 55006/37) remained in traffic by 1961. No 55006 was last seen at Eastleigh in 1962, while 55037 was noted at Templecombe in 1961, being repaired at Eastleigh in 1962 and at Polegate in 1963. Despite its age, it was still getting around! *R. C. Riley*

Table 3

Some examples of numbering of 20-25 ton goods brake vans are as follows:

SR Diagram	Official Tare	LSWR No	SR No	Recorded Tare (1950s)	Remarks
1543	20 tons	10408	54987	20-0	Always 20 tons
1543	25 tons	1782	55010	22-10	Noted in 1948
1543	25 tons	3343	55025	21-2	See note 1
1543	25 tons	4699	55032	20-0	See **Plate 72**
1543	25 tons	5359	55040	22-13	
1543	25 tons	15208	55074	20-7	Noted in 1948
1544	20 tons	3566	54952	20-8	
1544	20 tons	5698	54961	19-17	Ashford 1948 photo
1545	20 tons	4759	54958	20-18	Ashford 1948 photo
1545	20 tons	6996	54985	19-13	See note 2
1547	25 tons	4133	55084	23-16	See note 3
1547	25 tons	5104	55086	25-18	See note 3
1549	20 tons	None	55101	19-6	Noted in 1946
1549	20 tons	None	55118	20-0	Allocated to Lyme Regis branch, 1953

Note 1: Became internal user No 080673 at Andover Junction 2/58-1/61.
Note 2: Seen at Wimbledon 8/48 in SR post-1936 livery but without Venetian red ends.
Note 3: LSWR number is that of the china clay container wagon. This may not have been carried as a brake van.

Bolster and timber wagons

SR Diagram 1594 was allocated to cover the 417 single bolster wagons that became Southern stock in 1923, but such was the decline in timber traffic that within 10 years less than 50 remained in service. Indeed the decline had started well before the Grouping, as no less than 554 were listed on 31 December 1913. Of these, 11 were then Engineer's stock, this total rising to 23 at the Grouping — although they were to last no longer than the traffic department vehicles and all had been withdrawn by 1939. The 11 allocated to general ED stock were numbered in the Engineer's series (LSWR ED Nos 109/10/3/4/8, 240-2/4/6/7), painted red oxide and labelled 'Empty to Redbridge', however some older examples were specifically labelled for bulk timber traffic between Redbridge and Eastleigh — presumably supplying the works with materials — and these retained traffic department numbers (LSWR Nos 2088, 2101/13, 3099, 3302, 4154/73/4/81, 4306, 5221/38) and possibly brown livery. After the Grouping

these distinctions were not kept and all were allocated as service stock regardless, numbers now being 2s-13s (Bulk Timber, Redbridge to Eastleigh) and 14s-23s, 57s (general ED vehicles). We will encounter the 'bulk' (or baulk — sic) timber traffic again.

The oldest wagon extant in 1923 was LSWR No 5866/SR No 57328 — probably the last survivor from a batch of 50 built by Metropolitan in 1877 and numbered 5831-80. From their date of construction they are likely to be as drawn in *LSWR Carriages Volume Four*, Figure 1.31 and not exactly as shown by SR Diagram 1594; being slightly shorter although this difference fails to be recorded in the SR registers. All the other wagons in this number range had been replaced by newer construction by 1911, when production of single bolster wagons ceased at Eastleigh Works and Diagram 1594 would have rather more accurately depicted these.

The next recorded construction occurs in December 1884, when just three pairs were ordered specifically for Redbridge-Nine Elms baulk (sic) timber traffic — clearly a similar duty as the later wagons recorded above. At this time Redbridge Wharf had recently been purchased by the LSWR and was being developed as a landing point for timber and later as the main rail and sleeper depot for the company. These three pairs were LSWR Nos 7703-8 and are listed in SR registers as being 13ft long and to Diagram 1594. Another 30 pairs ordered early in 1885 as a result of Wagon Master Leigh's request for additional vehicles, LSWR Nos 7709-68, followed them and were presumably identical. Note that the vehicles were all ordered in pairs, although they could be used singly, in trios or more as required.

Constructionally they were not permanently coupled but by using their screw couplings could effectively be treated as single vehicles for loading purposes. Some (perhaps all?) of these had normal buffers instead of the more usual self-contained pattern fitted to such diminutive wagons (see **Plate 73**). By 1923 some of these had been replaced by newer construction charged to the renewal account and in some instances double or bogie bolster wagons replaced the earlier vehicles, but carrying the same running numbers, however a few of the 1885 construction survived to carry their SR numbers.

Only one further batch is recorded specifically in the minutes — charged to capital account — these being as follows:

LSWR Nos	Total	Survivors to SR Nos	Date built	Brake gear
9842-9941	50 pairs	57385-57423	1895	Single block

These were certainly 13ft long, built to a general arrangement drawing dated 1892.
As may be seen, only 39 of the 100 wagons remained in service at the Grouping and of these only Nos 57389/92/3/7, 57413/9 were still in traffic after 1933.

Above:
Plate 73 Three Diagram 1594 single bolsters loaded with sawn timber baulks, seen at Exeter St David's, *circa* 1910. This would have been a typical load at the time and would need careful securing to ensure that it could negotiate curves without derailing the wagons. Southern Railway working appendices give no less than 15 pages of instructions related to the loading of goods wagons and at least 11 are concerned specifically with the loading of single, double and bogie bolster wagons with logs, timber baulks and rails. In this instance at least 6in clearance was required between the load and the stanchions of the centre wagon in order for the load to traverse curves satisfactorily. The vehicles are, from left to right, LSWR No 5233 (built in 1898), 9914 (built in 1895) and 4340. Only No 5233 survived the Grouping to become SR No 57289, running until February 1928. Note that wagon No 4340 has normal buffers instead of the self-contained pattern, so probably dates from *circa* 1885-7. *BR/OPC Collection*

Above:
Plate 74 Single bolster LSWR No 9922 (later SR No 57418, renumbered in May 1929), photographed somewhere in the Manchester area about 1919. It is serving as a guard truck or runner to the ex-SECR double bolster wagon just visible to the right, loaded with round timber and reproduced previously in *Volume Three*, **Plate 173**. This was a common use for a single bolster, the screw couplings allowing it to be securely coupled to the wagon carrying the load—although in this instance the runner has no physical contact with the load, so any low open wagon or road vehicle truck could have served the same function. This wagon was one of the batch of 100 built in 1895 and charged to capital account, running until April 1932. *HMRS Collection*

Right:
The first ten double bolster wagons were ordered from Messrs Cravens in 1878 — probably in the nature of an experiment. They were delivered in 1879 and took LSWR numbers 6285-94. These differed slightly in appearance from all later LSWR double bolsters but despite this two of the 1879 vehicles lasted long enough to be allocated to SR Diagram 1595 in 1923. These were SR Nos 57428/32, although only the former (ex-LSWR No 6285) actually carried its Southern number, finally being withdrawn in July 1931. Figure 1.32 in *LSWR Carriages Volume Four* gives details of these prototypes, while one is just visible to the right of **Plate 75**.

All later double bolster (batten) wagons were to a slightly different design as typified by LSWR No 11716 (later SR No 57534), the main subject of **Plate 75,** photographed at Nine Elms in 1918. This was one of 100 completed in 1898/9 and equipped with Panter's cross-lever brake gear; the brake handle of which is just visible at the right-hand end of the wagon, together with the 'off/on' instruction and arrow. Note also the overhaul date of 24-7-18 and the location number (15-denoting Eastleigh Carriage & Wagon Works) above the overhaul date. This vehicle ran until June 1928. And could the wagon in the left foreground be one of the six aeroplane truck conversions to SR Diagram 1672? It is certainly a very featureless flat wagon. *J. Tatchell Collection*

Right:
Plate 76 This rather interesting photograph shows Fox Eliott & Co batten truck No 6, built by the Midland Railway Carriage & Wagon Company. Private owner bolster wagons are extremely uncommon so to find one from the LSWR area is a bonus. To be fair, the company's home depot was in the Great Western Dock at Plymouth Millbay — and the wagon may have been registered by the GWR as well. However, on examination it appears very similar indeed to the LSWR design of 1888, save for different axleboxes and livery. Just how many were built for the firm is not known, however the company were in business from at least 1896 and were still trading over 30 years later. The livery is definitely

not black, as the (presumed) white lettering has black shading and the ironwork is also picked out in the same colour. Perhaps it is finished in brown, purple brown or red oxide. *R. S. Carpenter copy negative*

Above:
Plate 77 The demise of the batten truck was almost as rapid as the single bolster — just a few years later in time. Of the 352 wagons taken into SR stock at the Grouping this total had reduced to 70 by the end of 1935 and just 19 (plus 12 in service stock) remained to become British Railways stock in 1948. Remarkably, one was included in the Ashford 1948 series — SR No 57566, formerly LSWR No 11748. One of the 1898/9 vehicles, it has now acquired Freighter brake gear in place of the Panter cross-lever pattern and was, almost certainly, the last survivor in capital stock; being withdrawn in 1955. Even more remarkably, an eagle-eyed enthusiast photographed and measured it up at Stevenage in 1951! Some of the 12 departmental examples may have survived longer, as these replaced the single bolsters allocated to the Redbridge-Eastleigh sawmill baulk timber traffic between 1932 and 1939. Departmental numbers of these were 625s, 626s, 1154/5s, 1187/92s, 1259-61s, 1347s, 1423/6s. *BR Official*

Above:

Plate 78 From 1916 production of bogie bolster wagons replaced the earlier types and 100 were put into service between then and 1926. SR No 57809 is seen at Axminster on 2 May 1960, freshly outshopped in BR light grey with black solebars and number patches. Note also that the bolsters, stanchions and headstocks are picked out in grey and that the BR code 'Bogie Bolster (C)' has been applied. It is parked in the siding adjacent to R. J. Luff's wood yard so has probably delivered a load of timber for that undertaking. Built by the Bristol Wagon & Carriage Company in 1921, its former LSWR number was 5833, SR Diagram 1597 being allocated. The five original wagons of 1916 were eventually allocated the sub-diagram 1597A and it is believed that these had normal buffers instead of the Spencer pattern fitted to the rest and the end bolsters did not have the facility to be moved to a position adjacent to the headstocks. Examples of numbering were given in *Volume One. A. E. West*

Left:

Plate 79 A close-up of the bolsters on wagon No 57809, showing the textbook stowage of the binding chains. The fact that the nearest bolster could be moved is evident by the gouges in the floor planking. Withdrawal came in July 1963.
A. E. West

Road vehicle trucks

This class of wagon goes back to the earliest days of the railways but as far as the South Western was concerned, there was perhaps just one design prior to 1893, when a range of different types were introduced. This may have been due to the acquisition of Southampton Docks a year earlier or possibly as a result of a general upsurge in traffic during the early 1890s. The 267 vehicles comprising LSWR stock at Grouping remain poorly covered by photographs — the six-wheeled types especially so, therefore much of what is presented here comes from a study of diagrams and the renumbering registers.

The original design came in several variants and was built over a long period, but all were 16ft long with capacities of, progressively, 6, 8 and 10 tons. It seems likely that the early

wagons carried LSWR numbers 1880-99, followed by 2157-86 and 3341-60, as most numbers within these ranges were subsequently re-used by newer road van trucks — of various different lengths — including updated 16ft examples that were later included on SR Diagram 1641. In January 1883 a batch of 25 were ordered from Midland RCW Co. — described in the minutes as 'precisely the same as the last van trucks', which had been ordered in 1876. However, the minutes then go on to record that a revised drawing was submitted and the vehicles (LSWR Nos 7198-7222) were built using these drawings. Just what the changes were is not known as none of these wagons remained in service at the Grouping; all their numbers having been reallocated to 17ft and 18ft trucks built between 1893 and 1910 and later allocated to Diagrams 1642 and 1643 respectively

Right:

Plate 80 Diagram 1641 wagon No 4652 (withdrawn prior to 1923) acts as guard truck to Diagram 1595 double bolster No 8427 (later SR No 57459, withdrawn in April 1928), well laden with round timber at Basingstoke, *circa* 1908-10. At the other end, single bolster No 9896 (which, remarkably, features in *Volume One*, **Plate 112**) is providing the same function. Note that the road vehicle truck has its hinged end dropped down to clear the load. A single block brake is provided on the far side, so this wagon must date from before 1892.
Wallis & Steevens, Basingstoke

Right:

Plate 81 Diagram 1641 truck LSWR No 9318 at Lydd Camp, *circa* 1912. This was part of a batch of 25 ordered in March 1892 and built in the following year. It failed to become SR stock in 1923, but at least 20 of the batch did so. Numbering details of these (and others charged to capital account) are as follows:

LSWR Nos	Date	No built	Survivors to SR Nos	Brake gear
8653-8682	1890	30	60021-38	Single block
9295-9319	1893	25	60039-58	Double block

Some vehicles charged to renewal account included LSWR numbers in the ranges 2157-86 and 3341-60, later becoming SR Nos 60003-15. Most vehicles to Diagram 1641 were withdrawn in the 1930s—on the mainland only Nos 60008/10/9/48/51/8 remaining after 1935. The later vehicles are represented by **Figure 12,** differing in detail by having a continuous top rail along the sides for roping and for positioning wheelbars.
Author's Collection

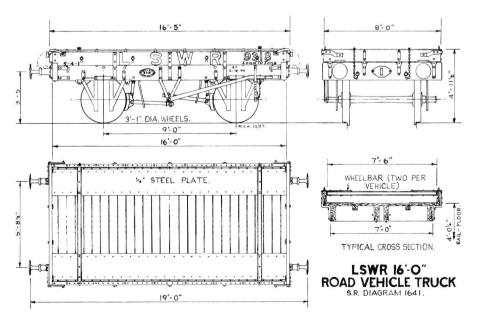

**LSWR 16'-0"
ROAD VEHICLE TRUCK**
S.R. DIAGRAM 1641.

Right:

Plate 82 From 1893 until 1901, 60 replacement 17ft vehicles were built, all taking numbers formerly allocated to 16ft trucks. LSWR No 2161 dates from 1895 and became SR No 60077 after 1923, running until April 1930. Photographed at Nine Elms in 1918, it is loaded with a horse van belonging to James Schoolbred & Company — the furnishers who had a store in London's Tottenham Court Road. This would make a delightful model, however the livery of the van is not known with any certainty. As already noted, all wagons to Diagram 1642 were charged to renewal account, other examples being LSWR Nos 304-13, 2159/86, 3358, 5816, 7199 and 7218. Like Diagram 1641, most were scrapped in the early 1930s, with only Nos 60065/73/90/9, 60103/6 remaining in traffic after 1935 and only No 60103 survived World War Two. *J. Tatchell Collection*

Right:

Plate 83 The 18ft design was built from 1902-10, using the same Fox pressed steel underframe as had been used under covered goods wagons since 1899. A total of 36 became SR property and all were charged to renewal account. Examples of LSWR numbering include 375, 1886/98, 2180, 3349, 5825, 7219-22, 8662 and 9307 — all replacing older 16ft vehicles. All 36 were still in traffic in 1936 and 23 remained at the end of World War Two. The final survivors of these were Nos 60131/5/51/2, withdrawn in 1956. Just two entered departmental stock in 1944, for conveyance of bulldozers — so road mechanisation was creeping up, even on the railway! These were allocated service stock numbers 1998/9s — the highest departmental numbers applied before Nationalisation. No 1998s is seen at

Stewarts Lane in August 1949 and was formerly SR No 60132/LSWR No 5321, dating from 1908. Morton brake gear is provided. The metal racking is behind the wagon, not on it. *The Lens of Sutton Association*

The vehicles ordered in March 1892 included, along with 16ft and 17ft trucks, some of various other lengths, including 22ft, 26ft, 28ft and 31ft examples — two designs running on six wheels. The 28ft four-wheeled vehicles were specifically ordered for Southampton Docks-Nine Elms meat cart traffic and were the first of 88 primarily dedicated to this service, later allocated SR Diagram 1645. They (and the meat carts themselves) have been well covered in both *Volume One* and *LSWR Carriages Volume Four*, but without full numbering details. These are as follows:

LSWR Nos	Total	Date built	Survivors to SR Nos	Remarks
9402-21	20	1893	60169-85, 61003/4	No 9411 lost in accident
1880	1	1895	60168	Replacement for above
11701-8	8	1898	60186-92, 61007	
12484-93	10	1899	60193-60202	
13551-75	25	1904/7	60203-25, 61005/6	
13756-80	25	1907	60159-67, 60226-40, 61008	

SR Nos 61003-8 were converted to aeroplane trucks in 1918, SR Diagram 1672.
Once new SR container wagons were built in the 1930s these wagons were rapidly withdrawn and only Nos 60175/80, 60203/9/16/27 remained at the end of 1935.

Above:

Plate 84 Photographs of the six-wheeled vehicles are rather elusive, however three to Diagram 1646 and one to Diagram 1649 (far left — identifiable by the deeper side rails without the wheelbar rail atop) are visible in this view of Thornycroft's motor factory adjacent to the Alton line near Basingstoke, prior to World War One. All are loaded with packing cases — probably lorry and trailer parts destined for the army. *IAP*

Figure 13 A drawing showing two types of six-wheeled road vehicle truck, SR Diagrams 1646 and 1649. The former became extinct around 1933 while only one vehicle to the latter (SR No 60155) remained after 1935.

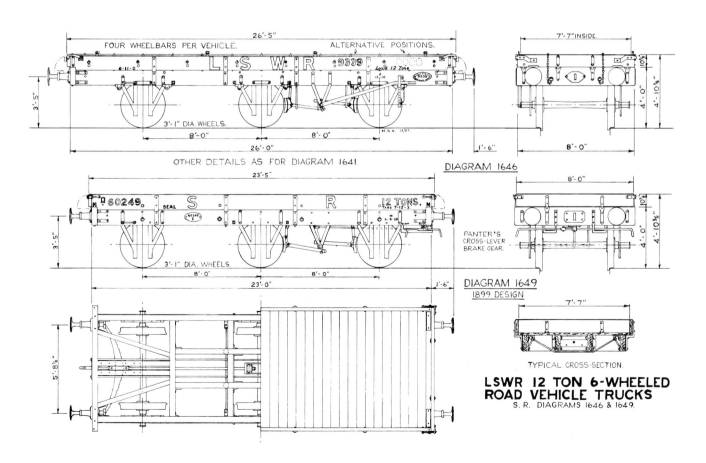

Special vehicles

Right:

Plate 85 Diagram 1674 machinery wagon LSWR No 1196, seen at Nine Elms in 1918, loaded with a marine buoy — an interesting and unusual load that has clearly stretched the ingenuity of the loaders. The consequences of a rough shunt are not worth thinking about! This wagon was built on renewal account in 1906, replacing an earlier wagon of similar design. It differs slightly from **Figure 41** in *Volume One* — namely that the solebar is not notched out to accommodate the brake lever; instead this is shaped to clear both solebar and headstock. The drawing represents the five wagons built on capital account in 1902, LSWR Nos 13546-50. No 1196 later became SR 'Well E' No 61010, running until June 1943 — possibly a war damage victim. Ex-LSWR No 1200, formerly duplicate stock and allocated SR No 61029, listed in the Appendix to *Volume One* is now known to be an earlier example of this design, perhaps built in 1879. *J. Tatchell Collection*

Below:

Plate 86 There were a number of army camps within LSWR territory, including Aldershot, around Dinton, on Salisbury Plain, near Lulworth and on Dartmoor, so military hardware would have been a common load. A selection of machinery trucks are seen loaded with tanks belonging to the 5th Battalion Royal Tank Corps, who were based at Perham Down on Salisbury Plain and accessed via the MSWJR near Ludgershall. Ironically, this comes from a German publication of 1934 and shows two LSWR 'Well E' wagons either side of a SECR 'Well B'. Note that the LSWR wagons lack the notched out solebar/headstock ends, however by the time of this photograph most would have received a second set of brake gear on the other side, so we may be looking at the newer fittings. Provided a suitable tank model is available to the correct scale, these would make an attractive and unusual model load. The author is grateful to Mr David Fletcher of Bovington Tank Museum for identification of the military equipment in this and the next plate, also for permission to reproduce the photographs. *The Tank Museum*

Above:
Plate 87 Another view of tanks loaded onto LSWR machinery wagons, possibly taken at Lydd Camp between 1925 and 1935. However, it is known that tank traffic to Lulworth was dealt with on the Bovington Camp branch at Wool until 1928, where army personnel were trained in the loading and unloading process, so such loads would have been seen regularly at this location. The tanks are medium Mark II models and may belong to the 3rd Battalion Royal Tank Corps. The wagons are a wonderful LSWR collection, from left to right being 'Well D' No 61026 (ex-LSWR No 13545), 'Well E' No 61018 (ex-LSWR No 13550), followed by another to Diagram 1674 and two more to Diagram 1675. *The Tank Museum*

Right:
Plate 88 The later generation of LSWR machinery wagons are covered by SR Diagrams 1673 and 1676 — of 12 and 20-ton capacities respectively. The former is illustrated by SR No 61019 at Sidmouth, circa 1930-34. This was previously LSWR No 13856, built in 1908 and the only one of the five examples to be charged to capital account. Notice the presence of two more machinery wagons — whatever the reason for their appearance at Sidmouth, it needed several of them — so even a small branch line terminus could see these unusual wagons from time to time. *HMRS Collection*

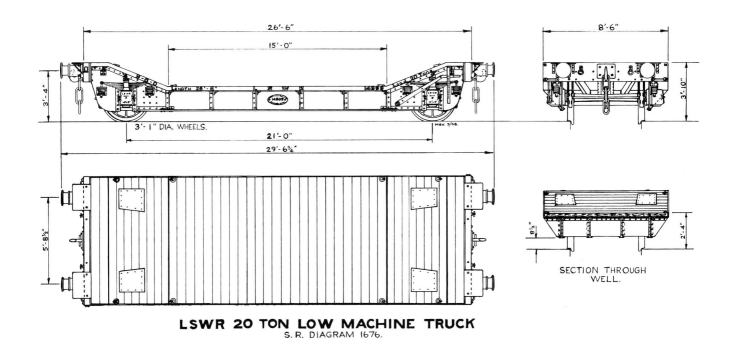

LSWR 20 TON LOW MACHINE TRUCK
S.R. DIAGRAM 1676.

Figure 14 The final design of LSWR machinery wagon, SR Diagram 1676, built in 1921. The late Frank Foote noted all three of them together at Hamworthy Junction in July 1923, so the presence of more than one at a location was clearly not unusual. All were charged to renewal account, as nominal replacements for the bogie wagon No 11813 (by then transferred to the Signal Engineer) and ex-SDJR implement trucks 14996/9.

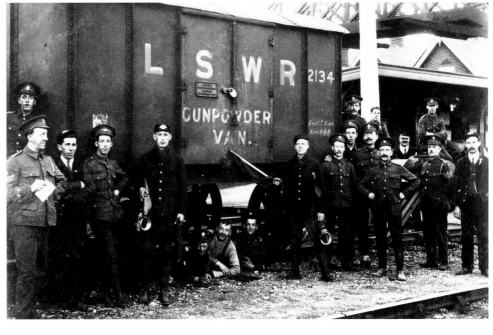

Right:

Plate 89 Diagram 1701 gunpowder van LSWR No 2134, built in 1904, surrounded by railway and military personnel, probably some time during World War One. The location was originally thought to be Dinton but is now confirmed as Redbridge, where the Shultz Gunpowder Works was set up in 1897, adjacent to the rail and sleeper works. This was served by its own siding until the works closed in 1922, so gunpowder vans would have been a regular sight here during this period. Once the various cordite works had been set up on Holton Heath, near Wareham from 1914, gunpowder vans would have been seen there as well. The South Western suddenly found itself short of sufficient vans for this traffic during World War One, meeting the need by hurriedly converting 103 brand new Diagram 1409 vans, including Nos 263, 2665 and 5929, as 'improvised gunpowder vans', but whether they were described as such on the vehicles is unknown. An invitation to would-be terrorists that seems unimaginable today, but in those days visible warning of the contents was considered of far greater importance. History repeated itself in 1938/9 when the Southern Railway took 100 ex-GWR 'iron minks' on loan for the same reason, as illustrated in **Plate 154** of *Volume Four*. However, it is now known that the reference quoted therein to their numbers being SR 59001-100 is incorrect and the wagons retained their random GWR numbers. Other known examples are 11016, 58710/87, all noted during 1940/1. The livery of LSWR gunpowder vans was also the subject of conjecture in *Volume One*. Frank Foote's boyhood sketches shed some light on this, as included is a drawing of a gunpowder van, lettered exactly as seen in **Plate 89** but finished in standard brown rather than red oxide livery. Wagon No 2134 later became SR No 61210 and was condemned in 1953. *The Lens of Sutton Association*

Right:

Plate 90 The LSWR shunting truck was mentioned briefly in *Volume One* and well covered in both its forms in *LSWR Carriages Volume Four* — in the chapter entitled 'Miscellany'. This close-up shows the vehicle running as SR No 61321 at Exmouth Junction in September 1936, coupled to a 'Z' class 0-8-0 tank. This shows yet another change to the brake gear — namely a centrally placed vee hanger and, presumably, two brake blocks on this side, although these are hidden by the foot guards — and again these appear different to the 1926 photograph. Was this brake arrangement a replacement of the original single block gear or in addition to it? If the latter, then this would give the most unusual situation of three brake blocks on the truck. An additional step is also just visible at the left of the picture. The visible repair date is 24/2/36, with the location code 13 (appropriately for Exmouth Junction) above. Remarkably, the wagon remained in service until November 1951, being replaced at this yard by Southern-built truck No 61322, to Diagram 1712, formerly used at Clapham Junction. *H. C. Casserley*

Engineer's Department ballast and rail wagons

Some railway men would say that these wagons were a law unto themselves! They carried their own number series in LSWR days; the number 508 being the highest allocated, to one of the bogie hopper wagons of 1911. It is likely that some numbers were allocated more than once, especially as many earlier ED vehicles were traffic department cast-offs with short life expectancy, but a study of the number series yields only about ten gaps in 1923 and no obvious trends beyond stating that the lowest numbers were for the most part allocated to two and three plank dropside wagons. Not surprisingly, however, these made up 70% of the Engineer's fleet anyway.

Above:

Plate 91 A typical two-plank ballast wagon to SR Diagram 1731, SR No 61633/LSWR No 255, as running just prior to withdrawal in 1950 and still finished in SR red oxide with post-1936 lettering. This was one of many originally provided with second-hand wheelsets and axle boxes (now replaced with ones to Warner pattern), as evidenced by the self-contained buffers — compare with No 224 in **Plate 128** of *Volume One* — and most of these were rated at either 7 or 8 tons capacity. Wagons to this diagram varied somewhat, as those built before about 1902 were three planks high, those built thereafter had only two, despite the fact that some of them were of 10 tons capacity. The three plank wagons were generally lettered as shown in **Figure 1** and many carried a 'When empty return to Woking' (or Eastleigh, Meldon or Redbridge, etc.) branding to the left of the company initials. *Author's Collection*

Several batches of new dropside wagons were ordered in the 1897-1900 period, including 50 eight tonners in 1897, 75 more in 1899 and 25 specifically for the main line widening works in 1900. Some further examples of Diagram 1731 are given below while the relevant drawing appears as **Figure 44** in *Volume One*.

LSWR No	SR No	Date built	Capacity	Journal spacing	No. of planks
3	61753	1910	10 tons	6ft 8 in	2
18	61515	1896	7 tons	6ft 6 in	3
34	61525	1901	7 tons	6ft 6 in	3
47	61537	1904	7, later 8 tons	6ft 6 in	2
62	61723	1900	8 tons	6ft 8 in	3 (steel u/f)
68	61762	1911	10 tons	6ft 8 in	2
99	61766	1912	10 tons	6ft 8 in	2
149	61593	1888	7 tons	6ft 6 in	3
208	61610	1897	7 tons	6ft 6 in	2
275	61647	1903	7 tons	6ft 6 in	2
337	61657	1898	7 tons	6ft 6 in	3
443	61711	1900	7 tons	6ft 6 in	3

All the above were still in service in 1935, but of 360 in service in 1913 only 29 remained in stock by 1948. It appears that most ED numbers in the ranges 337-89 and 430-53 were 7 or 8-ton, three plank examples built in 1897-1900, although not every number in these ranges was actually occupied by a Diagram 1731 vehicle and at least three were on steel underframes. Most wagons would have been built with double block brake gear on one side only, altered to Freighter pattern if still running in the 1930s. None received Panter's cross-lever gear, as the drop door would have fouled the brake lever.

In addition, some 80 examples to Diagram 1301 were allocated to the Engineer's department, as described at the beginning of this chapter, while after 1914 up to 32 former SDJR dropsides joined the LSWR examples, the latter taking random ED numbers between 15 and 450, formerly carried by wagons to Diagram 1731. See Chapter Two for more details of the SDJR stock.

Below:
Plate 92 The need for greater mechanisation in ballasting methods was felt as early as the 1890s, leading to the introduction of hopper wagons and plough brake vans. SR Diagram 1734 was allocated to the small 12-ton hopper wagons, three batches of which were built by contractors between 1898 and 1903. The six from R. Y. Pickering were delivered in 1902 and, as No 473 shows, arrived with another version of non-standard lettering, including full stops. Either-side brakes were fitted to this wagon in July 1932 and, as SR No 61877, it continued to serve until June 1964; probably the last survivor. *R. Y. Pickering*

Above:
Plate 93 Another of the Pickering wagons, SR No 61873/LSWR No 469 is seen at Delabole *circa* 1937, carrying SR pre-1936 lettering. Once the bogie hoppers were delivered, these smaller wagons were generally reserved for ballasting jobs to the west of Exeter.
E. L. Scaife

Above:
Plate 94 In 1903 tenders were invited for the construction of 16 large bogie ballast hoppers. Prices were received from no less than seven contractors, ranging from £299 to £403 each. That from G & R Turner was accepted, with the proviso that vacuum brake gear would be fitted at Eastleigh on delivery — presumably before the wagons entered traffic and at an additional cost of £50 per wagon. In fact they were booked out of Eastleigh Works at £366 each. Notice that the lettering on this wagon appears to be shaded black — another non-standard refinement applied by the builders. Interestingly, Turner's publicity material for these wagons shows them to be lettered 'L&SWR Co' in very large characters spread across the centre six panels, but it is unlikely that any entered service in this livery. The four additional wagons delivered in 1911 (for the same price) were equipped with vacuum brakes at Eastleigh in just the same manner.
LSWR Official

Above:
Plate 95 Diagram 1735 hopper SR No 61903 ex-works at Woking in red oxide livery in 1935. Evidence of strengthening plates may be seen over the bogies — part of the constant maintenance problems caused by regular fast journeys up the main line from Meldon Quarry under full load. No 61903 was formerly LSWR No 499, running from 1904 until June 1958, then becoming internal user No 081275 at Newhaven Harbour, along with 11 others until 1964. *F. Foote*

Above:
Plate 96 To work with the various ballast hoppers, five plough brake vans were ordered from Hurst Nelson & Company. This shows LSWR No 29 (later SR No 61940) at Meldon Quarry, at the end of a rake of 40-ton bogie hoppers, also photographed on the same occasion. The P. Way man obligingly demonstrates the lowering of the ballast plough mechanism. By now (post-April 1906) the lettering follows standard practice with a round-topped 'S' — compare with **Plate 133** in *Volume One*. *J. Tatchell Collection*

Above:
Plate 97 An early ballast brake van, duplicate No 019, is seen at Strawberry Hill on 1 October 1921. This is one of three such vehicles known, LSWR numbers being 017-019 and was presumably the precursor to SR Diagram 1736, illustrated and drawn in *Volume One*. Features of note include the self-contained buffers, timber brake blocks and old-style spring hangers, axle boxes and brake rigging. The van appears to be a reconstruction, incorporating 1870s materials along with a slightly more modern body and probably dates from the mid or late 1880s, although this has yet to be confirmed. Van No 019 was withdrawn soon after being photographed and failed to be allocated a Southern Railway number. *H. C. Casserley*

Right:
Plate 98 Similar van, LSWR duplicate No 018 is seen at Strawberry Hill on 28 April 1923, showing the other end. This was allocated SR No 61944 but scrapped later the same year without being renumbered. LSWR No 017 actually received its SR number (61943) and lasted until August 1930, being included on SR Diagram 1736. Note that the wagon number has been incised into the crib rail and, above it, the white circular symbol — the exact significance of which remains unclear. However it has only been noted on unfitted Engineer's Department stock (i.e. not on the bogie hoppers or plough brake vans), so may serve to indicate this.
H. C. Casserley

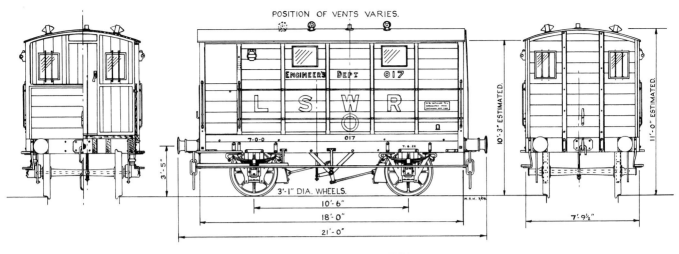

POSITION OF VENTS VARIES.

ENGINEERS DEPT ⊙17

L S W R
017

3'-5"

7-0-0
7.6.21

3'-1" DIA. WHEELS.

10'-6"
18'-0"
21'-0"

10'-3" ESTIMATED.

11'-0" ESTIMATED.

7'-9½"

LSWR 7 TON BALLAST BRAKE VAN
ONE VAN LATER ALLOCATED TO S.R.
DIAGRAM 1736.

Figure 15 A drawing of the earlier ballast brake van, based on the two photographs available to the author, together with other standard dimensions. Several assumptions have had to be made, not least in the overall length, which could be 18ft or 18ft 6in. Only one renumbering register consulted gave the wagon diagram as 1736 — the same as the later Panter vans — but others are silent on details. If this information is correct, then the former length applies, however LSWR goods brake vans built prior to 1886 are 18ft 6in long, so absolute accuracy cannot be guaranteed.

Left:
Plate 99 The older rail and sleeper wagons remain almost absent in photographs. This rather cruel enlargement was taken at Bournemouth Central around 1920 and shows a Diagram 1784 long sleeper wagon with what appears to be Morton brake gear. It is the only known illustration of any of these wagons.
Author's Collection

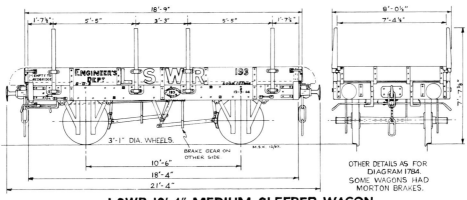

LSWR 18'-4" MEDIUM SLEEPER WAGON
S. R. DIAGRAM 1783.

Figure 16 A drawing of the medium sleeper wagon, to SR Diagram 1783.

Above:
Plate 100 In contrast, the bogie rail wagons built by Cravens in 1902 were well photographed. LSWR No 454, later SR No 64558 was the last survivor and is seen at Yeovil (Hendford) in February 1965 while working out of Broad Clyst permanent way depot. The livery was recorded as black, with red side rails. This was not quite the end of its life, as it was later transferred to the Western Region's Taunton depot and was last seen there in July 1966. *A. E. West*

Above and left:

Plates 101 and 102 LSWR Goods Department travelling cranes were seldom photographed and in *Volume One* all that could be provided was a list of them, taken from the Southern Railway service stock register. Goods Department crane No 5, allocated to Exmouth Junction, is seen at Exeter Queen Street about 1924, together with its match truck, LSWR Diagram 1301 7-ton dropside wagon No 01745, before they were renumbered as SR 44s and 44sm respectively. The livery is probably red oxide. Outline diagrams of these cranes appear in *LSWR Carriages Volume Four*. Both G. P. Keen

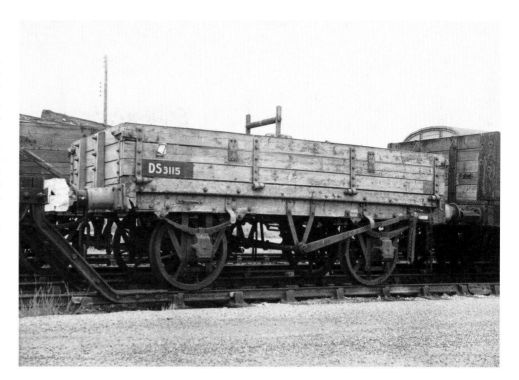

Right:
Plate 103 Match truck 44SM/LSWR 01745 again, photographed some 30 years later at Newhaven and now numbered in the Southern Region departmental series as DS3115 — a renumbering dating from June 1952. The vehicle was originally built in 1899, using second-hand wheelsets and axle boxes, as LSWR traffic department wagon No 1745. Warner axle boxes are now fitted, together with Morton brake gear. The livery is probably pale grey with black number patches and white lettering.
E. B. Trotter

Above:
Plate 104 Goods Department crane No 6 (later SR No 45s) deals with the result of a rough shunt, perhaps at the back of Woking yard, circa 1910. This crane was allocated to Nine Elms. The wagons are to Diagram 1311 (LSWR No 2019, which failed to become SR stock), type 7 in our survey of open wagons and Diagram 1309, type 14 (LSWR No 5597, later SR No 3215). *J. Tatchell Collection*

Chapter 2.
SDJR Wagons

Shortly after the LSWR and Midland Railway take-over of the line, the Joint Committee minutes report that the total number of goods wagons stood at 917 — at that date (December 1876) being considered sufficient for all purposes. Samuel Johnson of the Midland Railway estimated that a renewal programme of around 52 wagons per year would be sufficient to keep the stock in good order and abreast of current practice. This was more or less adhered to until 1885 when, on his recommendation, the programme was accelerated to 80 per year for the next three years, returning to the original renewal rate from 1889 onwards. In theory, this would result in all pre-1876 wagons being replaced by 1892. However, increased traffic levels soon presented themselves — probably as a result of better management — and tenders for additional stock were being sought as soon as 1879. By the time that the revenue-earning wagons were divided between the two parent companies in June 1914, the total wagon fleet had increased by 440 to 1357 vehicles.

Open goods wagons

Below:
Plate 105 By far the most numerous SDJR goods vehicle was the Midland Railway style five plank open goods wagon, which accounted for almost 40% of the stock. These came with several detail variations but were sufficiently alike for all to be allocated to SR Diagram 1304 after the Grouping. SDJR No 602 was one of a small number with round ends and a timber sheet rail, officially photographed in less than pristine condition around 1905/6 (the overhaul date of 25/4/05 is visible over the left-hand axle box). Just how many of these round-ended wagons were built is not known, but none appear to have been passed to the LSWR in 1914, since the South Western diagram makes no mention of this detail. However, two drawings of the type exist, dating from 1894 and 1899 — the main difference being an invisible one — namely the position of the buffer springing. On the earlier design this is between the middle cross-members, on the later it is directly behind the headstocks. **Figure 17** (opposite top right) represents the 1899 design. *MR Official*

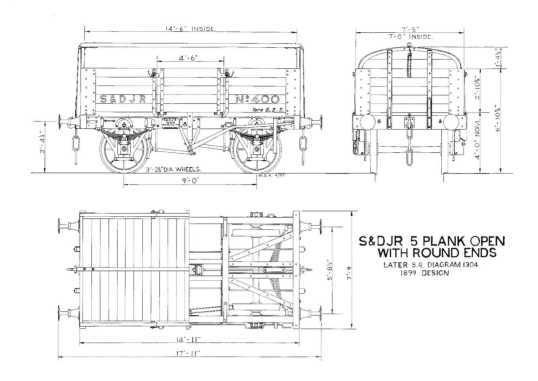

14'-6" INSIDE.

4'-6"

S & D J R   Nᵒ 400

Tare 5.2.2.

3'-4½"

3'-2⅜" DIA. WHEELS.

9'-0"

M.S.K. 4/07.

7'-5"
7'-0" INSIDE.

1'-4½"
2'-10⅝"
6'-10⅝"
4'-0" NOM.

S&DJR 5 PLANK OPEN
WITH ROUND ENDS
LATER S.R. DIAGRAM 1304
1899 DESIGN

14'-11"

5'-8½"
7'-9

17'-11"

Below:
Plate 106 The SDJR kept a fleet of 34 duplicate loco ash, coal and sand wagons and these were amongst the 221 vehicles retained by the Joint Committee until 1930. At Templecombe shed on 12 June 1926 we see round-ended open No 539A, stencilled 'For loco ashes only', together with square-ended open No 514A just visible to the right, but probably similarly lettered. Both date from 1895. Note the reversed position of the number and company initials compared with **Plate 105** — a layout adopted during or just after World War One. Those wagons relegated to the duplicate list; indicated by an 'A' suffix to the running number, included all these loco ash wagons — other examples being Nos 7A, 54A, 191A, 204A, 486A, 730A and 810A. In 1926 the minutes record that six of these were beyond repair and were replaced by a similar number converted from open carriage trucks, although just how this was achieved is not known. All these ash wagons passed into LMS ownership in 1930. Further down the line is a three plank dropside wagon, No 636, lettered 'Engineer's Department' along the top plank and this became SR stock in 1930 as the latter's No 62957. A few of the loco ash wagons were three plank dropsides as well, recorded numbers including 126A, 347A and 727A. Perhaps these were some of the former open carriage truck conversions? *H. C. Casserley*

Right:

Plate 107 What may be termed the 'standard' version of SR Diagram 1304 is represented by SDJR No 141, built at Highbridge in 1886 and photographed after overhaul in 1904, probably when the Williams patent sheet rail was provided. Fifty wagon renewals ordered in 1903 were to have these from new, but it seems that some were fitted to existing wagons at overhaul as well. A further 50 sheet supports were purchased through the LSWR in 1906 and these were to be fitted to wagons as they passed through shops, although it is likely that many of these were actually new wagons to SR Diagram 1305 instead. The first SDJR wagons built to what later became SR Diagram 1304 were probably the 100 ordered from

S. J. Claye in March 1879 — the first bulk additions to the stock since LSWR/MR takeover. Further batches of 50 each were ordered on capital account in 1882 and 1898, the latter again being built by Claye. SDJR numbers of the 1898 batch were 1072-1121. Two of these later became MR Nos 70465 and 74490, both being rare examples of SDJR wagons whose later MR numbers are known. Presumably, if they survived in 1923 they would have retained these numbers in LMS ownership. It is also worth recording that the Midland Railway built more than 63,000 of its own version of this diagram between 1879 and 1917 — the most numerous wagon design in the British Isles prior to 1948, so it is perhaps not surprising that the former Joint line examples were lost amongst all these! Some SDJR wagons built on renewal account had self-contained buffers similar to those seen on wagon No 689 in **Plate 153** of *Volume One*, however no Joint line numbers are known for these. *MR Official*

Above:

Plate 108 Photographs of SDJR wagons in Southern livery are equally uncommon, however this is Diagram 1304 open No 284 at Looe in the early 1930s. This was built at Highbridge in 1912 as SDJR No 250, one of the last wagons to be built at the works, becoming LSWR No 14951 after June 1914 and renumbered as seen in May 1928. It was one of 73 to the diagram still in traffic in 1936. Just 10 remained in ordinary service at Nationalisation, including SR Nos 258/9/70. *S. C. Fox, courtesy D. Gould*

Above:
Plate 109 Alexander's siding, between Ashcott and Shapwick on the Burnham branch, serving the Eclipse Peat Company's works, which dealt in this commodity between 1912 and 1964. The photograph dates from *circa* 1920 and the original formerly hung in the Eclipse Peat Company's staff canteen. Amongst the wagons visible, most of which are of LSWR origin, are three of the SDJR peat wagons, their loads protected by tarpaulin sheets. The nearest of these is fourth in the line behind the locomotive tender and is either No 561 or 568, with SDJR tarpaulin No 1119 overall. Another SDJR sheet, No 1043, may be seen covering the LSWR open second in the train. Both are presumed to be black with white stencilled lettering, the company initials, number and overhaul date being repeated four times on the sheet. This is one of very few photographs to show Joint Line wagon sheets in any detail, however it is known that both the MR and LSWR provided some between 1875 and 1907, so it is likely that these were lettered SDJR in the style of the providing company. Maintenance of them was undertaken at Burnham until April 1929, when the wagon sheet shop was closed down. Thereafter as the existing sheets wore out those of LMS or SR pattern replaced them. Returning to the peat itself, this was cut extensively on the Somerset levels, being widely used for fuel, as horse bedding and for horticultural purposes and it was transported all over the country by rail, as well as going by sea from Highbridge Wharf, where the Eclipse Peat Company also had a siding dedicated for their use.
The Eclipse Peat Co, courtesy R. Dagger

Figure 18 A drawing of the SDJR peat wagon, showing the extension rails fitted in 1911/2 to what were otherwise standard 8-ton open goods wagons. Fourteen were so converted and these remained the sole revenue-earning wagons to carry Joint line livery between 1914 and 1930, then passing into LMS ownership. SDJR numbers are given on page 86 of *Volume One*. From the limited evidence of **Plate 109**, the drawing is lettered 'When empty return to Evercreech Junction', although this is not confirmed, nor is it known if all 14 wagons were so branded. Some may also have been lettered 'Peat Wagon', 'Peat Traffic' or 'Peat Only' in 6in capital letters on the top plank of the drop door. Again, from the evidence of **Plate 109**, it is obvious that ordinary LSWR wagons were also used for peat traffic, with a variety of tarpaulin sheets overall.

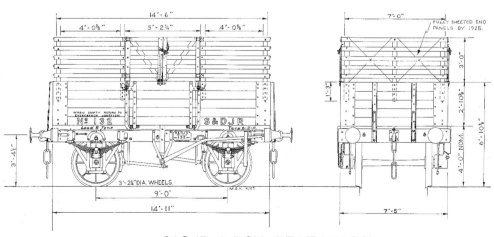

S&DJR 8 TON PEAT WAGON
AS CONVERTED IN 1911/12. TO LMS IN 1930.

Right:

Plate 110 Another group of wagons, albeit not revenue-earning, retained by the Joint line in 1914 were the 65 six-plank opens reserved for loco coal supplies and they again passed into LMS ownership in 1930. The Midland Railway had built a total of 80 of these wagons in 1902 and the balance of 15 was allocated to the traffic department. These had been divided between the parent companies in 1914, later being allocated SR Diagram 1306. SDJR No 1124 is seen at Radstock, *circa* 1905, carrying a cast iron plate that reads 'For loco coal only. When empty return to Midsomer Norton' — or Radstock or Highbridge Wharf — depending on the allocated supplier of the coal. *P. C. Dewhurst*

The Joint Committee retendered its loco coal contracts almost without fail on an annual basis and, unlike most of the other pre-Grouping SR constituents (and indeed the Southern Railway itself), usually awarded anything from three to eight separate small contracts to various suppliers. These ranged from the usual big names such as Stephenson Clarke, William Cory and Tredegar to small local collieries — the latter usually supplying the coal in either their own or SDJR wagons. The Joint line, of course, had the Somerset coalfield right on its doorstep and this process may have enabled it to obtain the keenest possible prices. From 1902, these Diagram 1306 wagons usually supplied the locomotive sheds at Highbridge, Radstock and Templecombe. Coal for Branksome and Wimborne sheds were supplied through the LSWR, usually in their own wagons, while that at Bath normally came from the larger firms, plus Kingswood Colliery, later renamed The East Bristol Colliery Company. Sea borne coal was also landed at Highbridge Wharf and this was distributed in Joint Committee wagons.

Above:

Plate 111 Two Diagram 1306 loco coal wagons at Templecombe on 5 July 1930, that on the left already carrying LMS initials in addition to Joint line livery. Whilst the wagon numbers are not visible, they are from the range 1122-86, but the lettering style may be seen, as well as the cast iron plate on the left-hand wagon, now reversed and stencilled 'Empty to Highbridge Wharf'. *H. C. Casserley*

Right:

Plate 112 Photographs of SDJR wagons carrying LMS livery are as rare as those in SR colours. Loco coal wagon LMS No 358377 is seen at Highbridge Wharf some time during the 1930s, but clearly still based on the line. Negotiations regarding the supply of locomotive coal passed to the LMS in 1930, along with all other motive power matters, so perhaps no immediate changes were apparent. Note SDJR Crane No 2 just visible behind, still carrying its Joint line number. This vehicle appeared previously in **Plate 172** of *Volume One* and has had some safety guards applied to the gear wheels since original construction. Presumably the three plank wagon visible to the right is one of the match trucks, now carrying LMS lettering. The number of the loco coal wagon does provide a clue to the likely range of numbers allocated by the LMS to former Joint line stock in 1930, as what few that have been noted are all in the 358XXX series. *LMS Official*

Above:

Plate 113 Probably the last SDJR wagon to survive in BR stock was Diagram 1307 two-plank open SR No 423, which was converted into crane match truck No 202sm in March 1932. It was based at Stewarts Lane and later Gillingham (Kent), along with former SECR crane No 202s. For this it was fitted with a large timber trestle to support the crane jib in the running position and an extra side plank above the fixed portions of each side. The original appearance may be deduced by reference to **Figure 55** in *Volume One*, where it can be seen that this was one of the wagons built with a drop flap door. The wagon dates from 1912 as SDJR No 158, later LSWR No 15059 and remained in departmental service until February 1962, after 1952 carrying the number DS3089. Five different numbers in 60 years — no wonder the railways had to keep meticulous records! *The Lens of Sutton Association*

Covered goods wagons

The earliest mention of these in the minutes occurs in 1863 and it was not until October 1882 that they feature again, when 49 were to be converted from cattle trucks. It is unlikely that any of these survived beyond 1900. In November 1891, the minutes again mention 'box wagons' — presumably covered goods vehicles — when 40 were to be built on renewal account to replace scrapped open wagons, at an additional cost of £15 per wagon.

Right:

Plate 114 Covered goods wagon No 750, probably one of the 40 referred to above and built in 1892-4, photographed at Highbridge carrying a high-specification paint finish with blacked-up ironwork and black shading to the lettering. It is one of a few Joint line wagons so finished and undoubtedly contrasts with similar van No 741 illustrated in **Plate 155** of *Volume One*, perhaps finished in 'smudge' grey. Just whether it ran in traffic in this livery is not known. *SDJR Official*

Devon County Prison from Northernhay.

Plate 115 A general view of Exeter Queen Street, from a commercial postcard, *circa* 1910. Just why anyone would wish to send a card depicting Exeter Gaol is beyond the author's comprehension — the caption 'wish you were here' is not exactly the greeting that comes to mind! However, in our context a good selection of wagons is on view, including two SDJR 16ft 6 in covered goods wagons as built from 1896 onwards. There were perhaps as many as 140 of these, 80 of which were charged to capital account, as follows:

Date of order	Date built	Total	SDJR Nos	Built by
Nov 1895	By July 1896	50	891, 1003-41 plus ten other random numbers	MR (Derby)
Feb 1899	By Dec 1899	30	1042-71	S. J. Claye

The rest were completed at Highbridge between 1903 and 1912 and charged to renewal account, so took further random numbers below 890. Presumably Nos 293 and 549 visible in **Plate 115** are amongst them. These (or other SDJR covered goods wagons) would have been a regular sight at Exeter, as well as at Bristol, Eastleigh and Nine Elms, since Joint line goods working timetables list up to 43 regular duties for 'road boxes' covering the entire SDJR system and beyond, providing a small consignment service to wayside stations. Other wagons visible include examples to SR Diagrams 1301, 1310 and 1410, a Varwell Guest coal wagon, one GWR and two MR covered goods wagons.
Commercial postcard by S. A. Chandler

After the February 1899 orders to Claye, the next orders for new wagons appear to have caused some prevarication, as the matter was discussed and deferred at meetings in May and August 1901, finally being approved in November for the construction of the 80 loco coal wagons from Derby (already discussed), plus 20 covered goods and 20 cattle wagons to standard LSWR designs from Eastleigh, delivered during 1902 and noted in *Volume One*. This proved to be the last substantial wagon order placed by the Joint line committee, all subsequent references concern mere single figure quantities.

Livestock vehicles

In 1893 the minutes record that movable partitions were to be provided for the 103 large and medium sized cattle trucks, at a cost of £134-6-7d, giving an idea of the size of the fleet at that time. The stock total rose by only 32 wagons before division in 1914 and little more can be added to what has already been written about the ordinary wagons, other than to suggest that the SDJR numbers from 1-30 still remain as possible Diagram 1505 wagons, plus numbers in the range 84/5/7-114, although this cannot be stated with certainty. However, two wagons in this number range are confirmed as prize cattle vans by the SDJR working timetable appendix dated 1914, Nos 89 and 102.

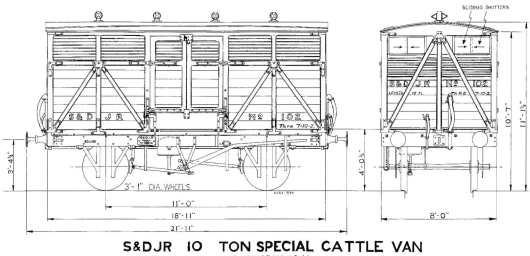

S&DJR 10 TON SPECIAL CATTLE VAN
S.R. DIAGRAM 1041.
DRAWING BASED ON S&DJR/LSWR DIAGRAMS.

Figure 19 LSWR and Southern records confirm that one prize or special cattle van passed to the South Western in 1914, becoming LSWR No 15123 and SR No 3670 (in the passenger van series). The latter also confirms that the van was built at Highbridge in 1910 and ran until September 1929, SR Diagram 1041 being allocated. This drawing is based on both the LSWR and SR diagrams but has not been confirmed by photographic evidence. Both show a van similar in overall dimensions to SR Diagram 1505, but differing in framing and other bodywork details. It is therefore less likely that the vans were rebuilds as was previously suggested but were built as special vehicles from new. It is not known which van became LSWR property, but presumably the other went to the Midland Railway in 1914. Both were vacuum-braked, with a through Westinghouse pipe.

Goods brake vans

Right:

The origins of the 10-ton four-wheeled vans described on page 94 of *Volume One* may go back to six rather ancient-looking vehicles ordered in 1876 from Bristol Wagon Works and built to a drawing supplied by the Midland Railway, rather reminiscent of brake vans built during the 1860s by the Birmingham carriage and wagon industry. One of these, SDJR No 20, is seen in **Plate 116** at Highbridge in the early 1880s. On the face of it, these were hardly likely to last for very long on a line as exposed or with gradients such as found on the SDJR, however the original 1876 general arrangement drawing survives, as does a later (undated) version showing their reconstruction with a much needed full length roof and covered verandas at each end. These drawings give the body length as 15ft with a wheelbase of 9ft — both dimensions being common to the later four-wheeled vehicles. It is not clear whether the 1876 open brake vans were reconstructed as proposed, but comparison with **Figure 59** in *Volume One* shows some remarkable similarities; not only in overall dimensions but also to the underframe details shown on the reconstruction drawing, complete with the external brake standard on the end. *R. Tarpey Collection, courtesy R. Dagger*

Right:

Plate 117 A later 10-ton van, coincidentally No 20 again, which according to the records was built in 1885. This exhibits almost the same underframe as the '1876 reconstruction drawing', but with a somewhat improved bodywork — now with external timber framing — and retaining the same overall length together with the rather characteristic narrow 'gate' entrance to the veranda, in exactly the same position as previously, as well as the external brake standard, albeit now at one end only. If the open veranda had been repeated at both ends, we would arrive at the 1876 reconstructed van almost exactly, save for a 6in increase in overall height — another well considered improvement. It is probably unlikely that the second No 20 is a rebuild of the first, especially as this van managed to last to LMS takeover in 1930, but it does contrast with the mere 9-year lifespan of the original vehicle in **Plate 116**. These 10-ton vans were built in batches, the first 10 being ordered in April 1879 (running numbers not known), while some of the later ones were numbered as follows:

Built 1884 — Nos 22, 23 (later 23A)
Built 1885 — Nos 20, 37, 39
Built 1886 — Nos 1, 4, 12, 24 (later 24A), 34
Built 1887 — No 14
Built 1888 — Nos 2, 10, 11, 21, 33

The minutes record that six additional vans ordered in 1885 increased the stock of brakes from 34 to 40, however it is not clear if these took the logical numbers from 35 to 40; although if No 20 listed above was judged a rebuild then this may be so. *SDJR Official*

Above:
Plate 118 In October 1887 two 20-ton, six-wheeled brake vans were ordered specifically for a proposed goods train mail service between Bath and Bournemouth. Thomas Clayton of the Midland Railway prepared the design and the vans were constructed at Derby in 1888 at a cost of £201 each. They shared the same 18ft 1 in underframe as employed on standard MR 15 and 20-ton goods brakes built from 1886 onwards, but had a specially designed full-length body divided into two compartments for the guard and the mail respectively. Numbered 41 and 42, the latter van is seen at Bath, *circa* 1890, before they were renumbered as SDJR 26 and 27. The date of renumbering is not clear, but both vans passed into LMS ownership in 1930. *SDJR Official*

Figure 20 A drawing of the 20 ton goods brake and mail van of 1888. The side lookouts were cut down and a fixed side lamp added by about 1905. Exact details of the roof skylights are uncertain and only the four longer ones appear on the general arrangement drawing.

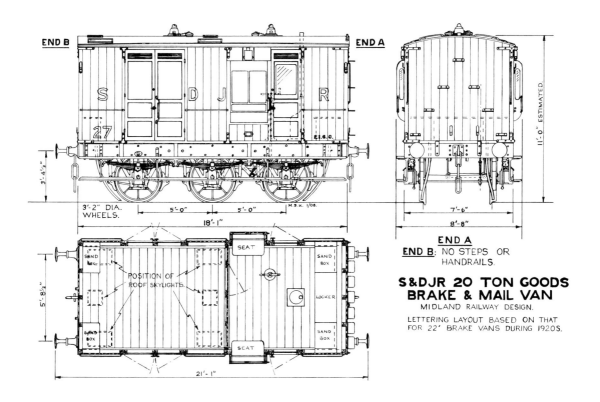

Right:

Plate 119 The two 20-ton vans soon proved their worth in braking power, especially over the Mendip Hills and from November 1888 all renewals were of the enlarged 22ft six-wheeled pattern — in many cases two 20-tonners replacing three 10-ton vans on renewals, so it seems double provision of brake vans was already becoming necessary. SDJR No 6, dating from 1890, is seen in photographic grey livery, complete with shaded lettering after overhaul about 1904, in original condition with full height side lookouts. The drawing for these is reproduced as **Figure 60** in *Volume One*. *SDJR Official*

A total of 22 were built between 1889 and 1923, as follows:

Built 1889 — Nos 43, 44 (later 13, 17)	Built 1910 — No 18
Built 1890 — Nos 3, 6, 16	Built 1912 — No 5
Built 1894 — Nos 30, 32	Built 1913 — Nos 19, 34
Built 1898 — No 15	Built 1920 — No 38
Built 1903 — Nos 9, 36	Built 1921 — Nos 29, 35, 40
Built 1908 — No 7	Built 1923 — Nos 2, 28, 31

The last seven were the only new wagons authorised after 1914. While on the subject of goods brake vans it is also worth recording the long hours regularly worked by goods train guards. The minutes contains several references to a reduction in hours — in February 1899 from 72 to 66 per week and in November 1907 to 60 hours per week. Tough times indeed!

Above:

Plate 120 One of the two original 22ft vans of 1889, by now renumbered as SDJR 17, is glimpsed at Bournemouth West in 1923, revealing the post-World War One lettering style, with approximately 10in company initials and numerals. On the original print the letters SDJR are only just visible level with the centre of the 'X' bracing, the letter 'D' being above and to the right of the number. The actual position of the numerals seems to vary, as some have been noted low down in the centre panel instead of at the end. Equally, some vans may have carried the number low down near both ends. The original subject of this picture, LSWR brake van No 1499, appears as **Plate 104** in *Volume One*, and it was only when the negative was obtained that the larger SDJR lettering revealed itself. *F. Foote*

Right:

Plate 121 In *Volume One* there was speculation as to how long these brake vans may have lasted. All passed into LMS ownership in 1930 and were renumbered into their 358XXX range. Proof that some at least survived to the 1950s comes from this view of M358319, taken at Wells in 1953. It is lettered 'To be returned to S & D Section' on the crib rail below the wagon plate. Several other views of these vans in goods trains are now known, many dating from the early 1950s and all but one is clearly on the Joint line, so it seems that the 'Return to' instruction was generally obeyed. Note the modified lookouts and the fixed side lamp over, plus the fitting of oil-lubricated axle boxes, necessitating the step board to be lowered by a few inches. Although not of the best technical quality, the photograph has been included for its historical interest. *P. Fry*

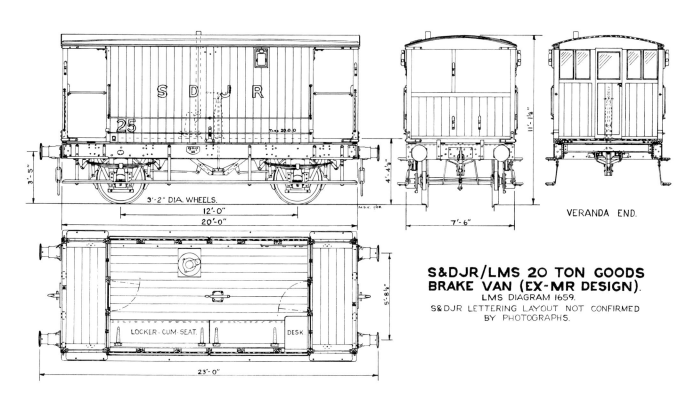

S&DJR/LMS 20 TON GOODS BRAKE VAN (EX-MR DESIGN).
LMS DIAGRAM 1659.
S&DJR LETTERING LAYOUT NOT CONFIRMED BY PHOTOGRAPHS.

Figure 21 By 1925 three of the 16 remaining 10-ton vans (Nos. 23-25) were in need of replacement — all being around 40 years old — but no renewals were authorised. Instead three standard Midland Railway 20-ton vans to LMS Diagram 1659 were sent from Derby in July 1925, at a cost to the Joint Committee of £396 each. As SDJR Nos 23-25 they served until returned to LMS ownership in 1930. No photographs of them in SDJR service are known so the livery shown here is based on the six-wheeled van layout. On their return to LMS property one is left to speculate whether they would have reverted to their old MR/LMS numbers or were allocated new ones in the 358XXX series. It may be mere co-incidence that identical vans M357491/3 were noted at Templecombe in 1961, lettered 'Not in common use'. The LMS numbers included a block from 357401-700.

Timber, bolster, rail wagons & machinery trucks

Plate 122 This magnificent picture shows no less than 13 SDJR single bolster wagons at Highbridge Wharf and quadruples our knowledge of these vehicles at a stroke! The original is so sharp that almost all are identifiable, from left to right, as follows:

Vehicle No	SR Diagram type	Remarks
597	1592	With sprung buffers
1001	1591	With dumb buffers
369	1591	With dumb buffers
403+362	1593	Twin bolsters, with sprung buffers
118?	1592	With dumb buffers
361	1591	With dumb buffers
81	1592	With dumb buffers
124	1592	With dumb buffers
?	1591	With dumb buffers
376	1591	Ex-works — with dumb buffers
?+?	1593	Twin bolsters, with sprung buffers
76	1591	With dumb buffers — not seen in picture

The photograph was taken from the cab of the wharf crane (its bucket is seen hanging in the foreground) and the wagons are loaded with 30ft rails destined for either the S&D Engineer at Glastonbury or the LSWR at Redbridge. In later years bogie bolsters to SR Diagrams 1597 and 1789 would have replaced the Joint line wagons. Note also the stacks of timber in the background and the coal wagons visible in the distance. The wharf must have been a busy place prior to closure in 1965 and would make an interesting model. *SDJR Official*

From the evidence of **Plate 122**, plus information from the Somerset & Dorset Railway Trust at Washford, some further suggestions may be made concerning the numbering of SDJR bolster wagons. Most appear to be numbered in the following areas of the list:

64-83	Nos 64-75 possibly double bolsters to SR Diagram 1596.
115-124	SR Diagrams 1591/2/3.
358-377	SR Diagrams 1591/2/3.
580-599	SR Diagrams 1591/2/3.
991-1002	Possibly a batch of 12 to SR Diagram 1591.

This is by no means certain, but only Nos 262, 329, 403, 781 and either 802 or 862 have been confirmed and fall outside these ranges. A total of 72 traffic department bolster wagons of all types were divided equally in 1914, but it is not known if the four diagrams were spilt evenly between the Midland and LSWR.

Above:

Plate 123 A broadside view of Diagram 1592 type bolster No, 118, possibly seen earlier at Highbridge, but officially photographed after lifting in 1895, according to the branding on the left-hand end of the solebar. This dates from July 1888, according to the wagon plate. There is only one reference to ordinary bolster wagons in SDJR minutes: concerning the purchase of 13 10-ton timber and rail wagons from a Mr. Kitson in December 1881, along with 17 high-sided 10-ton open goods wagons, for £38 each. *SDJR Official*

Figure 22 In February 1903 authority was given to construct four 10-ton bolster wagons and one 31ft rail truck at Highbridge, for the use of the Engineer's Department, at a cost of £389. These were destined to be the last wagons ordered on capital account and took the highest SDJR numbers, 1242-6. This is the rail & sleeper wagon, almost identical to a Midland Railway design. All five passed to the Southern in 1930, becoming their numbers 64590-4, however the rail truck was withdrawn in November 1930 and all except No 64591 of the bolsters had gone before the end of January 1932.

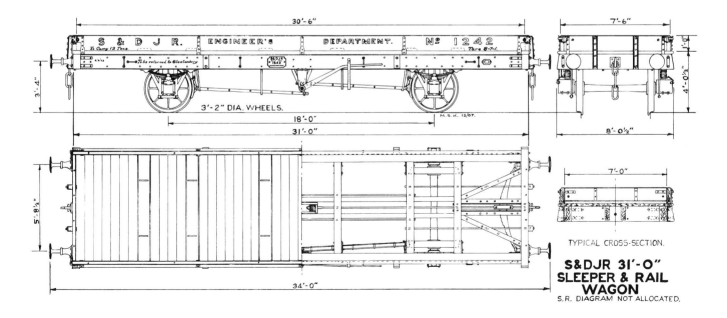

Above:

Plate 124 Four numbers in the LSWR wagon list (14996-9) were allocated in 1914 to implement/machinery wagons — perhaps giving the impression that eight such vehicles were in existence at that time. For the purposes of accounting and division, these vehicles appear to have been grouped with the open goods wagons. Only two wagon numbers were known back in 1983 and this situation has not changed up to the time of writing, although if there were indeed eight of these, SDJR numbers 637-44 might have been allocated. Joint line No 642 was photographed *circa* 1903 and differs in detail from No 641, illustrated in **Plate 171** of *Volume One*. Although the body length in both cases is 20ft, the proportions of the wagons differ as No 642 has 3ft diameter wheels necessitating the provision of raised metal covers over the wheels in the floor of the wagon. A South Western diagram was prepared and is correct for wagon 641 and it is known that LSWR numbers 14996/9 were reallocated to new machinery trucks built on renewal account in 1921, so it seems likely that at least two wagons of the type became LSWR stock in 1914. *SDJR Official*

Figure 23 A drawing showing both versions of machinery truck, based on two surviving (but indistinct) SDJR general arrangement drawings dated 1888 and 1890, backed up by the LSWR diagram. Both the GA's are described as 'standard implement wagons'. Note that the drawgear is mounted at a slight angle to horizontal to keep it clear of the well. On the original drawings the buffers are as drawn, but would need to be mounted on 3in packings to achieve the stated overall length of 23ft. The Midland & South Western Junction Railway also had some very similar vehicles.

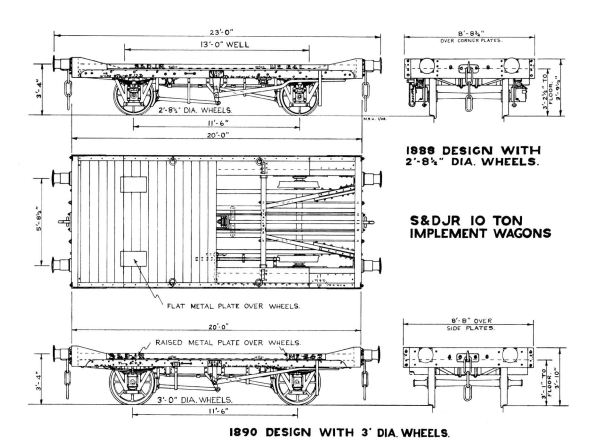

Ballast wagons

Right:

Plate 125 A point perhaps not made clear in *Volume One* was that by no means all SDJR three plank dropside wagons were allocated to the Engineer's Department. No 649 is a traffic department wagon dating from April 1904 and photographed at Highbridge when new. Just whether it was one of the 32 passed to the LSWR in 1914 is not known, as these were transferred to the LSWR Engineer's Department by 1918, receiving ED series numbers in place of their 14701-32 range LSWR traffic numbers. As a result of this change, their former Joint line numbers have been lost. However, it appears that not all SDJR ED wagons were branded 'Engineer's Department', as the dropside shown in **Plate 167** of *Volume One* later became a Southern ED wagon, yet it carries no such branding. Compare this with SDJR No 636, visible in **Plate 106**. *SDJR Official*

The Joint Committee minutes refer to ballast wagons just twice — firstly in 1884 when 12 old traffic department wagons were to be transferred to Engineer's use. Shortly after it was recorded that 12 ballast wagons were purchased from the LSWR for £120, but whether this was in place of or additional to the former traffic wagons is not clear. No more specific records appear until as late as July 1927, when seven second-hand wagons were provided by the LMS to replace some Joint line wagons that were beyond repair — at a cost of £243, including some spare parts. Their construction dates are recorded as 1926, but almost certainly they were older MR dropsides to their Diagram 305. These reused SDJR numbers 212, 662/98, 869, 489A, 711A and 899A, all becoming Southern Railway ED stock in 1930 as the latter's Nos 62945/60/2/5/80/7/91 respectively.

In 1914 the minutes also record that 24 dedicated ballast wagons were to be retained by the Joint line, together with 26 others, part of the 63 duplicate service vehicles 'for use only on the Joint line until they become unfit to travel'. The latter all carried numbers with an 'A' suffix, to denote their restricted use status. Contrary to what might be expected, many of these duplicate ballast wagons were actually newer than the others and all 50 lasted to become SR stock in 1930, allocated the new numbers between 62943-92. Examples of SDJR numbering are:

    Duplicates — Nos 3A, 57A, 397A, 402A, 546A, 686A,
    708A and 875A.
    Remainder — Nos 206/27, 395, 620/96, 709. 816/92.

Whilst withdrawals commenced immediately on receipt by the Southern some, including Nos 62948/67, lasted until British Railways days.

The only other references to ballast in the minutes concern the supply of the material itself. At various dates parcels of land were purchased near Corfe Mullen, to be used for ballasting purposes, while in 1910 a five-year contract for the supply of stone ballast was signed with John Wainwright of Shepton Mallet. This firm had wagons of its own (one is visible at Yeovil Junction in the foreground of **Plate 11** in *Volume One*) based at Vobster Quarries, near Frome, as well as at Shepton Mallet. This company later became part of the Roads Reconstruction group.

Right:

Plate 126 Typical of those wagons passed to the LSWR in 1914 is the company's ED No 260, just visible at Eastleigh around 1920. This was allocated to Diagram 1732 after the Grouping, becoming SR No 61743 and lasting until September 1953. It then received a reprieve as internal user No 080276 at Redbridge sleeper works until 1958, along with about 25 other LSWR/SDJR dropside wagons. Note the canvas flap over the axle box, the LSWR wagon plate and the 'Return empty to S & D Section' instruction to the left of the company initials. *H. C. Casserley*

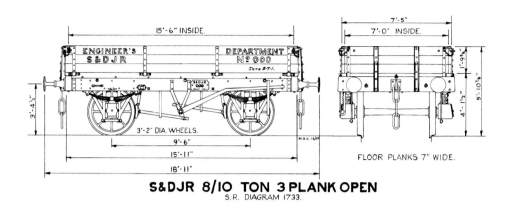

S&DJR 8/10 TON 3 PLANK OPEN
S.R. DIAGRAM 1733.

Figure 24 Just seven of the ballast wagons passed to the LSWR in 1914 were 15ft 11 in long — allocated to SR Diagram 1733. These were built in 1907-12 and included LSWR Engineer's department numbers 96, 147, 341 and 372. No SDJR numbers are known.

Below:

Plate 127 Joint line crane No 1, built by Stothert & Pitt of Bath in 1887, having a capacity of 5 tons. The match truck, lettered 'Pilot No 1' was built at Highbridge in 1910, almost certainly replacing a similar original vehicle built in 1887. This match truck appears to be a standard MR design. Both vehicles passed into LMS ownership in 1930. *SDJR Official*

Chapter 3.
LBSCR Wagons

Above:
Plate 128 Rebuilt Vulcan 0-6-0 No 545, ready to leave Willow Walk with a goods for Brighton, probably in July 1908. This was the first 'C2X' rebuild and these locomotives powered most of the heaviest LBSCR goods trains until the arrival of the 'K' class moguls from 1913. Note the make-up of the train, with a high proportion of sheeted open wagons and just four vans plus one or maybe two brake vans at the rear. All appear to be of Brighton origin — a typical scenario prior to World War One. *H. Gordon Tidey*

In Volume Two of *Southern Wagons* it was suggested that LBSCR wagon diagrams often failed to record differences between the wagons and also that the accuracy of some records were doubted. Readers in possession of the 2003 reprint will be aware that this was later proven by the Isle of Wight Steam Railway when restoring its LBSCR single bolster wagons, as some of these failed to conform either to diagram or to the register entries. Just how, when or why this came about is now impossible to determine. LBSCR diagrams regularly ignored such minor details as different roof profiles, number and provision of ventilators, Westinghouse brakes, etc, or, in some cases, carrying capacities and it is no surprise that the Southern Railway staff attempted to redress this after 1923. However, it seems that the information to enable this to be recorded correctly was not always available and whilst some errors were corrected, many others were not while, for good measure, one or two more were added! With this in mind, we will now take a second look at LBSCR wagons.

Open goods wagons

Right:

Plate 129 This view, one of several taken at Battersea Wharf between 1905 and 1910, shows a selection of 'Open A', 'Open D' and 'Open D2' wagons, although only two may be identified further. The 'Open D2' in the foreground, No 1192, is actually labelled as such; confounding the comment made on page 10 of *Volume Two* doubting whether this classification letter was actually applied to the wagons. It dates from 1903 and ran until March 1927, failing to receive SR livery or its allocated SR number of 20841, despite being allocated to Diagram 1367. It is coupled between two 'Open D' wagons and these were the predecessors of the D2 class, a handwritten note in the front of the LBSCR wagon register stating, 'After December 1898 only D2 wagons will be built instead of ordinary D wagons'. LBSCR numbers for these spanned from 21 to 5887 and all were charged to renewals. The first wagon in the background is 'Open A' No 9126 — a steel underframed example built by BRCW in 1897 and was allocated SR No 26488 but withdrawn in January 1925 without being renumbered. SR Diagram 1371 would have applied. The recorded costs of these two wagons are remarkable for their variance: No 9126 was charged to capital account at £102-10-0d while No 1192 was a renewal costing just £45-6-1d — clearly reusing existing wheelsets and ironwork. For this reason it was rated at only 8 tons capacity. *J. Tatchell Collection*

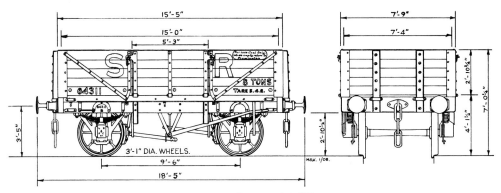

LBSCR 5 PLANK 8 TON OPEN GOODS WITH SQUARE ENDS
S.R. DIAGRAM 1367. THE EXAMPLE DRAWN WAS A LOCO COAL WAGON.

Figure 25 A drawing of the 'Open D2' wagon to SR Diagram 1367, showing an example transferred to loco coal traffic and seen at Wadebridge in 1937. Withdrawal of the 1,100 examples passed to the Southern began soon after Grouping and only 56 remained in ordinary traffic by 1947, the last being scrapped ten years later. Some final withdrawal dates are as follows:

1951 — Nos 20725, 21437
1952 — No 21550
1954 — No 21760
1957 — No 21599

No withdrawals to this diagram are listed for 1953/5/6. There may have been some still remaining in departmental use at this time.

The equivalent 'Open A' version of Diagram 1367 was SR Diagram 1370 — having round ends and a wheelbase of 9ft 6in. Production of these began in 1874 and most LBSCR numbers between 4051-4500, 4701-7000 and 9001-50 were in use by 1881, although any in these number ranges surviving in 1923 were replacements built from the 1890s onwards. Most early wagons would have resembled No 6627 illustrated in **Plate 17** of *Volume Two*, with either a timber or chain sheet 'rail'. A few wagons dating from the mid-1870s appear in photographs having low raised ends only one plank higher than the sides, known examples being LBSCR Nos 4878 and 5007.

Right:

Plate 130 LBSCR No 5006 is seen at Lancing Works on 27 March 1924, the occasion being the trial of the Gearlock-Reynard auto coupling, also seen in **Plate 8** of *Volume Two*. Clearly, this is the left-hand portion of the same photograph, but shows this wagon in greater detail. According to the SR registers, this was built in 1897 and was allocated SR number 23641 and Diagram 1370 — both matters being slightly academic as the wagon was scrapped in November 1925 without being renumbered. Note the last repaint date of N+ 5.9.21 below the tare weight inscription. Despite enthusiastic write-ups in the contemporary railway press, the auto coupling seems to have found little favour in Britain, but why has someone been at pains to remove the identities of the SR wagons in the background, yet has left those lettered LBSC untouched? *T. A. Barry Collection*

Left:

Plate 131 Relatively few wagons to Diagram 1370 carried post-1936 Southern lettering, never mind the wartime 'economy' 3in style seen on No 24853 — although where the initials 'SR' are is unclear — perhaps just out of sight under the wagon sheet? Notice also that the tare weight is painted in italic script, rather in GWR style. Formerly LBSCR No 6501, it ran from 1904 until June 1946. Double block brakes are now provided on each side, but grease axle boxes remain. By 1948 only 33 wagons to this diagram remained in traffic, with another 31 to Diagram 1363 (round ends removed) and the last two were withdrawn in 1953 (Nos 24208 and 24649), but without photographic evidence it is impossible to state whether these retained round ends at withdrawal. *H. V. Tumilty Collection*

Right:

Plate 132 From 1905 the wheelbase was shortened to 9ft 3in, this remaining standard for all timber-underframed 'Open A's' until production ceased in 1926. Some 5,000 were built, making this variation of the design by far the most numerous LBSCR wagon. Individual variants were few, however 1,400 built between 1905 and 1912 utilised second-hand wheelsets and were rated at only 8 tons capacity, the LBSCR numbers spanning from 2 to 2679. LBSCR No 1923 was one of these, completed in 1908 at a cost of £52 and was photographed in post-1911 livery shortly before being renumbered as SR 20383 in July 1929. It remained in service until April 1941. Diagram 1366 was allocated to the 8-ton wagons and this records that 303 were still running in September 1946. Two withdrawals from 1956 are known, Nos 19476 and 20477, however the January 1961 census records five still in service at that date and one wonders how reliable that figure might be? See **Plate 29** in *Volume Two* for the typical appearance of one of these wagons in their later days. *J. Tatchell Collection*

Left:

Plate 133 An early 10-ton example of Diagram 1369, No 24032 at Guildford in 1937. Built in 1905 as LBSCR No 5579, with double block brakes on one side only, these were duplicated on the other side in September 1931, while No 7 oil axle boxes were fitted in place of the grease ones seen here, some time after 1937. Withdrawal came in December 1946. Notice the pre-1912 style of body strapping, with inside knees and 'J' or 'hockey-stick' shaped external straps either side of the drop door. Wagons built from 1912 onwards had outside knees and a simplified strapping arrangement — compare with **Plate 136**. *E. Jackson*

Above and right:

Plates 134 and 135 Another early Diagram 1369 wagon, SR No 25652/LBSCR No 10585 at Cardington (Bedford) in October 1938. This was built in 1906 — one of more than 500 similar wagons built at Brighton between 1905 and 1908 — this example running until December 1944. Some number batches were given against **Plate 31** in *Volume Two*, to which may be added LBSCR Nos 9551-9850, most of which survived the Grouping to be allocated SR Nos 25332-25621. This batch had oil-lubricated axle boxes from new; possibly the first Brighton opens to have this feature, but were, in fact the second allocation of these LBSCR wagon numbers. The last repaint date of January 1932 is visible on the solebar and the pre-Grouping lettering is just beginning to show through this coat of SR brown. The wagon was renumbered and presumably repainted in SR livery in November 1926, indicating an overhaul cycle of about 5-6 years. *Both A. E. West*

Right:
Plate 136 A later Diagram 1369 wagon carrying faded post-1936 SR lettering, one of 10 sold to the Kent & East Sussex Railway around 1939. SR No 23468 is seen as KESR No 1, *circa* 1947/8. Built in 1913 as LBSCR No 4805, it was repainted and renumbered in SR livery at Ashford in December 1929. This has the later style of strapping, with external side knees as introduced on Diagrams 1366/9 in 1912. Double block brakes were provided on each side when built, with the second vee hanger mounted on the middle longitudinal timber — a common arrangement for wagons built between 1912 and 1918. *C. J. Binnie*

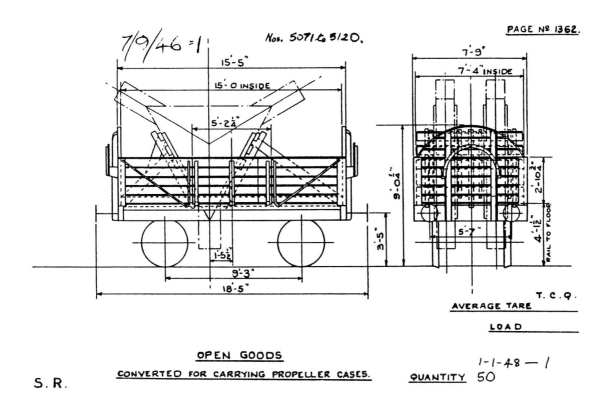

Figure 26 Fifty Diagram 1369 wagons were converted to carry propellers in cases during June-August 1941 — this being the Southern's contribution to an REC order placed with all the 'Big Four' companies in March of that year — the wagons being renumbered into the now vacant LSWR series 5071-5120. Presumably they also carried some form of suitable lettering and routing instructions. No photographs are known, so for this reason the conversion has been illustrated using a copy of SR Diagram 1362. This also usefully shows a reasonably well-drawn example of a Southern diagram — not all were as good as this. The conversion involved cutting two holes in the floor of the wagon and the fitting of a cradle to support the propellers — which were loaded in purpose-made cases. It is not known why Diagram 1369 wagons were selected; perhaps the round ends afforded some protection for the load or maybe it was simply a good way to utilise 50 otherwise surplus LBSCR wagons. Although the tarpaulin sheet support brackets are shown on the drawing, the rail itself is not — it would have almost certainly got in the way of the loading process and may not have been retained. The original conversions were undertaken on order E1489 and a similar order, number A3114, was issued for reconversion back to open goods wagons, dated December 1944. This order was closed in May 1946, yet the diagram is annotated to say that one wagon remained in stock until at least 1948 — or had it got lost in the meantime?

Right:
Plate 137 The final 600 Diagram 1369 wagons were completed at Lancing under Southern Railway auspices, many without the round ends. These should have been recorded as Diagram 1364 but this did not always happen. Isle of Wight transfer No 28404 is seen freshly outshopped in SR brown, but simply with an 'S' over the number, at Newport on 28 June 1949. This style of lettering was used on several Island repaints during 1948/9. Formerly SR mainland No 27528, it was one of order L8 completed in 1924 and was sent to the Island in June 1928, part of a batch of 70 (IOW numbers 28389-28458) and is typical of the final construction, having double block brakes each side (the SR Freighter brake) with the second vee hanger mounted on the inside face of the solebar. Note how the timber doorstop on the right is notched out to clear the brake lever — this being an almost universal detail on Brighton open wagons. *A. E. West*

Right:
Plate 138 Many LBSCR wagons entered departmental stock from 1924 onwards and this diagram 1364/9 open seen at Newhaven in January 1949 is typical. Built in 1915 as LBSCR No 4382, it became SR No 23263 at Lancing in January 1924, remaining in ordinary traffic until January 1948 — losing its round end and sheet rail at some date in between. Then transferred to docks use and renumbered 01060s, it then served for another four years. It is standing at the far end of the East Quay branch, near Bishopstone beach — hence the rather light permanent way. *G.A. Hookham*

SR Diagram 1369 states that 1,064 wagons remained in ordinary stock at 1 January 1948, plus a further 282 square-ended examples to Diagram 1364. Withdrawals continued apace such that the combined total had reduced to 383 just two years later — 36 only retaining sheet rails by this time. By the January 1961 census a mere 162 remained — probably all in the Isle of Wight. Some late running mainland examples are as follows:

Withdrawn in 1955 — Nos 18784, 22314, 22455, 22567, 24159, 26050
Withdrawn in 1956 — Nos 18867, 22375, 22389, 22485, 23328, 23898
Withdrawn in 1957 — Nos 22432, 23673 (the only two listed)

Probably none of these still carried round ends. Eight Island vehicles were rebuilt in late 1967 as ballast dropside wagons, utilising the sides from withdrawn Price & Reeves/SECR wagons to Diagram 1352 and these served the Island railway for a few more years. Numbers may be found in the Appendix. At least two of these rebuilds, plus an original Brighton open has been preserved at Haven Street. A few others were sold to the War Department and survived into the 1960s at Longmoor, Bicester and other WD establishments, some later passing into preservation.

Right:

Plate 139 Steel-underframed 'Open A' No 9212, officially photographed by the builders in late 1897. The finish is a special one, with all below solebars picked out in grey and the body ironwork blacked up — probably not typical of the production livery. Note also the full company initials 'LB&SCRY' as used around the turn of the 20th century, this being its earliest recorded use. Wagon 9212 just failed to become SR stock in 1923, however roundly 900 were allocated Southern numbers and Diagram 1371. The company always held a stock of wagons 'surplus to requirements' (i.e. probably classed as duplicates on other lines) and this

stood at the rather high total of 663 in December 1922, so possibly did include some departmental vehicles in the total. Two-thirds of these were open wagons and Diagram 1371-type vehicles probably accounted for many of them. Some of these were later added to SR stock to replace early withdrawals or wagons transferred to departmental or other restricted uses in 1923-5. The last traffic department survivors were SR Nos 26412, 26819, 26902 and 27031, all withdrawn in 1936-8. *BRCW*

Right:

Plate 140 Another BRCW steel-framed wagon, in SR livery doing duty as a loco coal wagon at Plymouth Friary in December 1927. Built in 1898 as LBSCR No 9533, this was at first allocated SR traffic number 26802 and Diagram 1371 in 1923, but was instead down rated to 8-tons capacity, allocated SR Diagram 1375 and number 64468, all in November 1926. The board over the number may read 'For loco coal only. When empty return to Fremington Quay' — although only the first line is clear enough to make out. Non-common-user 'N's appear on the corner plates — just to make sure the wagon was not appropriated for other purposes! All numbers in the SR 64401-500 range were allocated to ex-LBSCR wagons transferred to loco coal or other restricted coal duties between 1926 and 1929 and many of them were ex-Diagram 1371. Note the Mansell wheels — relatively uncommon on LBSCR wagons and probably fitted when downrated to 8-

tons — thereby releasing a better set for use on a traffic department vehicle. The withdrawal date for No 64468 was August 1931 and by 1936 only loco coal wagons 64441/57/64 to this diagram remained in use. *H. C. Casserley*

While discussing loco coal wagons, it is worth recording that further open wagons were transferred to this traffic in the years after 1929. At the Grouping, just 200 former SECR RCH mineral wagons were allocated to these duties, their SR numbers being 63751-950. From 1926 ex-LBSCR vehicles took numbers 64401-500, as noted above, while more were transferred after 1930, taking numbers 64291-347/52-91. Not every wagon in these ranges was of Brighton origin, as some in the 63452-71

batch were ex-SECR, however very few LSWR wagons were similarly renumbered. Most were elderly and failed to last for long, allowing some numbers to be allocated more than once. The numbers 64348-51 and 64393-400 were allocated to former Isle of Wight Railway loco coal wagons and some additional details of these appear in Chapter 4, while No 64392 was an additional Diagram 1369 loco coal wagon sent to the Isle of Wight in 1937.

Right:

Plate 141 The last new Brighton open wagon design to appear was the 500 Metropolitan vehicles built on renewal account in 1920/1, taking random LBSCR numbers between 1 and 3216. They were charged out at £315-17-6d each, giving some idea of the spiraling inflation that had taken place since 1914. SR No 22156 is seen at Kentish Town on 24 March 1934, loaded with locomotive coal (despite being an ordinary traffic department wagon — these things happened not infrequently) and was formerly LBSCR No 2434. Being of more modern construction and with the benefit of RCH wheelsets they lasted better than other Brighton open wagons and 360 to Diagram 1368, plus three to the square-ended equivalent, Diagram 1365, remained

in service in September 1946. The total for Diagram 1365 may be understated, as not all wagons were re-diagrammed when the round ends were removed. The January 1961 census states that three to Diagram 1368 remained in traffic, although several were still in internal use at either Littlehampton or Redbridge at that date. Other sample LBSCR numbers were 50, 299, 1477, 1791, 2729 and 3099, all of which retained their pre-Grouping livery until 1930. *H. F. Wheeller*

Mineral wagons

Neither of the two LBSCR designs could be illustrated when *Volume Two* was published — fortunately this omission can now be rectified. One other batch of mineral wagons also deserves mention, these being allocated LBSCR Nos 9551-9850. They were second-hand purchases of 1897/8 and were formerly Stephenson Clarke coal wagons, built originally by Harrison & Camm in 1882/3, SC numbers 1001-1100 and 2101-2300. Purchased specifically for coal traffic from Deptford Wharf, they ran until 1904-8, their numbers then being re-used by 'Open A' wagons to Diagram 1369.

Left:

Plate 142 At Fremington Quay the staff pose for the camera in front of Diagram 1374 open goods wagon No 64422 or 64423 — it could be either — some time between 1926 and 1930, this being the running period for both wagons. A former 'Coal C' mineral, either LBSCR No 8359 or 9867, which were originally allocated SR open goods wagon numbers 27100 and 27139 respectively in 1923, along with Diagram 1372. In 1926 both were downrated to 8-tons capacity and allocated to loco coal traffic — although clearly here the load is anything but coal. The board reads, 'For loco coal traffic only. When empty to be returned to Fremington', similar to the wagon illustrated in **Plate 140**. This was one of about 15 wagons to the diagram allocated to this traffic. Note again the Mansell wheels and the steel backstay across the end of the wagon, characteristic of all the 1896-1900 steel underframed wagons. Another wagon to this diagram appears in **Plate 145**. *H. Mock Collection, courtesy J. Nicholas*

Once the North Devon & Cornwall Junction Light Railway opened between Torrington and Halwill in 1925, a number of wagons were reserved for clay traffic from Peters Marland to Fremington Quay, including several of LBSCR origin. Numbers noted in the registers are SR 21108 and 21421 (to Diagram 1367) and 26575, 26655/87, 27048/66 (to Diagram 1371), but from the evidence of **Plate 142**, perhaps some of the loco coal wagons were used as well. In later years more modern wagons were substituted and by the 1960s the various SR five and eight plank opens were being used. Other LBSCR open wagons were allocated to such specific locations as the Crumbles ballast sidings at Eastbourne and the various gasworks on the system and were to be returned empty to these locations.

Right:
Plate 143 The elusive Hurst Nelson RCH mineral wagon to SR Diagram 1373, SR No 27320/LBSCR No 10953 is seen at Whitstable Harbour in 1937, carrying post-1936 SR livery. Apart from a fragmentary view of one in LBSCR livery, taken in 1922, this remains the only known illustration of the Brighton version of the design. The SR diagram tells us that 16 of the 225 wagons remained in service in 1946 and what may well be the final survivor, SR No 27250, was withdrawn in 1952. Presumably by then it had been uprated to 13 tons capacity along with most other 12-ton mineral wagons. That these were regarded as non-standard wagons by the LBSCR is demonstrated by the fact that a quantity of spare parts were ordered from the builders in 1912, a year after the wagons themselves entered service. *J. W. Sparrowe, courtesy R. S. Carpenter photos*

Covered goods wagons

Like the open goods vehicles, these were also extremely standardised and most variations were covered in *Volume Two*. However, there are a few matters that need to be followed up; mostly concerning the more specialised vehicles for 'Grand Vitesse', butter, poultry, refrigerated and gunpowder traffic.

In **Plate 5** of *Volume Two*, 'Grande Vitesse' van No 1507 was illustrated. Readers in possession of the 2003 reprint or *Volume Three* will be aware of the similarity between this van and the SER equivalent drawn in the latter volume as **Figure 41**. Fortunately, LBSCR wagon registers and working timetables from the 1880s now provide a little more information. The WTT's list 12 'large' and 34 'small' vans dedicated to this traffic. The latter were to LBSCR passenger stock diagram 50 and were 20ft long. The former were goods wagon numbers 1501-12 (although not all twelve have the annotation 'GVV' — Grande Vitesse Van — in the register), but clearly include the van illustrated. Closer examination of **Plate 5** yields the possible conclusion that it is also either 20ft or 20ft 4in long, with a wheelbase of around 12ft, although none of these dimensions have yet been confirmed. Even if only approximately correct, this fails to explain the large and small descriptions, since both types were of similar length.

Readers' attention is now drawn to the Wild Swan publication of 1989 *E.J. Bedford of Lewes*, by John Minnis where, in Plates 50 and 62 two unidentified vans appear at the head of Newhaven Continental boat trains. These have very high-pitched roofs and perhaps a droplight in one door, but are otherwise very similar to van No 1507. It should also be explained that the roofline in **Plate 5** has been retouched and on other copies of the same print, the roof is entirely lost in the background, so could be of a higher profile. This may account for the 'large' van description — although the possibility of the vans in the Bedford photographs being from another company cannot altogether be discounted, but why would these find themselves in a Newhaven boat service? This was, after all, the regular route for the vans, although the 1895 working timetable details one overnight working to Portsmouth Harbour, for which purpose No 1501 may have been equipped with vacuum brakes in addition to Westinghouse gear.

All this proves somewhat academic for true Southern enthusiasts, as the Grande Vitesse vans were all withdrawn in 1903-5, their LBSCR numbers being re-used by standard covered goods wagons built in 1909 and these became SR stock as Nos 46192-203, to Diagram 1433, at the Grouping. This diagram applied to by far the most common design of LBSCR covered goods wagon built between 1878 and 1915, very nearly all being 8-ton unfitted vehicles without any specialised or dedicated use. The later 10-ton equivalent to SR Diagram 1436 was almost identical and these were completed on renewal account in 1920-3. A combined total in excess of 1,000 were built, with two basic variants of roof profile depending on pre/post-1893 construction date, however it is unlikely that the total extant at any one time exceeded 600, as most true Stroudley vans were replaced by newer stock from 1903 onwards. Within these numbers were a small minority dedicated to more specialised duties, of which more anon.

A summary of the LBSCR and SR numbering blocks, with original construction dates, is as follows; -

Table 4

LBSCR Number Blocks	Original construction Dates*	Survivors to SR numbers	Remarks
1501-1600	1877-80	46192-46267	Includes Grande Vitesse and gunpowder vans. SR vans were all replacements.
3301-5/9	1915	46268-73	
3601-3740	1889-93	46274-46335	Includes poultry & butter vans. SR vans were mostly replacements.
3741-85	1896-1900	46336-53	Includes refrigerator vans
7996-8000	1900-2	46354-6	
8001-8258	1880-89	46357-46587	Includes poultry vans. SR vans were mostly replacements.
8259-70	1899-1900	46588-96	
8331-9	1900-2	46597-46602	
9002-31	1901-5	46603-20	Includes bogie refrigerator and gunpowder vans.

* By 1923 virtually all pre-1893 non-specialised vans had been replaced by newer vehicles with the sharper Billinton roof profile and most numbers in the 1501-1600, 3601-3740 and 8001-8258 blocks had been allocated twice. Some numbers between 1513 and 1600 were re-allocated to cattle wagons built in 1912-14.

Above:
Plate 144 This enlargement of part of a goods train entering Newhaven behind 'C2' 0-6-0 No 555, *circa* 1905, shows the usual selection of opens plus three vans. The nearest of these is a standard Stroudley vehicle, however the other two exhibit a number of unusual features. Most obvious is the double roof and six ventilators each atop. The middle van has the Billinton roof profile and eight ventilator bonnets in the side, the far van has only four side vents but has louvers in the doors, evident from the low position of the company initials and exactly as the ancient-looking van illustrated in **Plate 45** of *Volume Two*. LBSCR working timetables dating from 1892 state: '20 special ventilated box trucks numbered 3689-3708 are now in use for the conveyance of butter and other perishable goods from Newhaven. To be returned there without delay'. The far van and No 01183S in *Volume Two* are clearly from this batch, although the latter has lost its double roof and side ventilators by SR days. The middle van could be a meat van or one of the refrigerator vans, but comparison with **Figure 13** in *Volume Two* shows a number of unexplained differences. These two vans were also built for services to/from Newhaven but to date neither has been positively identified in a photograph. See also the caption accompanying **Plate 145**.
E. R. Lacey Collection

Apart from the poultry and butter vans, few Stroudley vehicles remained at the Grouping and probably the last of these, LBSCR Nos 1537/74, 3628 and 8111 were withdrawn in 1921-3. The 35 10-ton replacements to Diagram 1436 took random numbers between 1549 and 3713, later being allocated SR mainland numbers 46739-73, but all except seven were subsequently shipped to the Isle of Wight between 1927 and 1939, so the 10-ton vans would then have been a rare sight on the mainland.

Within the number blocks quoted opposite were just 31 vans dedicated to specialised traffic, as below:

Designated Traffic	LBSCR Numbers	SR Numbers	SR Diagram	Date Built
Poultry	3683, 8014/25/33	46311/70/81/9	1433	1880/1, 1891
Butter	3689-3708	46314-25 only	1433	1891
Refrigerated	3765/6	50594/5	1471	1898
Refrigerated (bogie)	9013	61072 (aero flat)	1685	1905
Gunpowder	1517/41, 9029/30	61261-4	1705	1903/4

In addition, 20 vans to Diagram 1435 were built specifically for egg traffic and these were described fully in *Volume Two*.

Alone of the above, just the poultry and refrigerator vans were Westinghouse fitted. An additional 21 ordinary vans were converted for gunpowder traffic between 1914 and 1920; examples including LBSCR Nos 1519/36/56/7, 3616, 9007/21 and all reverted to normal traffic later (see **Plates 146 and 147**). The four purpose-built gunpowder vans to SR diagram 1705 cost £244 apiece, whereas an ordinary van cost around £70-80 prior to World War One. Livery details and regular duties of the gunpowder vans remain unknown.

Figure 27 The butter van, based on known photographs and standard dimensions. Twelve became SR property but none received their allocated SR numbers, which would have been 46314-25, however four became departmental stock at Lancing Works instead, numbered 01160s/66s/70s/83s. All 12 traffic vans were out of service by mid-1927, the departmentals lasting another 10 years in semi-static use. None of the vans were allocated SR Diagram 1433 either, so had they lasted longer might the Southern have issued a different diagram for these variants?

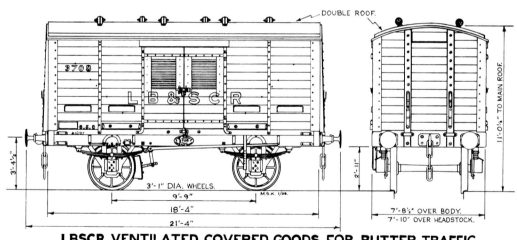

LBSCR VENTILATED COVERED GOODS FOR BUTTER TRAFFIC
A VARIANT OF S.R. DIAGRAM 1433.

Above :

Plate 145 'E3' class 0-6-2T No 459 heads a 'down' goods from Willow Walk to Norwood and probably beyond through Honor Oak Park, *circa* 1908-10. The rear brake of an 'up' goods may also be seen disappearing towards Willow Walk. Amongst the varied selection of opens in the 'down' train is a 'Coal C' (fifth in the line) with a left-handed brake lever — the first such sighting on one of these wagons — and this is loaded somewhat precariously with empty baskets, presumably roped in place through their handles. Five ventilated vans may also be seen but again these vary in their details. The first, second and fifth are certainly butter vans as **Figure 27**, however the third and fourth appear to be the refrigerator vans to SR Diagram 1471 — having the Billinton roof profile, double roof and no side or roof ventilators, as **Figure 13** in *Volume Two*, but in view of the distance and oblique angle this cannot be stated with certainty. It does bring further into question the identity of the van in **Plate 144**. As no definite view of a poultry van is known, could we be looking at one of these? Or was this a meat van, as a drawing exists dated 1901 showing such a vehicle with three end and eight side ventilators, four roof vents but without a double roof. Before moving on, note also the wagon sheets on the first two opens — with the small letters 'LBSC' stencilled diagonally on the lower corners — in addition to the lettering shown in **Figure 1** of *Volume Two*. IAP

The working timetables of the 1881-1910 period also detail the movements of the four poultry vans, as follows:

From the June 1883 WTT

Poultry — Heathfield to Willow Walk. Every Monday, Wednesday and Friday, van No 8014, with poultry, will be sent from Heathfield to Polegate by the passenger train leaving Tunbridge Wells at 6.7pm. At Polegate it will be attached to the 7.25pm up Hastings passenger train and sent on to Croydon, from whence it will be forwarded by goods train to Willow Walk. This van must be duly returned by goods train to Heathfield on Tuesdays, Thursdays and Saturdays.

Poultry — Uckfield to Willow Walk. Every Monday, Wednesday and Friday, van No 8033, with poultry, will be sent from Uckfield to Lewes by the 7.55pm passenger train. At Lewes it will be attached to the 7.25pm up Hastings passenger train and sent on to Croydon, from whence it will be forwarded by goods train to Willow Walk. This van must be duly returned by goods train to Uckfield on Tuesdays, Thursdays and Saturdays.

These timings varied somewhat over the years and by the mid-1890s both vans were being attached to the 10pm Newhaven-Willow Walk goods train at Lewes, travelling direct to their destination. By 1892 van No 3683 had been added to the Heathfield service, covering Tuesdays and Thursdays while by 1905 van No 8025 was also involved; two vans being dispatched on Mondays, Wednesdays and Fridays.

Each van was Westinghouse fitted to facilitate passenger train working, but apart from this it is not known if the vehicles differed from ordinary vans. By 1923 only Nos 3683 and 8033 remained fitted, although all four were still recorded in SR registers as being reserved for poultry traffic. By this date only the Heathfield working remained and this may have ended in 1927 when all except No 3683/SR 46311 were withdrawn from traffic. This van was then stripped of Westinghouse gear but continued to run in SR livery until 1932 — almost certainly the last Stroudley-style covered goods wagon in service. By 1930 the Heathfield poultry traffic was being handled using SR 'utility' vans.

Below and right:

Plates 146 and 147 Departmental No DS1913 at Archcliffe Junction (Dover) in May 1953, allocated to the motive power department and in use to distribute locomotive stores from Ashford Works to the various running sheds. It was one of 12 such transfers in 1943/4 and numbered consecutively as 1907s-1918s. Built in 1907 as LBSCR No 1519, it was one of the 21 temporary conversions to gunpowder traffic in 1914-20, although nothing of this remains evident in the photographs. It became SR No 46208 between October 1928 and February 1944. The livery was recorded as faded SR brown. Note that the metal ventilator cover high up on the end is missing. *Both A. E. West*

Below:

Plate 148 Another departmental conversion, this time allocated to the Bridge Examiner, Western Division Engineer, who was based at Exmouth Junction. No 1753s is seen at Axminster in March 1952, in grey livery and has had two windows cut into each side, plus a stove fitted near the right-hand end. It was one of several similar conversions from the early 1940s. Built in 1914 as LBSCR No 8086, it became SR No 46441 until transferred to departmental service in September 1942. Final withdrawal took effect in February 1954. *A. E. West*

Left:

Plate 149 If the records are to be believed, SR No 46380 was the last Diagram 1433 van in ordinary traffic outside the Isle of Wight, withdrawn in 1956. However, this was only part of the story. In fact the van entered internal use at Hackbridge before 1948 but was never renumbered either in the departmental or internal user lists and probably did not move for upwards of eight years. It was photographed *circa* 1950, finished in post-1936 SR livery, complete with the italic script stencil 'For internal use only, Hackbridge'. Several others were used similarly at this time, including a few returned from the Isle of Wight, but most were renumbered as appropriate. Another late survivor was internal user No 081032 (ex-SR 46488) at Gunnislake until 1966. No 46380 dates from 1910 and was formerly LBSCR No 8024. The last definite mainland traffic survivors to Diagram 1433 were Nos 46363 and 46582, both withdrawn in 1952. *The Lens of Sutton Association*

Centre left:

Plate 150 Isle of Wight Diagram 1436 transfer No 46974, seen at Sandown in August 1932, carrying pre-1936 SR livery. The last repaint date, 16-8-27, plus the depot location 41, denoting Lancing Works, may be seen on the solebar below the tare weight, this being just prior to island transfer. Built in 1922 as LBSCR No 3647, it was allocated SR mainland number 46760 but went to the Isle of Wight before receiving it. Freighter brakes and Westinghouse pipe are provided, the latter dating from island transfer. Some idea of World War One inflation may be gauged from the fact that this van was charged as a partial renewal costing £226 in 1922, while similar renewals in 1914/5 averaged £75. *E. R. Lacey*

Left

Plate 151 Diagram 1436 fully Westinghouse fitted van No 46959 is seen at Newport around 1960, carrying grey livery with black number patches. This was incorrect — as a fitted van it should have been bauxite. Also dating from 1922, the former LBSCR number was 3658 and it failed to receive its mainland SR number before transfer to the Isle of Wight in February 1929. Only eight vans to this diagram remained on the mainland after 1929, SR numbers being 46742/5/8/63/6/7/71/3. Most of these ran until 1943-6, except No 46771, which was the final IOW transfer, to M & T van 437s in 1939. The brake gear arrangement for this van may be seen in **Figure 37**. *D. J. Wigley*

Above:
Plate 152 100 steel-underframed vans were ordered from the Ashbury Railway Carriage & Iron Company in 1900, including LBSCR No 10388, seen at Battersea Wharf *circa* 1910 (part of the same view reproduced as **Plate 129**). This later became SR No 46658, to Diagram 1434. The lettering is shaded and in the form 'LB&SCRY', a feature of all these Ashbury vans when new; however this has discoloured badly and now appears very off-white. If the date of the photograph is correct, then the livery could be more than 10 years old. The last survivors to this diagram, SR Nos 46679/82, were finally withdrawn in 1951/2, after being reinstated in traffic around 1948. However, like van No 46380 in **Plate 149**, these may have been more static than mobile during their final years. *J. Tatchell Collection*

At least 150 former Brighton covered goods wagons entered departmental service between 1924 and 1948; about a quarter of the total inherited at the Grouping. A few were sold to the Government and survived at such locations as Chatham Dockyard, while many more were grounded as line side huts, etc. The SR allotment association expressed a particular preference for the vans and so as grounded bodies they could be seen at such diverse locations as New Cross Gate, Redhill, Ascot, Wingham (East Kent Railway), Staines, Fareham, Wool and Yeovil Junction. Preserved examples are few, confined to The Bluebell Railway and the Isle of Wight.

Livestock vehicles

Discrepancies in the records are a feature of the ordinary cattle wagons. All those passed to the Southern Railway had been classed as Diagram 12 by the LBSCR — the Southern separating them into Diagram 1527 (6-tons) and 1528 (10-tons) and in theory only the final 20 built in 1920-2 were to the latter diagram. However, some official records state that these were to Diagram 1527 and the other 400 were to Diagram 1528. Another version lists all of them as Diagram 1527! Both designs were almost identical save for carrying capacity so perhaps all this was rather academic, yet much more obvious differences such as roof profile and braking were totally ignored.

There appears to have been some attempt to keep LBSCR cattle wagons within defined numbering blocks and almost all fell within the 1601-1700, 4001-26/45-50 and 7103-7868 ranges. What may have been the prototype Stroudley vehicle took LBSCR No 1773 in 1877, replacing an 1852-vintage wagon of the type illustrated in **Plate 59** of *Volume Two*. The remaining 227 Stroudley wagons took numbers 1621-1700 and 7351-7497 but only a handful numbered between 7381 and 7400, dating from 1886, survived at the Grouping. All the others had been replaced by Billinton-style vehicles built between 1894 and 1917.

Left:

Plate 153 A Stroudley-era wagon, sold to Colonel Stephens Hundred of Manhood & Selsey Tramway. Despite a search through the LBSCR wagon register, the number of this wagon was not recorded but it is typical of the Stroudley vehicles with a shallow roof profile, grease axle boxes and single block brakes on one side only. The last vestige of LBSCR lettering is just visible, although that for the HMST is little better. The photograph was taken at Selsey in 1935, after the line had closed. *L. E. Brailsford*

Right:

Plate 154 Billinton-pattern Diagram 1527 wagon No 7192, built in 1895 at a cost of £89. Typical of the wagons built between 1894 and 1899, it was relegated to 'surplus stock' at the end of 1913 but reinstated owing to wartime conditions, contriving to give another 13 years' service and just failed to receive its allocated SR number of 53011. The photograph was taken at Lewes *circa* 1908 and is also an interesting portrait of Brighton company staff. *L. Marshall Collection*

35 wagons to Diagram 1527 were Westinghouse fitted in LBSCR days, to enable them to run in passenger trains. Some examples are:

LBSCR Nos 1596, 1690, 4004, 7105, 7418 and 7791.
SR Nos 52897, 52915, 53010, 53200/58-67/9.

All were equipped with through vacuum pipes soon after the Grouping but began to lose their Westinghouse gear from 1927 onwards. No photographs are known, so exact brake arrangements cannot be confirmed, but are thought to be as illustrated in **Plate 151** and **Figure 37**. This provision did not ensure longevity as the final mainland survivors, SR Nos 52901, 53063/283/6/93 were all unfitted and were withdrawn during 1951/2.

Left:

Plate 155 Although three Island transfers lasted longer, they saw practically no use after 1948. Diagram 1528 wagon No 53371 is seen at Newport in August 1936, having been shipped to the Island along with five others in 1927-9. This is certainly to the later diagram (it is of 10 tons capacity and has slightly wider corner pillars) and was formerly SR mainland No 53300 and LBSCR No 7529, one of the last Brighton cattle wagons built in 1922. The livery shows the typical pre-1936 lettering layout. *H. F. Wheeller*

LBSCR working timetables list allocations for the 24 passenger-rated 'cattle boxes' built in 1892 and 1894, as follows, this version coming from the WTT dated January 1895.

Cattle by passenger train — 24 cattle trucks, fitted to run in passenger trains are now in use. Eight will stand at Brighton, four at East Croydon, two each at Three Bridges, Horsham, Polegate, Lewes, Tunbridge Wells and Chichester. All have vacuum and Westinghouse brakes.

Nos 7161-3/5 marked Croydon
Nos 7164/6-72 marked Brighton
Nos 7173/82 marked Horsham
Nos 7174/81 marked Three Bridges
Nos 7175/6 marked Polegate
Nos 7177/8 marked Lewes
Nos 7179/80 marked Tunbridge Wells
Nos 7183/4 marked Chichester

Close examination of **Plate 64** in *Volume Two* will show a 'Return empty to …..' or similar instruction low down at the left-hand end of the vehicle.

Left:

Plate 156 The six special cattle vans with a drover's compartment were completed in 1921, although ordered and originally allocated goods stock numbers six years previously. Their recorded cost was £579-8-6d each. They could easily be mistaken for horseboxes and were always finished in passenger stock livery, both before and after the Grouping. SR No 3844 (ex-LBSCR No 528) is seen at Rotherhithe Road carriage sidings in April 1947, still carrying pre-1936 Maunsell green livery with black ends. It was withdrawn along with companion No 3848 in October 1949, possibly having seen very little use in their final years. Readers may wonder why horseboxes have not been included within this book, the simple explanation being that they were never goods vehicles and were always classed as non-passenger coaching stock. *D. Cullum*

Figure 28 The Diagram 1061 special cattle van, as running in the mid-1930s. The vans were originally Westinghouse braked with a through vacuum pipe and were gas lit. In later years Mansell wheels were substituted for the rather unusual Brighton nine-spoke pattern. After 1938 the letters 'XP' and 'WB 11ft 6in' were added in white in the bottom right-hand corner of each side (see **Plate 65** in *Volume Two*).

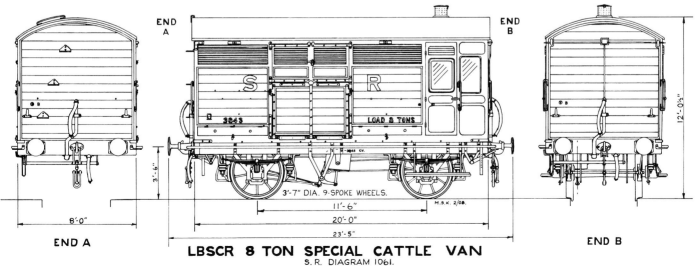

END A

END
A

END
B

END B

LOAD 8 TONS

3843

3' - 6"

3'-7" DIA. 9-SPOKE WHEELS.

M.9.K. 2/08.

11'-6"

20'-0"

23'-5"

8'-0"

12'-0½"

LBSCR 8 TON SPECIAL CATTLE VAN
S. R. DIAGRAM 1061.
DRAWN AS RUNNING IN 1930S WITH VACUUM BRAKES & OIL LIGHTING.

Goods brake vans

Even the LBSCR, not usually given to allocating many different wagon diagrams, managed to issue at least eight (and probably nine) for these vehicles. The Stroudley brakes came in a number of varieties, even if one ignores the different tare weights, however with one exception, these differences would not be obvious from photographs.

Above:

Plate 157 Craven 0-6-0 No 465 at Ford in 1895. The brake van is a typical Stroudley vehicle, complete with very obvious lantern lookout. Apart from the 1882 official photograph reproduced as **Plate 66** in *Volume Two*, there is a dearth of photographs showing this feature and it is not known how many of the 200+ examples were originally so provided, nor is it known for how long they were retained. The well-known Brighton historian, L. E. Brailsford, stated that Billinton commenced their removal, substituting end windows in their place. Certainly, LBSCR diagrams fail to record such a fitting by 1910, but it is thought that they had been dispensed with long before then and possibly only a minority of older vans had them in the first instance. *IAP*

Left:

Plate 158 Another general view taken at Battersea Wharf, *circa* 1910. The usual selection of open wagons may be seen, together with three 'standard' Stroudley brake vans, Nos 25, 33 and 157, all to LBSCR Diagram 21. No 25 was withdrawn in 1916, but the other two were allocated SR numbers 55610/85 and Diagram 1564 respectively. Neither was renumbered and this was typical of most of the 170 Stroudley vans passed to the Southern at the Grouping, being withdrawn during 1924. At just 7-tons tare, by the 1920s they were ineffective when used singly and it had become an expensive, but necessary provision to use two vans, with two guards on most services by this time. *J. Tatchell Collection*

Above:
Plate 159 The last 30 Stroudley brakes, dating from 1888-90 were some 2in narrower (7ft 5½in instead of 7ft 7¼in) and had cast-iron headstocks without self-contained buffers, but were otherwise exactly as their predecessors. LBSCR numbers were 85/6, 205-32 and most were later allocated to SR Diagrams 1567 or 1569. No 222 is seen in dirty 'illiterate mark' livery — being anonymous apart from the number and a chalked '8.20 ……' inscription on the solebar — a reference presumably to its next working. The date is somewhere between December 1894 and August 1909, when 'E3' *Blatchington* (just visible to the left) was running with its name — probably earlier rather than later. These vans tared either 9 or 10-tons so escaped the early cull of Stroudley brakes, being withdrawn between 1925 and 1931, probably kept in traffic for just long enough for Lancing to build some much-needed 25-ton vehicles as replacements. Van 222 was allocated SR No 55846, having been permanently coupled with van 221/SR 55845 just prior to the Grouping — one of three pairs to SR Diagram 1571. *T. A. Barry Collection*

LBSCR working timetables from 1910 onwards detail the requirement for provision of two goods brake vans on most services. In the majority of cases this was to be one at the front and one at the rear of the train, however certain routes required both vans to be at the rear, these being as follows:

Lillie Bridge and Battersea Yard (one 20-ton van only at the rear, if available)
Coal trains New Cross and Norwood Junction*
Willow Walk, Battersea Yard, New Cross, Norwood and Horsham, Littlehampton or Portsmouth*
Brighton, Uckfield and Tunbridge Wells
Brighton, Lewes and East Grinstead
Haywards Heath and East Grinstead
Brighton and Kemp Town
Eastbourne and Tunbridge Wells
Up Steyning line trains
* At the discretion of the local goods foreman, depending on the load.

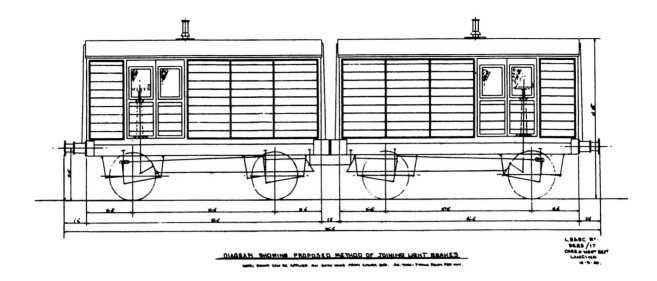

Figure 29 In September 1920 a proposal to utilise the Stroudley brake vans as close-coupled twins was put forward, this being a copy of Lancing drawing No 3225/17, showing how the brake rigging was to be arranged. This would allow single manning as all brake blocks could be applied from either van, in the same manner as the SECR 'combination brake vans' described in *Volume Three*. Two pairs of 7-tonners and three pairs of 10-ton vans were dealt with between 1922-4, SR Diagrams 1570 and 1571 respectively being allocated. Details were as follows:

SR Diagram	LBSCR Numbers	SR Numbers	Date renumbered	Withdrawn
1570	32 + 113	55609/50	3/24	1/26
1570	112 + 149	55649/79	3/24	12/24
1571	209 + 232	55842/48	4/29	4/31
1571	213 + 224	55844/47	3/24	2/26
1571	221 + 222	Not carried	-	8/27

Figure 30 Another idea was to convert the wagons into covered goods vehicles and to this end, brake van No 126 was stripped of its internal brake wheel and stepboards in April 1923. The drawing is based on a sketch taken by Guy Hemingway in 1926. However this solution was not considered worthwhile either and most of the 7-ton Stroudley vans went for scrap during 1924 without receiving their allocated SR numbers. Five became departmental stock as Nos 362s, 379s, 381s, 385s and 386s, lasting into the 1930s. Five are recorded in the LBSCR register as having been sold — one in 1897 to the Hundred of Manhood & Selsey Tramway, the rest found their way to the Isle of Wight Central Railway in 1902-7. A final mystery surrounds the eventual disposal of van No 126. One SR register states that it was withdrawn in 1926 without being renumbered, yet two other official documents record that it became SR No 46191 to Diagram 1432, lasting until December 1940. Which version is correct remains unknown.

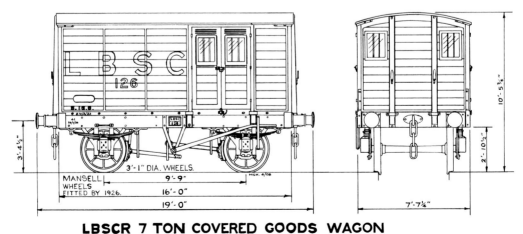

LBSCR 7 TON COVERED GOODS WAGON
REBUILT IN 1923 FROM A STROUDLEY BRAKE VAN.
S. R. DIAGRAM 1432.

The two vans allocated SR Diagram 1565, LBSCR Nos 143/82, were otherwise standard vehicles but had been rebuilt with the sharper Billinton roof profile, presumably in the mid-1890s. LBSCR Diagram 33 was allocated — which is surprising as a similar change on covered goods and cattle wagons failed to result in a new diagram being issued. Just whether any other significant alterations were made is not known, as nothing is apparent from either the LBSCR or SR diagrams and these two vans remained the only ones so modified.

Right:
Plate 160 The final illustration of a Stroudley brake van depicts the last Brighton livery style. LBSCR No 199 was photographed just prior to withdrawal in 1924. Built in 1882, this is one of 24 completed by the Midland RCW Co. at a cost of £160 apiece, LBSCR Nos 181-204. The allocated SR number, 55718, was never applied. *G. P. Keen*

Some further LBSCR numbers for these vans are as follows:

Date built	LBSCR Nos	Remarks
1873	95-105	See **Plate 67** in *Volume Two*
1876/7	117-29	
1878-81	3-6, 10, 143-80	No 143 later with Billinton roof profile
1882	1, 9, 12, 43, 57	See **Plate 66** in *Volume Two*
1886	24, 35/9, 48, 83/4	
1888	58/9, 62/3, 74/7	

Costs varied between £132 and £275, so presumably some were charged to capital account, others as renewals.

Left:
Plate 161 Production of the standard Billinton van to LBSCR Diagram 22 began in 1894, continuing until 1908, by which time no less than 111 were built and all except LBSCR No 66 became SR stock. These were then separated into 9, 10 and 12-tonners by SR diagram, although there appear to be few differences in construction apart from brake rigging. LBSCR No 250 (later SR No 55796) was photographed at Brighton upper yard in 1908 and is a typical 10-ton van dating from 1898, booked cost being £148-16-11d. It was a relatively early withdrawal, in October 1934. Most 9-ton vans went between 1927 and 1936, the 10 tonners between 1930 and 1947, the 12 tonners lasted to 1930-8. While some were renewals and so had widely scattered running numbers, LBSCR Nos 234-72/85-92/95-302/11-25 were all of this type, built in numerical order over the years 1896-1906. *L. Marshall Collection*

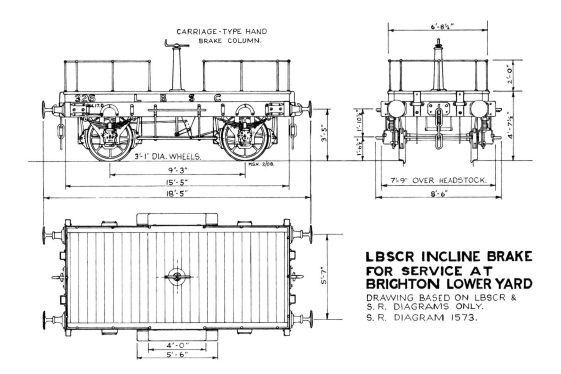

CARRIAGE-TYPE HAND
BRAKE COLUMN.

326 L B S C

3'-1" DIA. WHEELS.

9'-3"

15'-5"

18'-5"

3'-5"

6'-8½"

2'-0"

4'-7½"

1'-10½"

1'-6½"

7'-9" OVER HEADSTOCK.

8'-6"

5'-7"

4'-0"

5'-6"

**LBSCR INCLINE BRAKE
FOR SERVICE AT
BRIGHTON LOWER YARD**
DRAWING BASED ON LBSCR &
S.R. DIAGRAMS ONLY.
S.R. DIAGRAM 1573.

Figure 31 One odd vehicle numbered in the brake van sequence was the incline brake van used at Brighton lower yard. No photographs are known so this drawing is based solely on LBSCR Diagram 34/SR Diagram 1573, which shows a relatively standard 15ft 5in wagon underframe with a centrally mounted carriage-type brake column amidships. However, this position would have fouled the continuous drawgear (if fitted) so there is the possibility that it may have been mounted just off the longitudinal centre-line. The brake gear arrangement shown is entirely conjectural, but as the vehicle is described as an incline brake, presumably the maximum braking power would be required and that drawn would achieve this objective. Some form of scrap metal ballast must have been carried beneath the wagon floor to achieve the stated tare weight of 14tons 17cwt. Neither allocated SR number (55863/61361) was carried, the LBSCR number 326 being retained until withdrawal.

LBSCR minutes dated 4 August 1915 refer to the instruction to cease painting the ends of goods brake vans in red — at the recommendation of the General Manager and A.H. Panter — as a cost saving could be made. The cost of the raw materials used in the paint had risen sharply under wartime conditions (from 26/- to 45/6d per cwt). The colour was officially referred to as 'orange lead'. A cheaper alternative — vermilionette — had been tried in 1914 but was found unsatisfactory. The new Panter 4w and 6w brake vans of 1915/6 were probably the first not to carry this finish, although the monochrome film emulsions of the period fail to make this distinctive colour show up in photographs.

Right:
Plate 162 After a gap in new construction between 1908 and 1915, A.H. Panter's contribution to the wagon fleet appeared during World War One — supplying much needed braking power to complement the haulage capacity of the new 'K' class moguls. Two designs appeared, a four-wheel 15-tonner and a six-wheel 20-ton van. SR No 55867 at Lyme Regis in August 1948 illustrates the former design — proving yet again that these vans migrated off the Brighton section after the Grouping. Built in 1916 as LBSCR No 351, it ran until January 1949 and was allocated to SR Diagram 1574. Note the provision of a through vacuum pipe for working in the branch passenger trains. Nos 55865/6/9/74 were similarly piped by the 1930s. The final survivors were SR Nos 55870/3, withdrawn in 1950 and 1957 respectively. *E. R. Lacey*

Right:

Plate 163 SR No 55930, ex-LBSCR No 335, at Guildford in 1937, represents the 20-ton six-wheeled vans to Diagram 1577. This also carries post-1936 livery with Venetian red ends. It remained in service until April 1946, while the final survivors, SR Nos 55929/31/41/2 were withdrawn during 1948. *E. Jackson*

Left:

Plate 164 Diagram 1576 was Panter's final (and probably best) LBSCR design, appearing in 1922. This broadside view of No 43, later SR No 55898, was clearly taken at the same time as **Plate 81** in *Volume Two* and is a rather clearer original. *LBSCR Official*

Right:

Plate 165 Many Diagram 1576 vans were rebuilt as ballast brake vans between 1928 and 1937, so by Nationalisation only 12 remained in original form. Most were withdrawn during 1953, however DS55907 passed to the ODM (Outdoor Machinery) section in April 1960, being based at Three Bridges until 1971. During this period it is seen in all-black livery with minute white lettering. LBSCR numbers were 25, 43, 53, 66, 78, 102/9/52, 226/80 and 373-93. It is believed that Nos 373 onwards had steel-sheeted lower side panels from new. *T. A. Barry Collection*

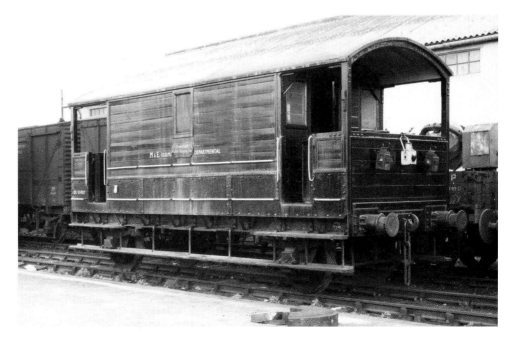

Bolster & timber wagons

Left:
Plate 166 Bridge girder renewal work is in progress near Selhurst *circa* 1895. Single-line working is in force and the Engineer's train occupies the 'down' line. Three dumb-buffered single bolster wagons are visible — all being of the short (12ft) pattern, although the nearest, LBSCR No 7247, is of an older design than the others, which are substantially of the type built until 1911, save for the dumb buffers. No 7247 dates from 1880 and was scrapped in 1895, being replaced by a wagon of later pattern in 1897. All three wagons have single block brakes on one side, probably with timber brake blocks. Traces of the 'illiterate' livery may be seen on all three. The crane match truck is a machinery wagon, while a Stroudley 26ft former brake third provides riding accommodation for the guard and bridge gang. *R. S. Carpenter Photos*

Centre left:
Plate 167 A much later 12ft single bolster, SR No 59038, one of 15 sent to the Isle of Wight in 1928-30 and seen at St Helens Quay in June 1949. The livery, as recorded by the photographer, was black without any company initials or 'S' prefix to the running number. The overhaul date of 1/48 is repeated twice on the solebar. Presumably at that date no instructions had yet been received at Ryde as to how to paint the wagons in British Railways livery. The vehicle was formerly LBSCR No 4659, built in 1909 and was allocated SR mainland No 58358 in 1923, but was transferred to the Isle of Wight before receiving that number. Originally a 6-ton vehicle to SR Diagram 1616, it was uprated to 10-tons and Diagram 1619 on transfer, not that the change of diagram is recorded in the registers. *A. E. West*

Below left:
Plate 168 A useful top view of Diagram 1616/9 single bolster No 59052, in grey livery at Newport in 1960. This shows details of the bolster itself, binding chains and deck. Again this wagon dates from 1909, formerly LBSCR No 4656 and was renumbered as SR mainland No 58356 before being sent to the Island in 1930. Again, originally to Diagram 1616, it was also uprated to 10-tons on transfer. Just visible to the right is Diagram 1661 machinery/road vehicle truck No 60571. *J. Eyres*

According to the registers, the 15 short single bolsters transferred to the Isle of Wight became SR Nos 59037-45/7-52, while the five longer vehicles were Nos 59033-6/46 and, again according to the records the latter five were scrapped in 1955. However, two acquired from BR by the Isle of Wight Steam Railway *circa* 1990, Nos 59043/5, turned out to be 13ft examples and should have carried numbers 59034/46. How and when these changes came about is not known, but it is definite proof that ex-LBSCR stock records are not always accurate (a similar discrepancy exists with the IOW covered goods wagons), so just whether any of the Island transfer records are correct is anybody's guess! However, in this instance it fortunately means that examples of both types of LBSCR single bolster have survived into preservation on the Island.

Above:
Plate 169 A 13ft single bolster wagon, LBSCR No 2917, officially recorded at Lancing around 1913/4. This was ordered in the second half of 1912, part of a batch of 50 completed in late 1912/early 1913. Originally of 6-tons capacity, it became SR No 58534 to Diagram 1617 when renumbered at Ashford in April 1929. Subsequently uprated to 10-tons and Diagram 1620 (this was recorded in the register), it ran until December 1947 — a late example of the diagram. *LBSCR Official, courtesy K. Marx*

Further examples of LBSCR single bolster wagon numbers are as follows:
Diagram 1616 type — LBSCR Nos 4502/30-3, 4661-3, 7222-4, 7497
Diagram 1617 type — LBSCR Nos 2822/42/87-91, 2910/67, 4535, 4620
Diagram 1619 type — LBSCR No 7238 only prior to 1923
Diagram 1620 type — LBSCR Nos 2864, 4519, 4611, 7322, 7930
Some final mainland withdrawals were: SR 58806 (1951) and 58545 (1953), both by then to Diagram 1620.

Right:
Plate 170 LBSCR double bolster wagons were all very similar, only varying with regard to axleboxes, brake gear and carrying capacity. No 7631 was built in 1899 at a cost of £87 and was photographed not long before receiving its SR livery and number (58721), which took place at Ashford in August 1929. SR Diagram 1621 applied, as this was a 10-ton example, running until January 1940. Double block brake gear is provided on each side, with twin vee hangers. *J. Tatchell Collection*

Left:
Plate 171 Another double bolster from the same 1899 batch, LBSCR No 7635 is seen at Bricklayers Arms, *circa* 1928. This wagon has lost its bolsters and is stencilled 'To be returned to Three Bridges'. The allocated SR number was 58723, although the wagon was scrapped in March 1930 without being renumbered. SR Diagram 1618 applied as this remained of 8-tons capacity. A Diagram 1661 machinery wagon is visible behind, loaded with plant belonging to the Limmer & Trinidad Asphalt Company.
E. R. Lacey

Further examples of LBSCR double bolster wagons are as follows:
Diagram 1618 type — LBSCR Nos 4693, 7327/33, 7539/51/60, 7712/34
Diagram 1621 type — LBSCR Nos 4028/44, 4512, 7566, 10460-5/91
The last withdrawal was No 58886 in 1949, to Diagram 1621.

Road vehicle trucks

These were described and labelled by the LBSCR as machinery trucks, despite often being used for the conveyance of containers, road vehicles and the like. Whilst mentioning container traffic, a note from LBSCR working timetables dated January 1910 is worth recording. This states: 'Class B trucks — to be treated as special stock and worked accordingly. To be used for loading furniture skips or vans without wheels in preference to machinery trucks.' **Plate 13** in *Volume Two* therefore shows this instruction being followed to the letter.

LBSCR machinery trucks were another group of vehicles that occupied a definite number series prior to the Grouping — most falling into the 7001-7115 block, with just a few in the higher 71XX, 72XX and 75XX ranges. Apart from buffers, brakes and axle boxes, their design varied little between the 1890s and 1924. In the period before 1890, some were to be returned to certain specific stations, this instruction being painted on the vehicles concerned.

Right:
Plate 172 An enlargement of the view originally reproduced as **Plate 96** in *Volume Two*, showing machinery truck No 7160, loaded with a container owned by Curtiss & Sons. The wagon has grease-lubricated axle boxes and dates from 1893, being withdrawn in 1912, part of a batch numbered 7147-60. Several such vehicles were still in service at the Grouping but all had been withdrawn by 1928. Examples included LBSCR Nos 7004/27/56/84, 7115/48/53-5/7, all scrapped without receiving their allocated SR numbers. Curtiss & Sons had depots in many South Coast locations from Chatham to Plymouth and may have specialised in removals for naval personnel. The Curtiss livery was chocolate brown, with a red name panel having a white or cream outline. The lettering was white

or cream, shaded black. Readers with the 2003 reprint of *Volume Two* will already be in receipt of this livery information. The company later merged with Pickfords and then adopted their livery of navy blue with white lettering. *Author's Collection*

Right:

Plate 173 A close-up of the end of Diagram 1661 cartruck No S60515 at Feltham in March 1950, also seen in **Plate 99** of *Volume Two*. From this angle it may be seen that the wagon has double vee hangers on the far side but only a single hanger this side. Almost certainly the last mainland survivor to the diagram, it was withdrawn in 1955. *A. E. West*

Right:

Plate 174 One of the 19 vehicles to Diagram 1661 transferred to the Isle of Wight, SR No 60582 (ex-mainland No 60499 in 1930) is seen at Ventnor in 1956, possibly still carrying SR brown livery. Built in 1909 as LBSCR No 7081, it remained in traffic department use until October 1960, then giving a further six years' departmental service. The 1961 census shows just one of the Island vehicles remaining in ordinary traffic, the other nine survivors then being departmental stock. *J. W. Sparrowe*

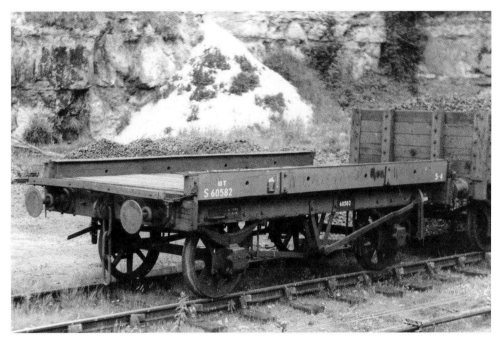

Engineer's Department wagons

One point that needs further discussion concerns the livery of these vehicles in LBSCR days. L.E. Brailsford noted, with particular reference to ballast brake vans, that these were painted red, however his notes are then slightly ambiguous as to whether this colour was applied to the ordinary ballast and rail wagons as well. Just why it might be thought necessary to paint the ballast brake vans alone in a distinctive livery, as opposed to the entire ED fleet (as was done on the LSWR) is not entirely clear. However, the various specification documents for the contractor-built ballast hoppers, bogie rail wagons and the convertible rail/sleeper/ballast wagons of 1897-1904 all call for lead grey bodywork with black running gear and it is now thought that this was general for all other Engineer's wagons except the brake vans, post-1896. Just whether red was used previously for all ED wagons remains uncertain.

Before leaving this matter, the following extract from the January 1888 and 1891 working timetables should be noted.

'Conveyance of creosoted sleepers and other permanent way materials, ballast and sand excepted: 30 ballast wagons painted a dark lead colour with the words 'To be returned to Norwood Junction when Empty' written upon both sides of each wagon, have been put into traffic and are intended solely for the conveyance of creosoted sleepers and other permanent way materials excepting ballast and sand. The distinctive numbers of the vehicles are 7518/23/50/60/96/7, 7613/8/9/25/7/31/49/58/96, 7707/13/44/8/54/8/62/81, 7809/26/57/71/2/87 and 7900.'

All are identified in the LBSCR wagon register as being dropside ballast wagons built between 1876 and 1881, presumably of the type that later became SR Diagram 1751. All were charged out at £50 each and none remained in service at the Grouping. The reference to 'dark lead grey' is in marked contrast to the then standard Brighton wagon livery of pale grey — or does this indicate that other ballast wagons of the period were red, as perhaps suggested by Brailsford.

Left:

Plate 175 This two-plank ballast wagon, LBSCR No 7798, was photographed in 1882 and dates from 1878, so could be similar to the 30 wagons reserved for creosoted sleeper traffic. Of 4-tons capacity, it differs somewhat from all other known two-plank wagons — appearing slightly shorter than sister-wagon No 7796 illustrated in **Plate 104** of *Volume Two* and having a round tiebar between the axle boxes. Apart from the wagon plate, no other lettering is visible, but presumably the 'illiterate' mark is present, if obliterated. The wagon was replaced in 1900 by a three plank vehicle that later became SR No 62633, to SR Diagram 1753. *LBSCR Official*

Figure 32 A drawing of the two-plank dumb-buffered ballast wagon, later SR Diagram 1751. These varied somewhat in their detail but despite their antiquated appearance and dimensions, 43 of them actually carried SR livery and numbers, including at least seven shipped to the Isle of Wight in 1927. The example drawn, No 7755, was one of the Island transfers but was never renumbered before scrapping. The livery shown is based on a photograph dated August 1922 and so may have been how the wagon ran until the end. The final mainland survivors were withdrawn in 1933. Examples of LBSCR numbering are 7504/32, 7600/82, 7722/80, 7831/79, 7920/66 and 8431/55. Numbering of practically all earlier LBSCR ballast wagons fell within the 7500-7999 range.

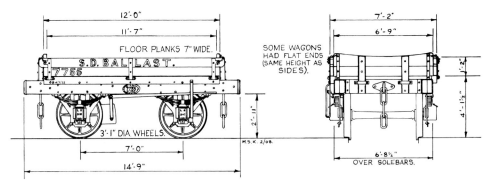

LBSCR 4 TON 2-PLANK BALLAST WAGON
S. R. DIAGRAM 1751.

Left:

Plate 176 This rather interesting print shows two dumb-buffered ballast wagons being used as makeshift inspection cars, possibly during the construction of Southampton New Docks in 1931/2. This enormous project could well explain why so many of these old wagons lasted until late 1933. SR No 62653 was previously LBSCR No 7880 of 1902, to Diagram 1753 — the later three plank design and cost £36-15-5d. Further examples of LBSCR numbering include 7526, 7651/90, 7705/77, 7810/61/83/97, 7912/58, all passing into SR ownership. The far wagon is one of the ex-SER dropsides purchased from contractor William Jones in 1897-1901 and described in *Volume Three*.
L. T. Catchpole

Right:

Plate 177 The post-1905 modern replacement LBSCR dropside ballast wagon to SR Diagram 1754 — not that the wagon looks very modern in this picture. One of the final survivors of the type is seen at Eastleigh permanent way yard in September 1959, showing not a trace of its former identity on its peeling Southern Railway applied red oxide paint finish. The drop door cappings are already loose and the left-hand timber doorstop is missing, so it seems doubtful if the wagon ever saw service again. The January 1961 census records just six remaining in use. *A. E. West*

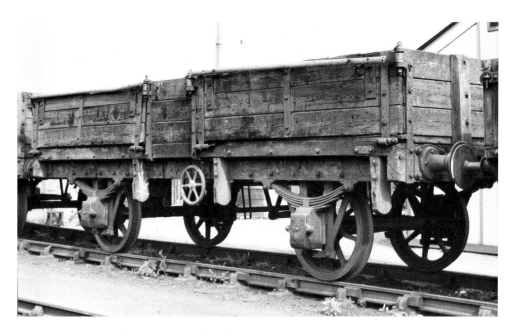

These wagons were not all built in numerical order, as LBSCR numbers between 8411 and 8500 (except Nos 8431/2/55/91, which were to other diagrams) date from 1905-14 and became SR Nos 62706-91, and only the earliest of these had metal doorstops. Those completed between 1914 and 1921 carried random LBSCR numbers between 7754 and 7971, became SR Nos 62680-62705.

By the early 1920s some were recorded carrying standard company initials, viz. LBSC, using 18 in high initials across the wagon, instead of the 'ND' or 'SD' and 'Ballast' markings of earlier years. One known example was No 7900, noted by Guy Hemingway in 1923. Regrettably, despite carefully recording the lettering, his notes are unclear regarding the base colour of the wagon.

Below:

Plate 178 Diagram 1755 Hurst Nelson ballast hopper No 62809, photographed at Eastleigh on the same day as **Plate 177** — looking in a similarly parlous state. The left-hand hopper control wheel is missing, but details of the drop door and interior are revealed. Despite everything, the 1930 Charles Roberts livery remains visible after almost 30 years! This wagon was withdrawn in 1960, but No 62800 was seen in service at Barnstaple Junction in 1965 — the last survivor to the diagram. It was still labelled 'Return to Broad Clyst'. *A. E. West*

Above:
Plate 179 The 20 sleeper wagons to SR Diagram 1798 could not be illustrated in *Volume Two*. In this somewhat poor print, at least four are seen on bridge widening works at Thornton Heath on 22 March 1903, complete with crane and Stroudley brake van, plus Engineer's staff in attendance. *R. C. Riley Collection*

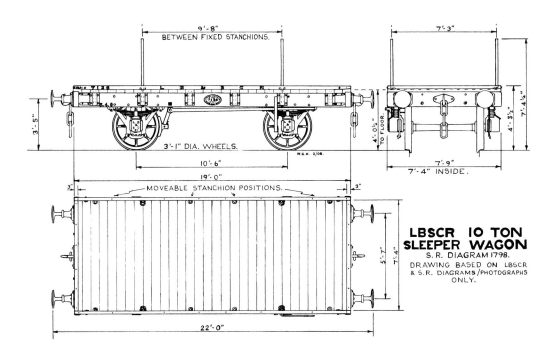

Figure 33 A drawing of the Diagram 1798 sleeper wagon, based on the details shown in **Plate 179** and the LBSCR/SR diagrams, so not guaranteed accurate on points of detail. LBSCR numbers were 7121-40 and the last, SR Nos 64645/6 were withdrawn in 1935/6. Some details are shared with rail & sleeper wagon Diagram 1800, this being the timber under-framed version of the wagon drawn as **Figure 38** in *Volume Two*.

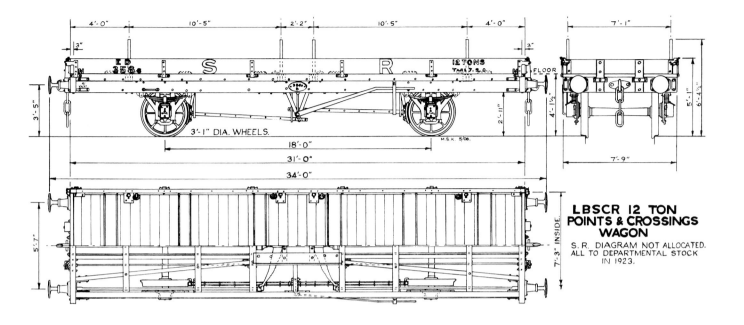

Figure 34 The 31ft points and crossings wagon was mentioned briefly on pages 67 and 70 of *Volume Two* and no photographs have yet been found, however the wagon was, in effect, the LBSCR version of the MR/SDJR rail wagon drawn in Chapter Two. Seven are listed in the LBSCR register, Nos 7829/32/5/7-9/49, all built in 1901. With the exception of No 7839 the rest became SR departmental stock as Nos 352s-357s.

Below:
Plate 180 A broadside view of Hurst Nelson bogie rail wagon SR No 64734, to Diagram 1802, at Bromley South in August 1934, carrying ED red oxide livery. The former LBSCR number was 10548 and the vehicle remained in service until January 1958. Sister wagon No 64735 was the last survivor, withdrawn in April 1961. *H. C.Casserley*

Chapter 4.
Minor Companies' Wagons

The Isle of Wight

Above:
Plate 181 The pre-Grouping Island scene. A Ventnor-bound Isle of Wight Railway goods train leaves Shanklin on 11 June 1910, hauled by 2-4-0T *Bonchurch*. The first, third and fifth wagons are five plank opens, the fourth is a three plank (there were relatively few of these on the Island), while the Chaplin's container is loaded on to a flat wagon that appears well down on its springs at the far end. The IWR was quick to develop container traffic, as it reduced the amount of double handling inevitable on an Island railway and most of the IWR stations could deal with this traffic. IWR goods brake No 2 (later SR No 56034) is at the rear. Just visible beyond the station is an IWR covered goods wagon. *K.Nunn Collection, courtesy LCGB*

When the Southern Railway took over the three Island companies they found very little standardisation amongst the goods vehicles. This was hardly surprising; as so much of the stock had been purchased second-hand from a variety of sources and by the time that local rebuilding had taken place there were very many individual variations indeed, even amongst wagons nominally the same when originally purchased. Readers with a specific interest in the pre-Grouping Island scene are strongly advised to consult the following document now housed in the National Archives at Kew: Reference: Rail 633/308 — SECR Wagon Register Part Five.

Despite the unlikely title, this includes a list of former Island company wagons as found by the Southern Railway during 1923, recording such details as former company running numbers, carrying capacities, body dimensions (length, width and height),

tare weights, brake gear and withdrawal dates. If used in conjunction with a known photograph, some attempt at drawing and/or modelling may be made. Such an approach will seldom give complete accuracy, nor will it answer all questions, but in absence of anything else may be of great assistance.

The information gathered was almost certainly the result of an initial survey undertaken by mainland staff, to see what had been inherited and was used by the Southern to formulate an action plan. This resulted, sooner rather than later, in the wholesale replacement of the stock with more modern vehicles of (mostly) LBSCR origin. The majority of the later transfers will also be found listed in the same document, together with renumbering and transfer details. Only post-1931 transfers fail to appear, but fortunately there were relatively few of these.

Above:
Plate 182 The changing Island scene. 'O2' class 0-4-4T No 25 *Godshill* is shunting a varied collection of stock at Ryde St Johns, *circa* 1934. Identifiable are:
Diagram 1541 LSWR goods brake van No 56053.
LCDR brake third No 4133 (one of three rebuilt as mail vans in 1933/4).
A Diagram 1433 LBSCR van reserved for fish traffic.
LCDR luggage van (one of either SR Nos 1008/9/13).
A Diagram 1436 LBSCR covered goods wagon, another fish van, and an LSWR passenger brake van, followed by at least seven diagram 1364/9 open goods wagons. Every item visible is a post-1923 transfer to the Island. *A. B. Macleod*

The Isle of Wight Railway four plank 17ft open wagons formed a group of around 65 vehicles, built between 1903 and 1920. Although by no means all identical, they were possibly the nearest approach to standardisation that the IWR could offer in 1923. The last four in ordinary traffic were as follows, all being recorded as 10-ton wagons with body dimensions (L x W x H) of 17ft x 7ft 1½in x 3ft:

SR No	IWR No	Built	Brake Gear	Tare (1923)	Withdrawn
27891	38	1914	DB both sides	5-1	2/33
27899	133	1914	SB both sides	4-12	4/33
27914	156	1912	DB one side	4-14	1/34
27936	189	1914	DB both sides	4-18	2/33

Their likely appearance, if not livery, was probably as **Plate 129** in *Volume Two*.

Figure 35 Between 1929 and 1932, 12 of these former IWR open wagons were reserved for loco coal traffic and survived long after almost all other Island company vehicles. Their original form is illustrated by **Figure 39** in *Volume Two*, but by the 1950s most had been rebuilt with various ex-LBSCR fittings. This shows S64397, which received the 5ft wide doors and strapping from a Brighton open, although still retaining its IWR axle boxes and buffers. Formerly IWR No 221 and SR traffic department No 27965, it became a loco coal wagon in September 1929. Finally downgraded to an ash disposal wagon in 1952, it was withdrawn around 1958/9.

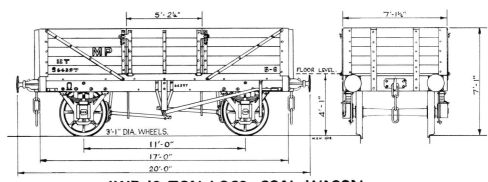

IWR 12 TON LOCO COAL WAGON
AS RUNNING CIRCA 1952.
S.R. DIAGRAM NOT ALLOCATED.

Left:

Plate 183 Similar loco coal wagon No S64350, one of the four 1931/2 transfers is seen at Brading in May 1952. This retains its original narrow side doors, now with five side planks, but still has four end planks as built. Formerly IWR No 226/SR traffic dept. No 27970, it now carries a black patch painted/unpainted livery. Also downgraded to a loco ash wagon in February 1952, it too lasted another five or six years before scrapping. *P. J. Garland*

Numbering of the 17ft loco coal wagons was 64348/50/1 and 64393-400, while No 64349 alone measured 15ft x 7ft 3in x 3ft 6in, possibly with a wheelbase of 9ft. After withdrawal most of these numbers were reallocated to LBSCR Diagram 1364/9 wagons that served the motive power department until the end of steam operation in 1966. Examples of these appear in *Volume Two* as **Plates 39** and **165**.

Figure 44 in *Volume Two* illustrated the Isle of Wight Central

Railway Harrison & Camm 10-ton open wagons delivered in 1897. These were actually obtained through a hire purchase agreement with an organisation called the Southern Counties Rolling Stock Company, for £1456-8-0d — a pretty substantial outlay for the IWCR. They lasted well and all except six carried SR livery, being renumbered as 28065/6 (by then downrated to 8-tons) and 28183-6/9-97/9-28201/4. The final survivors were SR Nos 28183/5/90/3/4-7/9, all withdrawn during 1931/2.

Left:

Plate 184 Photographs of Freshwater, Yarmouth & Newport Railway wagons are rare — this shows No 18 at Newport, circa 1920, during the period when it was running as a makeshift cattle wagon. This was the first of five such conversions, FYN Nos 18-22. The rather crude method of adaptation is obvious, but it does also serve to illustrate the standard FYN livery — if indeed there was such a thing! The Southern quickly returned the wagons to open goods status and this became SR No 28227, running until January 1932; one of the final Freshwater wagons in ordinary service. The SECR wagon register records the dimensions as 15ft long and 7ft 6in wide, with a carrying capacity of 8 tons. **Figure 36** (below) is a drawing of this wagon as it probably appeared after 1923. *P. C. Allen Collection*

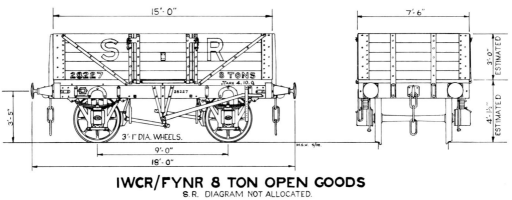

IWCR/FYNR 8 TON OPEN GOODS
S.R. DIAGRAM NOT ALLOCATED.

Volume Two included drawings of the former GER and MR covered goods wagons purchased by the IWCR in, respectively, 1904-9 and 1911. Some numbering details of these are:

Ex-GER vans

IWCR No	SR No	Capacity	Withdrawn
274	47007	10 tons	3/30
277	47010	10 tons	3/30
289	47018	10 tons	3/30
290	47019	10 tons	4/29
295	46991	8 tons	4/29
296	(46992)	8 tons	6/28
299	46994	8 tons	3/30

Ex-MR vans

IWCR No	SR No	Capacity	Withdrawn
323	46999	8 tons	4/29
324	(47030)	10 tons	6/28
325	(47031)	10 tons	6/26
326	(47000)	8 tons	1/28
327	47001	8 tons	4/29
328	(47002)	8 tons	6/28

SR numbers in brackets were never applied to the vans.

The GER vans were originally allocated IWCR numbers 274-82/6-91/5/6/8-301/3/5-7, however they were by no means all identical. The six MR vans were a rather more homogenous group and few later IWCR modifications were made, apart from minor alterations to convert at least two into ventilated vans.

While noting the ex-Great Eastern purchases, it is now known that two of the cattle wagons obtained in 1908 were large vehicles, 19ft long over headstocks, to GER Diagram 6. These were IWCR Nos 45 (8-tons) and 46 (10-tons), later SR Nos 53380/7, withdrawn in June 1928 and March 1930 respectively.

Below:
The last former Isle of Wight company covered goods wagons were replaced by LBSCR types in 1930/1, however the stock was augmented by three former cattle wagon conversions in 1935. These were unique to the Island and were allocated SR Diagram 1457 and running numbers 46924-6. **Plate 185** illustrates the only one to survive into BR days, as departmental No 1066s, at Newport soon after transfer to the Signal & Telegraph Engineer. Diagram 1434 van No 46938 accompanies the rebuild, by then also in use as a static stores van. *F. Foote*

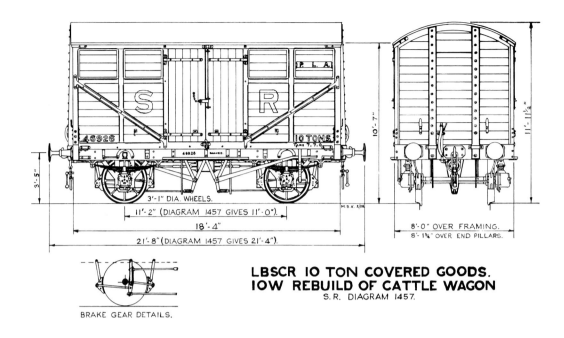

BRAKE GEAR DETAILS.

LBSCR 10 TON COVERED GOODS.
IOW REBUILD OF CATTLE WAGON
S.R. DIAGRAM 1457.

Figure 37 A drawing of the Diagram 1457 rebuild, also showing the arrangement of brake gear on Westinghouse fitted stock. The P.L.A. board (Passengers' Luggage in Advance) was red with white lettering.

Below:

Plate 186 IWCR goods brake vans 2 and 3 were nominally recorded as being of LBSCR origin, but were extensively rebuilt by their new owners into the form seen here (and drawn as **Figure 51** in *Volume Two*). They became SR Nos 56035/6 after the Grouping, the latter being transferred to departmental stock as Signal Section tool van No 445s in April 1929. This view shows the balcony end, now with additional diagonal and vertical framing, plus a flush-planked sliding door in the balcony partition, in place of that shown in *Volume Two*. Note also the substantial engineer's vice mounted on the balcony — an essential piece of equipment when working 'on site' away from workshop facilities. The location is Newport, on 18 May 1952. Withdrawal came in March 1954. *P. J. Garland*

Above:

Plate 187 The crew of 'O2' tank No 22, not yet christened *Brading*, pose with their immaculate locomotive at Ryde St Johns, *circa* 1926. In our context the two wagons visible to the left are of interest. Just seen is IWCR 8-ton five plank open No 16, not yet renumbered as SR 27991. Credited to 'North Central', it was probably built at Newport and measured 15ft x 7ft 4in x 2ft 11in, with a tare of 4-13-0, double block brakes on one side only and appears very similar to IWCR No 150 illustrated in **Plate 135** of *Volume Two*. The wagon was withdrawn in April 1929. The rather long 6-ton flat wagon, SR No 59016, was previously IWR No 88, built at Ryde in 1919. Its dimensions were 20ft x 8ft x 9in high side rails, tare 4-10-0 with double block brakes on each side. Constructionally it is an elongated version of IWR No 1 as drawn in **Figure 42** of *Volume Two*, with a wheelbase of about 14ft, having widely spaced solebars and second-hand Oldbury wheelsets. This wagon was withdrawn in February 1928. IWR No 53 was of similar dimensions. *E. R.Wethersett*

Right:

Plate 188 IWR flat wagon No 1, still showing its 'special' pre-Grouping lettering as applied on Mr Macleod's instructions in November 1931, but on the works side only, in 1948! The SR departmental number, 568s, is also carried. The other (more visible side) was lettered in orthodox SR style. Between 1928 and 1931 the wagon carried traffic department number 59021. The wide spacing of the solebars is again apparent, also evident from the wide buffer backing plate. IWR Nos 54-6, 89 and 90 (SR Nos 59013-5/7/8) were similar but 15ft long, while IWR No 2 was 15ft 5in long. Once the LBSCR Diagram 1661 vehicles arrived in 1928-30 the Island company wagons were quickly withdrawn. The wagon beyond is one of the ten LBSCR Diagram 1755 ballast hoppers transferred to the Island in 1947. *F. Foote*

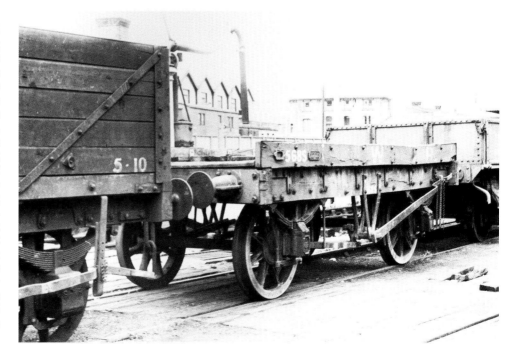

Right:

Plate 189 The Island weed killing train, formed during 1932 using the two former IWCR tar/water tanks, Nos 140/1. From right to left are SR No 443s (ex-IWCR No 140/SR traffic department No 61383), SR No 428s (ex-IWCR No 141, which does not appear to have ever been allocated a Southern traffic department number) and IWR goods brake No 2/SR 56034, not yet renumbered as departmental 472s, which took place in August 1932. Neither tank yet carries any form of identification on their black painted finish — they were later lettered 'Weed Killing Train' centrally

across the upper tank, together with their numbers, just visible in **Plate 134** of *Volume Two*. No 443s already has a second-hand underframe, ex-IWR tar tank No 61381, dating from 1896 and fitted in June 1932, so the picture must date from very soon after. *A. B. Macleod*

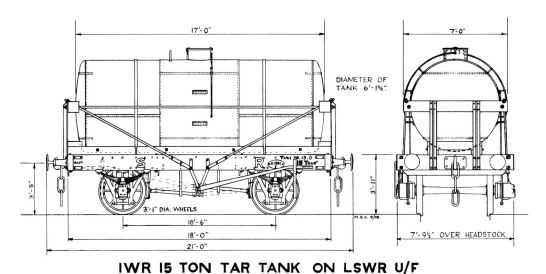

IWR 15 TON TAR TANK ON LSWR U/F
S. R. DIAGRAM 1713.

Figure 38 The two IWR tar tanks, Nos 202/3 and later SR Nos 61381/2, were unusual in at least two respects. Firstly, they were the only revenue-earning SR-owned goods tank wagons and, secondly, they were one of only two Island wagon types to receive a Southern diagram number — 1713 — in 1929 when they were mounted on former LSWR covered goods wagon underframes. This drawing is based on the SR diagram, standard LSWR wagon dimensions and photographs, so may not be accurate down to the last detail.

Left:

Plate 190 The LSWR underframe from Diagram 1713 tar tank No 61382 at Ryde St Johns in June 1949, prior to being reused under one of the weed killing train tanks 428s or 443s. In their later form, both appear in **Plate 155** of *Volume Two*. The replacement tar tanks (former LSWR 'A12' tenders Nos 61384/5) were only on the Island from May 1947 until November 1950, then being returned to departmental service on the mainland. *A. E. West*

The Plymouth, Devonport & South Western Junction Railway

Relatively little may be added to what has already been written, but two photographs will give some additional details.

Above:

Plate 191 Gunnislake station, probably soon after opening in 1908. Hawthorn Leslie 0-6-0T *A.S. Harris* hauls a goods train that includes PDSWJR three plank dropside wagon No 30 and, beyond the station building, five plank open No 43, both being ex-Midland Railway vehicles exactly as drawn in *Volume Two*. The last survivor of the PDSWJR wagons was SR departmental No 0240s at Eastleigh Carriage Works, withdrawn in 1936. Note the PDSW horse van, optimistically proclaiming 'Furniture removals to all parts' — well, all parts locally more probably! *The Lens of Sutton Association*

Right:

Plate 192 Goods brake van No 54, in the sidings at Bere Alston, *circa* 1910. Disc or Mansell wheels are now fitted, instead of the spoke pattern shown on Pickering's general arrangement drawing. This van later became SR No 56043. Both brake vans were proposed for transfer to the Isle of Wight in 1925, but this entry was later crossed out and the vans appear to have stayed on the mainland until withdrawal. One wonders if they ventured far away from the Callington branch after 1923? Behind is a selection of LSWR milk, fruit and meat vans, including (to the left) a Diagram 1483 meat van rebuilt with standard sliding doors. It is not known how many were so altered - for a picture of one in original condition see **Plate 55**. The area around the Callington branch produced much soft fruit during the summer season and this probably accounts for the presence of so many LSWR vans. *Author's Collection*

The Lynton & Barnstaple Railway

All 11 SR diagrams were drawn and detailed in *Volume Two*, so
the present information is confined to eight additional photographs.

Above:
Plate 193 Some idea of how small the L&BR wagons were may be obtained from this view of the transfer siding at Barnstaple Town, *circa* 1934. Four-wheeled open No 28304 (to Diagram 1394), SR bogie open No 28318 (to Diagram 1396), two more Diagram 1394s and another Diagram 1396, plus a van occupy the narrow gauge siding, while a GWR ' wooden Mink', a coke wagon belonging to J. C. Abbott of Birmingham and an LNER open are in the standard gauge siding. *D. E. H. Box*

Below:
Plate 194 An end view of one of the four-ton, four-wheeled open wagons at Pilton Yard, awaiting sale, in November 1935. The original body width was the same as the headstock width. *HMRS Collection*

Above:
Plate 195 Bogie open wagon No 28301, formerly L&BR No 12, to Diagram 1393. This was one of the original bogie vehicles built by Bristol Wagon & Carriage Company in 1897 and appears in original condition in **Plate 174** of *Volume Two*. Again, it awaits sale at Pilton Yard after closure of the line, in November 1935. *HMRS Collection*

Below:
Plate 196 One of the 1927 Southern Railway additions to the stock, built by J. & F. Howard of Bedford, bogie open No 28317 (to SR Diagram 1396) at Pilton Yard about 1930. Note that some repairs have been made resulting in the corner plates and one diagonal strap being repainted black. It is believed that the SR-ordered wagons were found to be out-of-gauge when first delivered and perhaps the substantial underframe trussing or brake linkage may have fouled the hand point levers in Pilton Yard and elsewhere on the line. As no obvious alterations seem to have been made to the wagons, presumably the point levers were modified. The very small lettering over the 8 Tons inscription reads 'Ballast not to be loaded beyond thin iron strip inside wagon' and was applied to all the bogie opens during SR ownership, to prevent overloading. *The Lens of Sutton Association*

Above:
Plate 197 Diagram 1456 bogie covered goods wagon No 47043 in its final form, outside Lynton goods shed on 17 August 1935, only six weeks before the line closed. No livestock vehicles were built for the line and when this had to be carried, the usual method was to jam a brick in the open door of the vans and tie the door almost closed to provide the necessary ventilation. Considering the tight regulations that applied to standard gauge cattle wagons, one wonders what officialdom would have thought of this practice.
H. F. Wheeller

Below:
Plate 198 Diagram 1590 goods brake van No 56040 and one of the Diagram 1396 SR open wagons stand in the bay platform at Lynton.
J. E. Hoyland

Above:
Plate 199 Goods brake No 56041, to Diagram 1589 and the only van built at Pilton Works, stands in the transfer siding at Barnstaple Town in 1934. In theory, the ends of the brake vans should have been painted Venetian red, mirroring standard gauge practice after 1923, but this has not been confirmed, nor is any tonality difference evident in photographs. Remarkably, this van was rediscovered on a farm locally during the 1990s and is now preserved by the Lynton & Barnstaple Railway Association at Woody Bay station, restored to its original 1908 grey livery. *A. B. Macleod.*

Below:
Plate 200 Crane No 441s and its match truck, 441sm, at the end of the headshunt at Pilton yard in 1935. This was one of two purchased from George Cohen & Sons in 1926 — the other (No. 442S) being used at Lynton goods yard. The match truck was converted at Lancing Works in 1927, using the identical underframe from a third crane purchased at the same time. *F. E. Box*

Chapter 5.

SECR Wagons

At the beginning of *Volume Three* of *Southern Wagons*, it was stated that the South Eastern & Chatham was a railway of contrasts. True to form, amongst the 12,100 or so wagons handed over at the Grouping could be found both the most modern and the oldest vehicles to become Southern stock in 1923. The Maunsell/Lynes new designs then accounted for a little over 20% of the total stock, yet there were a number of SER and LCDR wagons dating back as far as 1862 (and one or two that were even older) still running at that time. No doubt, without the restrictions of World War One, the proportion of new-build might have been doubled, as most of these wagons had been completed since 1918. In comparison, neither the LSWR nor the LBSCR handed over many wagons that were older than 1879 vintage.

Not surprisingly, withdrawal of the older wagons continued rapidly after 1923, some failing to even have SR numbers allocated, while many more had these allocated but were never repainted or renumbered into SR livery. Such was the rate of withdrawal that by the end of 1935 not one wagon of LCDR origin and just 470 wagons of SER design remained in capital stock. If one wished to be pedantic, four ex-LCDR ballast brake vans were still in use, however these were actually SR carriage stock conversions of 1927 and will be described in Chapter 6.

In *Volume Three* the decision to run down and close the former LCDR works at Longhedge was questioned — an odd decision in view of the perennial lack of capacity at Ashford. After much Directorial pressure this was finally accomplished late in 1912 or early in 1913 and shortly afterwards Harry Wainwright departed. Interestingly, wagon repair work restarted again at Longhedge in August 1917, after a break of just four years. Whilst the Great War had undoubtedly increased the volume of work, this sounds very much like an admission that the wrong decision had been taken back in 1912.

Open goods and mineral wagons

Below:
Plate 201 Photographs of LCDR wagons remain elusive and the few that are available appear as incidental subjects in locomotive or station views. LCDR No 730 is seen at Longhedge, probably around 1898 and was drawn as **Figure 4** in *Volume Three*. It is a three plank low round-ended open wagon to SECR Diagram S1093 and later SR Diagram 1330 or 1331, dependent on the height of the side. It is also, along with the wagon just visible to the right, one of few such wagons with external diagonal strapping. Later SECR No 10623, it was replaced by a new SECR wagon in 1908. Note also the end detail of the right-hand wagon, without the curved top section of body framing. Was this by accident or design? From the manner in which the end uprights are finished, it looks as if the wagon was built as seen and was not the result of accident damage or other modification. *Author's Collection*

Other known examples to the LCDR low open goods wagon design were as follows:

LCDR No	SECR No	SECR Dia	LCDR No	SECR No	SECR Dia
503	10398	S1093	548	10443	S1/1093
582	10477	S1093	632	10527	S1/1093
718	10611	S1093	760	10653	S1/1093
1110	10902	S1093	781	10674	S1/1093
			863	10756	S1/1093
Diagram S1093 is the original LCDR			1184	10976	S1/1093
design, S1/1093 is the SECR rebuild.			1194	10986	S1/1093

SECR Diagram S1/1093 reflects the rebuilding process started in 1912, as depicted by **Plate 14** and **Figure 5** in *Volume Three*. It therefore seems likely that SR Diagram 1330 was issued for the original version and 1331 for the rebuild, as SECR Nos 10398 and 10611 became Diagram 1330 (as SR Nos 14896 and 10035) and just SECR No 10674 became Diagram 1331 (as SR No 10036), not that these alterations are accurately depicted by the latter diagram.

Right:

Plate 202 A partial view of a four plank medium round-ended open wagon, possibly LCDR No 931 and again at Longhedge around 1898/9. This is to SECR Diagram S1092 and later SR Diagram 1325, although if correctly identified, this wagon ran from November 1897 until September 1920 only, being withdrawn as SECR No 10824. The side planking comprises four 8½in planks and it was rated at 8-tons capacity. Also visible is a goods-rated LCDR cattle wagon, of the type later allocated SR Diagram 1516. Another cattle wagon appears as **Plate 227**. *Author's Collection*

Some further examples of SECR Diagram S1092 are LCDR Nos 518/53/66, 628/81, 713, 884, 924, 1178 and 1222, later SECR Nos 10413/48/61, 10523/76, 10606, 10777, 10817, 10970 and 11014 respectively. All remained in traffic long enough to be listed in the SECR wagon register now at the PRO, Kew, compiled around 1919.

Left:

Plate 203 The high round-ended LCDR open goods wagon — SECR Diagram S1091 and later SR Diagram 1329 — is represented by this less than perfect view, again at Longhedge in the late 1890s. This is one of the short (15ft) examples of the design. Clearly ex-works, it is typical of the type with a single timber brake block on one side. Numbers of the seven survivors at the Grouping were given in *Volume Three*, to which may be added the following: LCDR Nos 509/50/60/61/71, 646/55/71, 778 and 1137, later SECR Nos 10404/45/55/56/66, 10541/50/66, 10671 and 10929 respectively, all of which were withdrawn between 1919 and 1923. Some of these were extremely ancient, having been built by The Railway Carriage Company in 1862. *Author's Collection*

Above:
Plate 204 A view of Staplehurst station, taken on 31 October 1887, showing a busy scene during the loading of hops and fruit in baskets. At least seven SER Diagram S1069 wagons may be seen, of which only No 7662 may be identified further. This was built a year earlier; one of a batch of 100 10-ton wagons (Nos. 7622-7721) completed at Ashford and costing £89 each. This wagon failed to survive the Grouping but SECR Nos 7661/4 did last long enough to be allocated SR Diagram 1327 and running numbers 11930/1. Note the wagon behind No 7662, with 'cut-away' or 'stepped ends'. These are now confirmed as SER Nos 4031-80, completed in 1863 by Brown Marshalls & Company. Also visible are two Diagram 1328 coal wagons and a Diagram 1421 covered goods wagon.
The Lens of Sutton Association

Below:
Plate 205 Diagram 1327-type open SER No 6485 at Marden in 1890. This was one of the last batch of 50 eight-ton wagons completed in 1880/1, SER Nos 6483-6532 and just six remained in service in 1923 to be allocated SR Nos 10015-20. One of these, in its final form, appears as a useful comparison in **Plates 26-28** in *Volume Three. The Lens of Sutton Association*

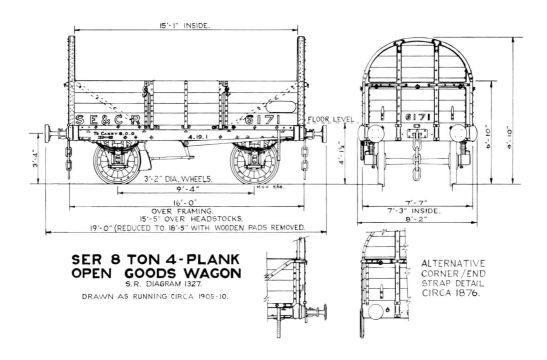

15'-1" INSIDE.

S E & C R   6171

FLOOR LEVEL

To CARRY 8.0.0   4.19.1

3'-4"

3'-2" DIA. WHEELS.   M.S.W. 5/68.

9'-4"

16'-0"
OVER FRAMING.
15'-5" OVER HEADSTOCKS.
19'-0" (REDUCED TO 18'-5" WITH WOODEN PADS REMOVED.

6171

4'-1½"

6'-10"

9'-10"

7'-7"
7'-3" INSIDE.
8'-2"

**SER 8 TON 4-PLANK
OPEN GOODS WAGON**
S.R. DIAGRAM 1327.
DRAWN AS RUNNING CIRCA 1905-10.

ALTERNATIVE
CORNER/END
STRAP DETAIL
CIRCA 1876.

Figure 39 A drawing of the Diagram 1327/S1069 wagons dating from 1878, depicting the first from a batch of 15, Nos 6171-85 and based on a photograph taken at Merstham cement works, *circa* 1905-10. Just one of these survived the Grouping (No. 6181) but was withdrawn in November 1923 before receiving its allocated SR number of 10008. This is typical of wagons built from 1863 until at least 1878. The detail shows one batch of 10-ton wagons built around 1876 that had a different arrangement of corner strapping, possibly some of SER Nos 5707-5856.

Below:
Plate 206 East Kent Railway No 29 was formerly a SER Diagram S1069/SR Diagram 1327 8-ton open wagon, seen at Shepherdswell on 6 September 1947. Apart from removal of round ends, it appears substantially as built, almost certainly before 1881. The former number and date of sale to the EKR are not known but the wagon was there by 1929 and may have been purchased some time in the previous five years. It failed to be recorded on the British Railways take-over inventory dated May 1948, so was presumably broken up during the previous six months. *G. A. Hookham*

Right:

Plate 207 A slightly more modern version of Diagram 1327, EKR No 24, at Shepherdswell station in August 1937. This was recorded by the East Kent Railway as having been built at Ashford and was of 10 tons capacity — not that there is anything on the wagon to this effect and it was one of at least a dozen former SER/SECR wagons purchased by the company. From its appearance it may be one of the early '6625-type' reconstructions from *circa* 1902-5 and retains a single timber brake block on the far side but has a simplified end detail retaining timber corner posts instead of steel corner plates used on the final Diagram 1327 reconstructions. EKR No 40, visible behind, was one of at least three ex-Midland Railway purchases. *J. W. Sparrowe*

Figure 40 Four Diagram S1069 open wagons of 1869 vintage were rebuilt as shunting trucks for use at Bricklayers Arms in 1914/5, SECR Nos 4793-6 and were illustrated on page 134 of *Volume Three*. This is based on general arrangement drawing No 436A, dated 1909.

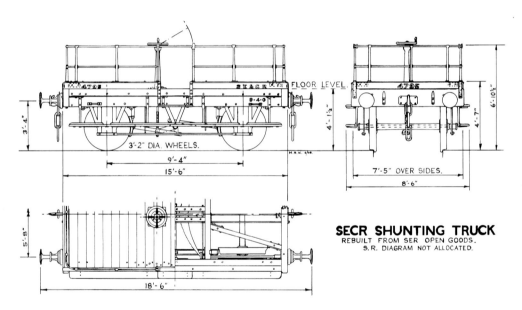

SECR SHUNTING TRUCK
REBUILT FROM SER OPEN GOODS.
S.R. DIAGRAM NOT ALLOCATED.

Left:

Plate 208 An enlargement of the photograph originally reproduced as **Plate 24** in *Volume Three*, showing a line of SER wagons allocated to marine coal traffic at Folkestone, on 13 September 1925. From left they are *(see above right)*:

Diagram 1328 coal wagon SECR No 4771/SR No 9699.
Diagram 1327 open wagon SECR No 5081/SR No 9956.
Diagram 1327 open wagon SECR No 2489/SR No 9809

All were allocated new numbers in the marine coal wagon series in December 1923 (SR numbers 63985/8/7 respectively) but none were ever repainted in SR livery before withdrawal between December 1925 and June 1926. Note that wagon No 5081 still retains round ends, while No 2489 does not. Diagram 1328 coal wagon No 4771 was drawn as **Figure 13** in *Volume Three*. *F. J. Agar*

Several Diagram 1327 open wagons were sent to Tilmanstone Colliery in 1925, including SECR Nos 4061, 4136, 4739, 5094 and 5137 (allocated SR numbers 9849/69, 9952/64/87 respectively). Just whether they were used internally at the colliery or on the East Kent Railway is unclear, however they stayed until 1931 but it is not known if they received SR livery or numbers, nor whether they retained round ends at this time. By January 1936 just 42 wagons to the diagram remained in ordinary traffic, some examples being as follows:
On steel underframe: Nos 11399, 11402/4/14 and 11652.
8-ton wagon No 9878 (ex-SER No 4171 of 1865, by then possibly the oldest SR open wagon in general service).

10-ton ordinary wagon No 11693 (ex-SER No 5799 of 1877).
10-ton 'express' wagons Nos 11491, 11502-4/9/11/2, 11693 (all built in 1890).
'6625-type' reconstructions Nos 11698, 11701/30/4/9/85/99, 11813/7/30, 11924/41.
8-ton marine coal wagon No 64001 (originally SER/SR numbers 4199/9885 respectively).
8-ton loco coal wagon No 64357 based at Fremington (originally SECR/SR numbers 6700/11736 respectively — one of the '6625' reconstructions of 1908).
By 1939 only a few of the reconstructed wagons remained in service.

Right:
Plate 209 What was almost certainly the last Diagram 1328 SER coal wagon in existence, EKR No 28 was photographed at Shepherdswell during the 1930s. Purchased from Ashford between 1924 and 1929, it was remarkable in lasting long enough to feature in the British Railways inventory of 1948 — to the point of being allocated BR number S21636 (by now vacant in the former LBSCR number series), although this was never applied. Clearly in good condition when photographed, it was formerly an 'express coal wagon' in SER parlance. The SR registers list just two such wagons remaining in ordinary stock at the end of 1935, these being SR Nos 9740 (ex-SECR No 7479 of 1885) and marine coal wagon No 64020 (former SER/SR numbers 7566/9753 respectively) at Dover.
M. Lawson Finch Collection

Right:
Plate 210 At just 14ft long, the Diagram 1328 wagons were small even in the 1880s and the design was superseded in 1889 by a 15ft coal wagon, later allocated SR Diagrams 1333 and 1334, depending on width. The narrower type is represented by SER No 1240, seen at Herne Hill sidings around 1900. Built in April 1891 it later became SR No 10223, to Diagram 1333, running until April 1928. Its recorded cost was £103-0-2d, charged to capital account. Notice the blacked-up body ironwork on, presumably, SER red oxide. The Williams patent sheet rail has seen better days! In *Volume Three* it was noted that wagon numbers 1 and 2 from this diagram were renumbered as 15 and 17 — the date is now confirmed as between July and December 1906, however the reason remains unknown.
Author's Collection

Plate 211 The wider version became SR Diagram 1334. EKR No 1 is seen at Shepherdswell during breaking up in June 1939 — it had been recommended for scrapping two years earlier, so there had been no hurry to comply with this instruction. Apart from stating that the former SECR number fell between 19 and 604, no further positive identification is possible. *Rev A. W. V. Mace*

Right:
Plate 212 One of the SER end-door loco coal wagon conversions, No 838 is seen at Herne Hill *circa* 1900. Completed in December 1889 and charged out as a renewal at £81-12-6d, when built it was identical to wagon No 1240 in **Plate 210**. Two other known conversions from this number series were SER 1296 and 1441. In 1898 the Locomotive Department had requested the provision of 400 new wagons suitable for loco coal traffic. What it got instead were 100 rebuilds allocated to SECR Diagram S1323 and later SR Diagram 1342. No 838 was scrapped in January 1924 without receiving its allocated SR number, which was 13336. The SER lettering style is now confirmed, complete with the 'Empty to Erith' instruction. *Author's Collection*

Left:
Plate 213 Captioned as 'the first wagon load of Kent coal to arrive at Tunbridge Wells', for coal merchant Thomas C. Allan, this shows Diagram 1342 loco coal wagon No 1204 with SECR lettering, *circa* 1911 at the earliest. Built in December 1890 and at that time identical to wagon 1240, it ran until October 1925, becoming SR No 13355. By this time the Locomotive Department had received some larger wagons dedicated for their use, allowing the end-door Diagram 1342s to be utilised elsewhere. *J. Arkell Collection*

Above:
Plate 214 An example of the final design of SER coal wagon and a rare find in SR livery. Diagram 1341 open No 13261 (formerly SECR No 8810, built by Ashbury in January 1898 at a cost of £101) is seen at Lyme Regis in 1927. In *Volume Three* it was noted that this design featured several detail variations depending on where the wagons were built and the SECR diagram for this particular vehicle is recorded as S1/1082, while others were just plain S1082. In theory it should appear exactly as **Plate 36** in *Volume Three*, but in fact has square ends and no sheet rail like the BRCW wagon in **Plates 38 and 39**. Withdrawal is recorded as December 1932.
P. Coutanche Collection

Right:
Plate 215 The SER and SECR often found themselves short of wagons and were forced to hire from time to time, usually from William Cory, Stephenson Clarke or Birmingham RCW Co. In 1900-2 no less than 450 of these hired dumb-buffered wagons were purchased from BRCW (at £41-10-0d each) and Metropolitan (at £42 each) and put to good use as loco coal wagons. No SECR diagrams have so far been traced and it is by no means certain that all were to the same dimensions. SECR No 12404 is seen in Ashford Works yard *circa* 1905 and appears typical of the 300 purchased from Metropolitan, having four side planks — the 150 from BRCW had six. Perhaps because of their dumb buffers and second-hand

status, they failed to last very long and withdrawal had already commenced by 1907. The arrival of the RCH-specification mineral wagons from 1910 onwards caused their rapid withdrawal such that only a handful remained by 1918. *SECR Official (part)*

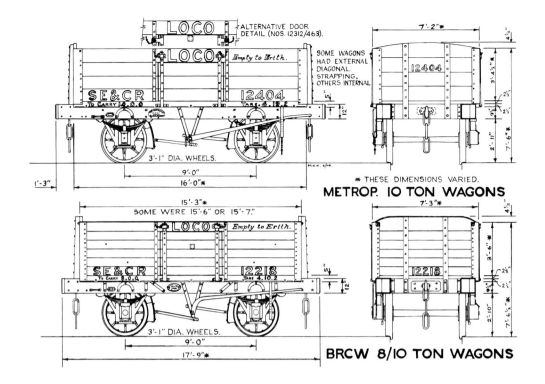

METROP. 10 TON WAGONS

BRCW 8/10 TON WAGONS

Figure 41 A drawing of the second-hand loco coal wagons from Metropolitan and BRCW, based on photographic evidence and standard private-owner wagon dimensions only. By 1907 just three of the BRCW wagons had been scrapped (Nos. 12097, 12196/7) and 36 from Metro had suffered the same fate. Just one wagon was allocated a Southern number (14895) but was scrapped in July 1923 before this was applied, although some remained in internal use at Angerstein Wharf and Whitstable Harbour at this time.

Below:
Plate 216 One of the elusive Diagram 1350 mineral wagons purchased from the Bute Supply Company in 1912/3, SR No 14722 was photographed around 1937 — location unknown but certainly at a Southern suburban station. Originally SECR No A14, it dates originally from 1900 and would have had an end door when purchased by the company — as shown in **Figure 26** in *Volume Three*. Reconstructed in 1919 and renumbered as SECR 12102, comparison with the later drawing shows some detail variations, viz. provision of sheet cleats, timber doorstops and side knees reversed (i.e. facing towards instead of away from the side door). By the time it was photographed, the wagon was in use for tarred stone only, as recorded by the boarded instruction.
J. W. Sparrowe, courtesy R. S. Carpenter Photos

Above:

Plate 217 Crane test weight truck SR departmental No 264s is seen at Ashford on 5 July 1950. Only the axle boxes and tie bar between give the former origin away — a Diagram 1360 15-ton mineral wagon, in this case SR No 18700 as drawn in **Figure 25** in *Volume Three*. It was converted in November 1929 (along with similar wagon No 265s) and ran until March 1964, easily outlasting the unmodified wagons. The livery was recorded as red oxide. *A.E. West*

Right:

Plate 218 Included more for the photographic record than for quality, this is Diagram 1351 type B reconstructed open wagon SECR No 13003, photographed somewhere in North Wales during 1923. It is the only known picture of these first 80 Maunsell/Lynes reconstructions on timber underframes, allocated SECR Diagram S2522/4 and was nominally a replacement for a Hurst Nelson Diagram 1344 type wagon of 1901. The later SR number was 14779 and it ran until November 1946. *J. P. Richards*

Left:

Plate 219 The later Maunsell/Lynes wagons are well photographed and some lasted in departmental service until around 1970. SR No DS19080 was built in October 1925; the second wagon on order A15 to Diagram 1347 and was photographed at Eastleigh on 1 August 1962, having been allocated to the Operating Department at Durnsford Road (Wimbledon) since November 1951. The January 1961 audit records just 14 still in ordinary traffic. *A. E. West*

Left:
Plate 220 Diagram 1355 seven-plank open SR No 15894, photographed at Newport (Monmouth) in the late 1920s exhibiting a slight variation in SR lettering layout, with the 12 Tons inscription on the lowest plank and the tare weight almost unseen on the solebar — a curious mix of late SECR and early SR styles. Built in 1920 as SECR No 12417, it ran until May 1944 — a fairly early withdrawal. *Edwards Bros*

Covered goods wagons

Most South Eastern covered goods wagons built before 1900 were quite small in their dimensions, indeed the last 6-ton vans to Diagram 1419 (SER Nos 6250/1, allocated SR Nos 44717/8 and both withdrawn in 1923) appeared as late as December 1878. However, just prior to this in August 1878 the company purchased four very much larger vans from the Metropolitan Railway Carriage & Wagon Company, SER Nos 6246-9. Just whether these were an experiment cannot now be stated, however, were it not for one remarkable survivor, this fact would probably be unknown, as none of the vans remained in ordinary traffic long enough to be included in the 1919 registers now at the PRO, Kew.

Below:
Plate 221 A serious collision between two goods trains occurred at Sevenoaks on 7 June 1884 and the clear-up operation was well recorded by a local photographer. Many wagons were destroyed, however several survived the accident, including those pictured. Nearest to the camera is one of the Metropolitan vans, No 6248, seen awaiting recovery and repair. The wagon number and company initials are visible on the fifth plank down, either side of the doors. What is remarkable is the similarity between this and the contemporary Stroudley LBSCR vehicles — which also date from 1878 — so was there some sort of connection between Stroudley, the SER and Metropolitan at this time? This style of van did not find favour on the South Eastern, except perhaps for the Grande Vitesse vans of 1881, where again the LBSCR built similar-looking vans as noted in Chapter 3. Also seen in the photograph are S1069 opens Nos 7347 and 5200, plus a standard SER goods brake van and the remains of a covered goods wagon. The final vehicle in the line is a dumb-buffered ballast wagon — one of several brought in to assist in the recovery operation. *Author's Collection*

Right:

Plate 222 Metropolitan van No 6246 was withdrawn from service as long ago as March 1913 but became a goods warehouse at Brasted yard two months later. Remarkably it was still there when the Westerham branch closed in 1961, its former number remaining visible on the solebar. It therefore became a Southern-owned wagon — of a sort! This shows the van as it appeared in June 1950, with sliding doors on each side in place of the hinged originals. Unusually for a grounded body, the 'W' irons are retained and the van is mounted on brick piers, presumably to assist in transferring goods from wagon to store to road vehicle — and to deter the rodent population from eating the contents! The author recalls seeing the

van but took it to be of LBSCR origin and failed to appreciate its significance or record its dimensions. However, scaling a broadside photograph, the van appears to be 18ft 4in long (as a Brighton van) with a wheelbase of 9ft (9in less than the LBSCR standard). From **Plate 221**, it is apparent that long springs and tiebars were also provided. *D. Cullum*

Some idea of the relative capacities of SECR covered goods wagons comes from a survey carried out and reported on 21 May 1918, as follows:

Carrying capacity	Internal dimensions L x W	Cubic capacity (cuft)	Relevant SR Diagrams
6 tons	14ft 0in x 7ft 3in	650	1419
8 tons	15ft 2¼in x 7ft 3½in	699	1420 and 1422
8 tons	15ft 0in x 7ft 3½in	684	1421
10 tons	15ft 5in x 6ft 11in	632	1423
10 tons	14ft 5in x 6ft 11in	591	LCDR 15ft vans
10 tons	15ft 9½in x 7ft 3in	697	1424
10 tons	16ft 5in x 7ft 5 in	891	1425
10 tons	16ft 10¼in x 7ft 8½in	1,000	1426 and 1427

The 1,000cu ft figure was achieved using the Maunsell/Lynes elliptical roof profile.

In comparison, the Metropolitan vans would have achieved a capacity of around 920 cubic feet, not a bad figure in 1878.

Right:

Plate 223 A more typical SER van, SR departmental No 915s at Nine Elms loco in February 1940. Built in 1890 as SER No 1048, it later became SR No 44792 to Diagram 1420. According to the records it had passenger-type running gear and double-block brakes but in fact has a single block on both sides. In July 1935 it was transferred to departmental service as a sponge cloth van, and marked 'To be returned to Ashford West'. The records also state that withdrawal occurred in July 1939 but perhaps due to the international situation the van was reinstated. Coupled behind it are a Diagram 1367 open and a Diagram 1433 van, both of LBSCR origin. *J. W. Sparrowe, courtesy R. S. Carpenter*

Right:

Plate 224 Messrs. H. Pooley & Son held the contract for maintenance of weighing machines and weighbridges throughout the SECR and later the entire Southern system. This was a large and important task, as each machine had to be tested regularly. On the SECR alone the number of appliances exceeded a thousand — locations such as Bricklayers Arms goods depot having over 60, while small wayside stations would have at least one each. The railway provided a number of vans for the purpose, equipped internally with full workshop facilities. Three new conversions were provided in 1919-22, using ex-SER Diagram 1422 vehicles, with three more added in 1925. One of the latter, SR No 45210, is seen at London Bridge in November 1932 and this appears to have retained its former SR traffic department number. When first converted in 1925 it should have carried departmental number 223S. Withdrawal came for this van in November 1934, but some of the others lasted until around 1943. SR Diagram 1428/9 conversions were then provided for Pooley's use, details of which may be found in Chapter 6. The van just seen on the left is departmental No 239s, illustrated in *Volume Three*, Plate 86. *R. W. Kidner*

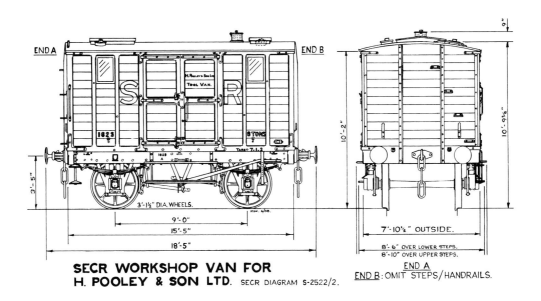

SECR WORKSHOP VAN FOR H. POOLEY & SON LTD. SECR DIAGRAM S-2522/2.

Figure 42 A drawing of the Pooley's weighing machine van, based on SECR Diagram S2522/2. Wagon numbers were:

Departmental Number	Former SECR number	Date converted	Departmental Number	Former SECR/SR number	Date converted
160s	9034	1922	221s	9117	1925
161s	9225	1919	222s	9185/45226	1925
162s	9291	1921	223s	9169/45210	1925

SR numbers 45210/26 do not appear to have received their allotted departmental numbers. Those converted prior to 1923 initially kept their SECR traffic department running numbers.

Above:

Plate 225 By the mid-1940s it was the turn of some Maunsell/Lynes wagons to enter departmental service. No DS1794 was formerly Diagram 1426 van SR No 45907/SECR No 16190, and was the last SECR van constructed, in March 1922. When photographed at Redhill shed it was allocated to the ODM (Outdoor Machinery) section and was painted light grey. The side windows were put in as part of the conversion in August 1949 and the van remained on these duties until March 1971. *J. H. Aston*

Right:

Plate 226 South Eastern ventilated covered goods wagons were a rare breed, but just visible at Dover Priory in 1924 is one of the six meat van conversions to SR Diagram 1489. This confirms that they were painted stone buff colour with Venetian red lettering after the Grouping and that they were vacuum piped and lettered 'Meat Van'. However, the footplate of LCDR 'M3' 4-4-0 No 474 obscures the wagon number, which fell in the range 51221-6. For a drawing see *Volume Three*, **Figure 42**. The three Diagram 1490 SER meat vans that remained in stock until 1938 are now confirmed as numbers 51230-2.
R. K. Blencowe Collection

Livestock vehicles

Right:
Plate 227 Former LCDR cattle wagons are equally elusive, however this shows a portion of Westinghouse-fitted LCDR No 1064, at Herne Hill sidings *circa* 1900. Just visible over the wagon number are the words 'To be returned at once EMPTY to HERNE HILL sorting sidings'. Presumably similar instructions were applied to all Westinghouse-fitted LCDR wagons, although the destination may have varied, as Faversham is known to have been another holding point for empty wagon stock. The two unfitted LCDR cattle wagons allocated Southern Railway numbers 52652/3 lasted until February 1924 and March 1927 respectively but may not have been repainted in SR livery. *Author's Collection*

Above:
Plate 228 Maunsell/Lynes special cattle van No 3748, ex-works at Southampton Old Docks on 17 May 1947. It still retains the pre-war lettering style and Maunsell green livery including the ends, so might just have been revarnished rather than given a full repaint. Nevertheless, it looks extremely smart, although the van may have seen little further use before scrapping in December 1950. Only van No 3752 lasted longer — until July 1951. *D. Cullum*

Whilst on the subject of livestock vehicles, four converted brake vans for cattle trains should be mentioned. These were SECR Nos 648-51, formerly four-wheeled passenger brake thirds or seconds Nos 1566/56/69/79 respectively and were built by Gloucester RCW Co. in 1866/7. Their dimensions were 19ft 6in x 7ft 3in and they were rebuilt in 1904/5, but while two Locomotive Publishing Company photographs show them as built, it is not known how they were altered for their new duties, but presumably some of the passenger accommodation was retained for the drovers. All were withdrawn in 1921, by which time they would have looked very ancient indeed.

Goods brake vans

Above:
Plate 229 This interesting picture was taken at Bromley South at Easter 1927 and shows an ex-WD Belgian ferry van along with two Diagram 1553 SER brake vans. The ferry van would have arrived via the Harwich train ferry, as the Dover-Dunkirk service did not start until October 1936, after which various continental wagons became a fairly common sight between the Channel ports and London. The two brake vans are standard SER/SECR vehicles, one still retaining pre-Grouping livery. Withdrawal of these accelerated after the Grouping such that by 1936 only 17 remained in service, SR Nos 55191/4, 55209/12/8/33/6/9/43/72/4/6-9, 55305/39. Most, if not all would have been allocated to some sort of 'local use' by this time, as noted in many instances in *Volume Three*. Comparison of building dates will also show that only the first five listed were actually of SER origin. *Rev. A. W .V. Mace, courtesy R.S. Carpenter*

Below:
Plate 230 A Diagram 1553 brake van sold out of service and almost certainly far from its home area. The recently applied National Coal Board initials suggest a date not long after 1947, but the location is unknown. Clearly, along with the two (possibly ex-Metropolitan Railway) coaches the train is providing a colliery workman's service of some sort. One early brake van, SECR No 6545, is recorded as having been sold to contractor J.F. Wake of Darlington in September 1920, along with several open wagons and four vans, but it is not this example, as this is of later construction, evident by the eight brake blocks. Quite possibly this was actually the last survivor of the type, despite what was stated against **Plate 153** in *Volume Three*, although a grounded body of one could still be seen in a field near Hamstreet, on the edge of Romney Marsh, until at least 1970. *T. A. Barry Collection*

Above:
Plate 231 One of the final batch of 'Midland style' six-wheeled brake vans to be built with one open veranda, SECR No 2026 of 1909, is seen in later condition as SR No 55381 at Guildford in June 1939. By this time it was possible to see these SECR vans on Central and South Western section duties, although the author has only seen evidence that those allocated to the Civil Engineer from 1950 actually reached the West of England. No 55381 was withdrawn in February 1950. *F. E. Box*

Some other withdrawal dates for Diagram 1558 vans were:

    1951 — Nos 55384/9, 55408/51.
    1952 — Nos 55392, 55405/35.
    1953 — Nos 55391, 55400/12/8/9/34/46/8.
    1954 — Nos 55369/76/93, 55415/29/31/3/42.
    1955 — Nos 55371 (now on the KESR), 55436/41.
    1956 — Nos 55397, 55401.
    1957 — No 55372 only.
The four ED vans, Nos DS55380/94, 55419/55 had through vacuum pipes added and lasted rather longer. Departmental series Diagram 1913 was issued for these, although apart from provision of pipes they were not otherwise altered.

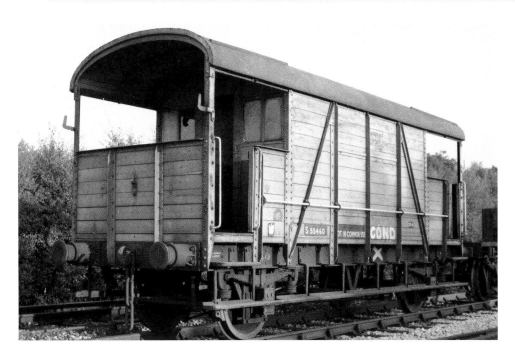

Left:
Plate 232 'Dance hall' brake No 55460, one of the Diagram 1559 vans completed in 1921 (in this case, SECR No 11896) on 12 inch channel underframes is seen marked condemned at Three Bridges in February 1963. BR unfitted grey livery with black number patches is carried — typical for those vans remaining in ordinary traffic during the 1950s. All bar one of the survivors (plus all except one SR-built example to Diagram 1560) were transferred to Engineer's service by 1961, including the van illustrated, but in this instance no repainting took place, save for the application of the 'Not in common use' stencil. *Author's Collection*

Bolster & timber wagons

Above:
Plate 233 Carriage of round timber by rail was once an everyday sight in southern England. Three ancient SER single bolster wagons are loaded and ready to travel at Westenhanger, some time in the late 1880s. The leading wagon, SER No 3816, dates from as far back as 1862, built to an 1859 design just 10ft long over headstocks with a wheelbase of 6ft. Despite its early build, it has self-contained sprung buffers, although construction of dumb-buffered single bolsters continued intermittently until 1897. Note the five-link coupling, typical of the period. In other details it is similar to the 13ft wagons drawn as **Figure 60** in *Volume Three*. This wagon was withdrawn before the formation of the SECR in 1899 but some of the type lasted until 1921. Behind is a coal/open wagon, SER No 2964, built in 1857. Note the corner detail — with 'L' angles bolted through the planking instead of conventional corner plates. This was a common early South Eastern feature, last seen on the Folkestone Harbour bank brake vans *Author's Collection*

Below:
Plate 234 East Kent Railway Class O1 0-6-0 No 100 comes off the Tilmanstone colliery branch at Eythorne with a coal train in August 1937. At the front is a pair of Maunsell/Lynes Diagram 1610 twin bolsters, numbers not identifiable. These probably went into the colliery loaded with steel or timber pit props, which would have been a regular inbound traffic at this location. *J. W. Sparrowe*

Road vehicle trucks

Left:
Plate 235 An early example dating from 1862, SER No 3892 is seen at Tonbridge some time before withdrawal in 1901. It was replaced by an almost identical vehicle carrying the same number two years later and this survived to become SR No 60345 to Diagram 1655, running until the early 1930s. By 1936 only four examples of the diagram remained in service, SR Nos 60343/7/52/62. *Author's Collection*

Centre left:
Plate 236 Diagram 1654 road vehicle truck SECR No 3332 at Bricklayers Arms loaded with Harrods furniture pantechnicon No 149 around 1905. The livery for this is presumed to be green with gold lettering, similar to that still used by the retailer today. The wagon carries the usual SECR description 'For Highway Vehicles' and later became SR No 60328; one of those built by Hurst Nelson in 1901 and ran until July 1929. By 1936 just three remained in traffic, SR Nos 60322/6/35. Express goods wagon No 7854, built in 1889, is just visible behind. This failed to survive long enough to be allocated to SR Diagram 1327. *SECR Official*

Below left:
Plate 237 Again perhaps of interest more for the load than the wagon itself, this shows Diagram 1654-type truck SECR No 3879 at Sevenoaks in either late 1911 or January 1912. This was built in June 1898 and ran until May 1919. It is stencilled on the solebar 'To be returned to B. Arms Immediately', as were many of these vehicles prior to the Grouping. S. Young's furniture container is marked 'To H. Nicholson Esq., British Embassy Constantinople per SS E_____'. Harold Nicholson travelled from Sissinghurst to take up his position there on 24 January 1912, so presumably his personal effects preceded him, hence the suggested date span. The wagon to the right is Diagram 1341 coal No 8875, that to the left appears to be one of the eight second-hand coal wagons purchased from J. &. B. Martin earlier in 1911 — No 3261 — and the only known illustration of these wagons. *J. Arkell Collection*

Engineer's Department wagons

In *Volume Three* the SER livery for the ballast brake vans was speculated upon. Two very poor photographs from the 1890s (regrettably not suitable for reproduction) have now surfaced and these perhaps show that the colour was darker than the ordinary wagons, suggesting the use of dark reddish-brown with bright red ends, similar to the traffic department brakes. The lettering layout

for the standard Diagram 1747 van is rather clearer and shows two lines of small writing on the upper planking either-side and symmetrically placed about the two centre windows (refer to **Figure 77** in *Volume Three*), as follows:

S.E.R	Engineer's	Dept.
3929	Ballast	Break

In addition, **Plate 204** of *Volume Three* is now confirmed as showing ballast brake No 11972 and for those readers with the original 2000 edition, the LCDR van illustrated in **Plate 206** and **Figure 79** is now known to be tool brake No 4, rather than a ballast brake van. There were two such vehicles, LCDR Nos 4

and 5 and they became SR departmental numbers 0604s and 0605s after the Grouping and lasted to 1935/6, thus being the final ex-LCDR brake vans in existence. Readers with the 2004 imprint will already be in receipt of this information.

Right:
Plate 238 Construction of the Tovil branch, to the south of Maidstone, provides the location for this period study, dated 1885. Seven two-plank dumb-buffered dropside wagons appear in the whole picture and this is a close-up of the nearest, SER No 4237 which was built by Metropolitan in 1864 and withdrawn before 1903. Note the somewhat unorthodox pre-1890 coupling arrangements — said to allow them to be 'coupled apart' and allowing ballast to be unloaded over the ends between the wagons, as well as at the sides. Note that the next wagon in the line has spoke, instead of Mansell wheels. There were a considerable number of these wagons in service in SER days and despite their obvious antiquity, some remained in service to become SR Diagram 1741. Relatively few were reconstructed with sprung buffers from 1913 onwards to be allocated to SR Diagram 1742. *SECR Official*

Right:
Plate 239 As a comparison, the Maunsell/Lynes design of 1919 is represented by No DS62461 to Diagram 1744 at Sidmouth on 25 June 1964. This probably has just two features in common with SER No 4237 — namely two planks and dropsides! This wagon was one of the 60 built in 1923 just after the formation of the Southern Railway, but probably appeared in SECR livery as their No 547. It was passed to the Western Region in March 1963 and ran until April 1966. The photographer recorded the livery as 'reddish-brown with white lettering'. Some were downrated to 10 tons capacity, including Nos 62373/4/8/81/7/9/90/7, 62400/2/4/6, as soon as 1928. Perhaps they were then equipped with second-hand wheelsets? *A.E. West*

Above left:
Plate 240 One of the 1915 Leeds Forge Company ballast hoppers to Diagram 1746, SR No 62495 (also illustrated in *Volume Three*, **Plate 211**) at Battersea Wharf in September 1952, at the end of a rake of hopper wagons awaiting return to Allington Quarry — the chalked destination almost obliterating the wagon number. Just visible to the left is one of the Diagram 1745 hoppers. Note that SR-pattern axlebox covers have replaced those lettered SECR since the 1946 photograph was taken and the wagon number plate is now incorrectly suffixed 'B' to indicate (wrongly) that the wagon is of LBSCR origin. The livery was still SR red oxide. *A. E. West*

Left:
Plate 241 Diagram 1794 30-ton bogie rail wagon SECR No 6077, completed by Charles Roberts & Co in November 1906, is seen at Ashford Works, probably when new. Just whether it is being subjected to a load test or was simply available to transport wheelsets around the works cannot be stated — however the 26 sets loaded on board could not travel far in the manner seen — certainly not on the main line without being shackled in place. The high standard of finish of the ex-works Mansell wheels may be noted, complete with varnished timber segments, gloss black centres and rims, together with blue axles, not that the latter is apparent from the photograph. The wagon became SR No 64604 and ran until June 1956. *SECR Official*

Above:
Plate 242 The later Maunsell/Lynes rail wagon design, SR Diagram 1795. No DS64621 is loaded with rails at Woking CCE yard in May 1974 — one of the most recent photographs of a pre-Grouping wagon in the book. This was the final survivor to the diagram and was withdrawn in November 1975. Behind is ex-LSWR Diagram 1597 bogie bolster No 57875, built in 1926 under SR order E108. This was one of the 32 reserved for Bertram Mills circus train until 1965, then being reallocated to the Civil Engineer. The Engineer's yard at Woking is now very much reduced in size and the location seen is now occupied by a well-known supermarket chain, so the author now visits this site for a very different (and far less interesting!) reason than 30-40 years ago. *Author*

Chapter 6.
Southern Railway Wagons

The Southern Railway inherited approximately 39,000 wagons from its pre-Grouping constituent companies in 1923, if one includes the 853 wagons actually on order at that time. Between then and 1951, when the last true Southern designs were completed, just over 30,000 new wagons had been constructed for the company. By 1949, the total wagon stock stood at around the 35,000 figure, so it may be reckoned that about 5,000 pre-Grouping SR wagons still remained in ordinary stock at that time. This total was probably in the proportions 40% LSWR, 40% SECR and 20% LBSCR. The ex-LSWR designs were still very well represented, with examples from in excess of 60 diagrams remaining in traffic, however only the Maunsell/Lynes SECR types remained in any quantity, while for the LBSCR almost half of its wagons would have been on the Isle of Wight. It should be stressed, however, that all these numbers are an approximate guide

only, as figures from the company could vary according to source as the status of some Engineer's wagons, loco coal wagons, departmental or duplicate stock was often debateable.

Until this chapter, there have always been (and probably always will be) gaps in our photographic and drawn records, however, because examples of most Southern Railway standard vehicles lasted until more recent times, it proved possible in *Volume Four* of *Southern Wagons* to illustrate all but a handful of types. This situation has only changed marginally since then and, of approximately 65 diagrams issued to cover the post-1923 productions, just two remain conspicuous by their absence — and these amount to single figure quantities in each instance! This chapter will therefore concentrate more on photographs of wagons in traffic or later in their lives, as most official portraits of the wagons when new appeared in *Volume Four*.

Open goods wagons

Below:
Plate 243 Where better to start than with Diagram 1379 — the Southern's most numerous wagon. No 32565 is seen in typical everyday condition around 1945, by now uprated to 13 tons capacity — this lettering alone having been repainted more recently. This was built as part of order A255 in 1928 and has Freighter brake gear. The load is rolls of chain link fencing, an unusual one and perhaps challenging to model in the smaller scales. It usually came in 3ft, 4ft or 6ft high rolls. Another contractor-built wagon to this diagram appears as the title page picture. *HMRS Collection*

Right & centre right:

Plates 244 and 245 Two views of Diagram 1378A (later 1899) cable wagon conversion No DS1667 at Eastleigh on 6 August 1949. The original pre-war cable conversions were allocated Diagram 1378 and only distant views of these have been found (apart from on Messrs Pirelli-General's advertising material!). Sixty were converted over the 12 months April 1936-7, numbers being widely scattered in the range 29079-36897 and all reverted to Diagram 1379 with the onset of war. By 1948 this requirement had resurfaced, so an initial 60 wagons were then rather more extensively adapted, with side and end apertures in place of the simpler pre-war expedient of removing the second plank from the bottom. The first 36 conversions, including this one, were renumbered into the departmental series, numbers being DS1657-83/9/90/3/5/6/9, 1704/8/13, however those converted after July 1949 retained their former running numbers, merely with a 'DS' prefix and this remained the norm for the many subsequent conversions into the 1960s. The livery is light grey, while **Plate 245** shows the drum cradle (almost certainly similar to or recycled from the earlier conversions) and the interior construction of the wagon. Most of the 1949 conversions were stencilled 'When empty return to Eastleigh', although this changed as the electrification and recabling schemes moved around the Region.
Both A. E. West

Left:

Plate 246 One of the somewhat elusive Diagram 1385 vacuum-fitted wagons of 1933, No 37042 at Carlisle Upperby in February 1960. This correctly carries BR fitted bauxite livery but is incorrectly stencilled 'XP' and WB 10ft 0in — it is actually of 9ft wheelbase. The sheet rail has now gone but otherwise the wagon remains very much as built.
D. P. Rowland

Above:

Plate 247 Diagram 1387 ferry wagon No 36873 at Salisbury in June 1936, during the period prior to the commencement of the ferry service in the following October. The overhaul date of June 1935 is visible on the solebar, so clearly these wagons were released to ordinary traffic in the 12-18 months before the ferry dock was ready, although the vehicle still looks ex-works a year after painting, so perhaps their movements had been restricted in some way. Note the use of 3-hole disc wheels on this wagon. *J. G. Griffiths*

Right:

Plate 248 One of the many 'rebuilds' utilising second-hand wheel sets and axleboxes — in this case a Type 3 with ex-SECR parts dating from 1934. Those wagons built against orders A638 and 737 with SECR parts were later allocated Diagram 1381A, to distinguish them from identical 10-ton wagons with LSWR wheels and axleboxes, allocated Diagram 1381B. However the first batch of wagons with SECR fittings, built in 1932, remained simply as Diagram 1381. The exact differences are not known but probably involve different wheel sets. No DS26261 remained of 10-tons capacity and was photographed at Paddock Wood in June 1961, another cable wagon allocated to the Signal Engineer. The livery may be 'gulf red'. Steel channels have replaced the two lower end planks — a common BR modification that helped to prevent loads bursting

through after a rough shunt. This wagon was cut down to five planks high in 1966, one of at least 20 known examples so modified, some of which are listed in the Appendix. *E. B. Trotter*

Right:

Plate 249 The equivalent 10ft wheelbase rebuild to Diagram 1400, No 27390 (built in 1937) at Torrington on 3 June 1965. This now has vacuum brakes, a flat metal tie bar between the axleboxes and modern hydraulic buffers — all typical BR 1950s/60s modifications and is now painted bauxite and rated at 13 tons. When built it would have had second-hand wheels and been of 10 tons capacity — a 'rebuild Type 4'. Because of their size, it was easy to overload these wagons, particularly the 10-tonners, as was found in later years when some were allocated to the Engineer's Department. This may be the reason why these were cut down to five planks high. *A. E. West*

Many eight plank open wagons entered departmental service from the late 1940s onwards, as a general rule the 9ft wheelbase wagons to diagram 1379 going first. Some idea of the survival rate in normal service may be gauged by the January 1961 census, which recorded the following totals still in traffic.

9ft wheelbase

Diagram	No. in stock
1379	510 (some in IOW)
1381/A/B	87
1385	96 (with AVB)
1387	30 (Dover ferry)

10ft wheelbase

Diagram	No. in stock
1377	724
1398	333 (with AVB)
1400	1295

As may be seen, 94% of the 10ft wheelbase wagons were still running, yet only 8% of the 9ft wagons remained — although almost all of the 130 vacuum equipped vehicles survived. Most Diagram 1377 and 1400 wagons received AVB under British Railways and these only became a rare sight into the 1970s. The last few survivors were withdrawn from departmental service around 1984 (including No DS11530, now on the Kent & East Sussex Railway).

Some of those noted cut down to five planks high (in the mid-1960s) include DS1660/76, 30385, 30624, 34616 & 36993. In addition, No 33453 was cut down to four planks high. For the sake of completeness, the survival rates of the other two Maunsell-era open goods wagon designs were as follows

Diagram 1380: 108 in stock at 1/1/1961.
Diagram 1388: 18 in stock at 1/1/1961.

Left:

Plate 250 The last Maunsell-era eight plank opens appeared in December 1939, to Diagram 1377 and were followed immediately by the first Bulleid five planks to Diagram 1375. Construction continued until 1948 with a total of 4676 being built for the Southern, 400 for the LNER, 465 for the LMS and 1600 for the Ministry of Supply (see **Frontispiece** picture). Rather belatedly therefore this became the Southern's second most numerous wagon diagram, despite the diversity of owners. SR No DS38182 is an early example dating from 1940 and is seen at Hoo Junction, probably in the late 1960s. It now has vacuum brakes, LNER axleboxes and other modifications similar to the wagon in **Plate 249** and was now included on Diagram 1389. Withdrawal took place in February 1976. *D. Larkin*

Above:

Plate 251 In 1970 a number of five plank opens were reconstructed as 'Coil S' wagons, to carry wire coils from the steelworks at Scunthorpe all around the country. Wagons from all four pre-Nationalisation companies, plus similar BR-built wagons were involved, including at least 86 formerly to SR Diagram 1389. No S12334 is seen at Battersea (Wandsworth Road goods) in November 1977 fulfilling this role. BR Diagram 1/450 was issued and the wagons had their sides completely removed, together with some portions of the end planks. One new side plank was fitted, raised on stanchions and angled outwards to support and restrain the coils. The wagon number and 'COIL S' were usually painted on this plank. Other examples include S11879, 11900/35, 12035, 13815, 38401/14 & 38742. None appear to have come from the lower-numbered batches between 5153 and 7120. All were out of use by October 1983. *D. Larkin*

Right:

Plate 252 A view of three 'Coil S' wagons from above, at Scunthorpe in August 1980, showing the floor detail. Two rolls were usually carried. These may not necessarily be SR vehicles, but all the conversions were very similar. *D. Larkin*

During the 1950s all except about 100 Diagram 1375 wagons were equipped with vacuum brakes. A few that missed the programme were Nos 5198, 5301, 5501, 5624, 6182, 6607, 6970, 7108, 11937, 12016, 12371, 12720/66, 13182, 13547, 14002, 38313/41, 38666 & 38716.

The 400 LNER wagon numbers are now confirmed as 262449-848, all completed during 1943/4 (to LNER Diagram 178), while the additional wagon allocated to Diagram 1389 during World War Two appears to be No 38417.

Being modern wagons, they lasted well and only 31 of the SR allocation had been scrapped by the January 1961 audit, many continuing to serve until the 1980s/90s and were amongst the last ex-Southern ordinary wagons to survive on BR.

Above:
Plate 253 The unique three plank conversion of a Bulleid open, DS13443, at Hoo Junction in the early 1970s. Converted to a crane test weight truck in August 1963, against order 5258 to replace a withdrawn Diagram 1360 conversion, it appears almost identical to the purpose-built vehicles 1085-8s, illustrated in **Plates 161/2** of *Volume Four*. The conversion was done very well, replacing the side doors with through planking and apart from the retention of the doorstops there is nothing obvious to show that the wagon had not been built thus. Such was the high standard of workmanship that almost invariably surrounded the SR workshops — even to the tradition of ensuring that all visible screw-heads lined up with each other and with the slots in line with the grain of the timber! *D. Larkin*

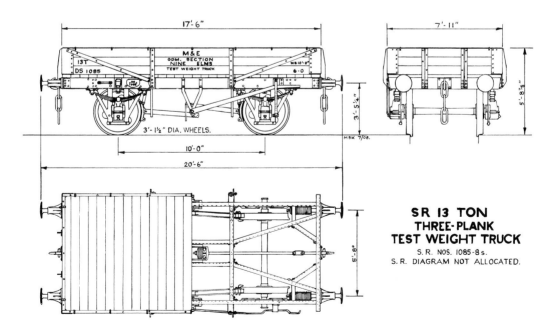

**SR 13 TON
THREE-PLANK
TEST WEIGHT TRUCK**
S. R. NOS. 1085-8 s.
S. R. DIAGRAM NOT ALLOCATED.

Figure 43 A drawing of the 1937 crane test weight truck, to general arrangement drawing A7432 and order A955. The dimensions were actually taken by the author from DS1085 at Eastleigh in October 1972, by which time the capacity had been reduced to 8 tons. One earlier wagon was completed in 1932, SR No 610S, built against order A696. The bodywork was identical, but mounted on the then standard 9ft underframe. Unusually, no diagram appears to have been issued for any of these wagons.

Right:

Plate 254 One of the originally unfitted shock wagons to Diagram 1392, No S14042, at Hoo Junction in the late 1960s, stencilled 'Empty to North End Sidings, Erith'. These were built with Morton brake gear (Nos 14033-51) and all except 14035/9 received AVB under British Railways. This example has replacement hydraulic buffers and has a protective cover over the spring mechanism. The January 1961 census records that all 50 SR shock-opens to Diagrams 1376/92 were still in traffic. This wagon was scrapped in December 1971.

The 'Return to' allocations for these wagons remained remarkably constant throughout the 1950s (and possibly longer), as recorded on some copies of the relevant diagrams, as follows:

Return to North End Sidings, Erith — Nos 14037-40/2/3/5-7/55/8/9/61-3/8/70.
Return to North End Sidings, Erith — Nos 38389/92-4/6-400.
Return to Uralite Siding, Hoo Jcn. — Nos 14051, 38390/1/5.
Return To Dartford — Nos 14033/49/52/6/66/7.
Return to Horsham — Nos 14034-6/44/53/4/60/4/5/9.
Return to Southampton — Nos 14048/50.
Return to Poole — Nos 14041/57.
D. Larkin

Figure 44 A copy of SR Diagram 1391, covering the solitary wagon built on a triangulated underframe in September 1945, No 6780. To date no official photograph has been found, which is surprising in view of the experimental nature of the vehicle. The bodywork shown appears remarkably ordinary, unlike the underframe, but note that the end is devoid of planking. Just whether this is significant cannot be stated. One other detail of the wagon is also a mystery. Some records state that it became departmental No 1430s at Lancing in June 1950 and to internal-user a year later, but BR withdrawal records give the date as December 1966, for traffic department wagon No 6780, built in September 1945. Was it reinstated in inter-depot service after 1951? The January 1961 census also records its presence. In the absence of a photograph, we may never know.

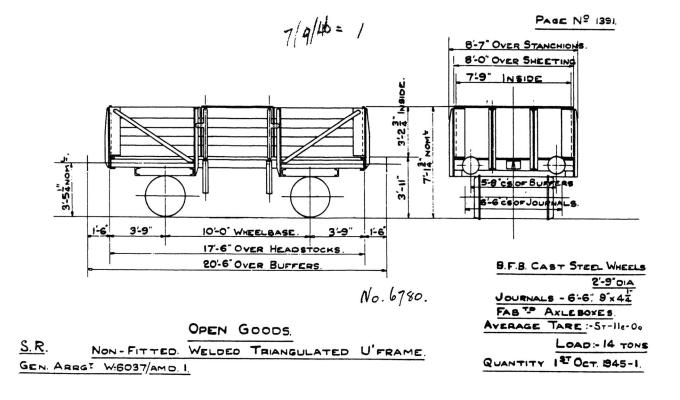

Right:
Plate 255 The prototype Bulleid three plank dropside wagon, B457100, at East Grinstead in September 1968 — carrying the ED 'green triangle' symbol. Had it carried SR numbering, presumably this would have been No 3941. Note the odd wheel sets and replacement hydraulic buffers.
E. R. Kemp

Centre right:
Plate 256 The other Bulleid dropside wagon, with the impossible-to-lift five plank door. No B483672 is seen ex-works at Honiton in September 1961, in grey livery with black number patches, but still with the 'On loan to Civil Engineer' marking. It is still as built, save for the replacement of the original wheels by those of spoke pattern. *A. E. West*

Below:
Plate 257 Some of these Diagram 1/33 wagons were upgraded with AVB, Morton brakes and new buffers. No B483706 is seen at Lingfield in July 1969 with more modern markings, but still with the 'On loan to Civil Engineer's' board — clearly still unwanted! Note how the brake lever is 'set' to clear the door springs.
E. R. Kemp

Container wagons and containers

It should be recorded here that the last batch of Diagram 1380 five plank open wagon rebuilds (order A577) were originally ordered in May 1930 'with whole drop sides suitable for conveyance of containers', so clearly it took a little while for a more suitable design to be worked out, two specific types being ordered in October 1931.

Left:
Plate 258 An interesting load for conflat 'D' No 39507 at Brighton station on Boxing Day, 1932. A replica Stephenson's *Rocket* forms part of an exhibition held at the station over that Christmas and New Year to mark the inauguration of full electrified services between London and Brighton on 1 January. The wagon is to Diagram 1383, part of the first 75 completed with AVB, eight brake blocks and short brake levers and was, at the time, less than two months old — quite possibly its first duty. *H. F. Wheeller*

Above:
Plate 259 The second batch of 75 wagons to Diagram 1383 were originally unfitted — coded conflat 'C'. These had long brake levers and lift-link brakes with only four brake blocks. No 39592 is seen at Southampton Docks in August 1936. It was soon found advantageous to equip every container wagon with vacuum brakes, so all examples of conflats 'A' and 'C' were fitted on order A884 between 1935 and 1937, all then becoming conflats 'B' or 'D' respectively. The Diagram 1383 vehicles all received the same brake arrangement as that seen in **Plate 258**. In the background may be seen an LSWR refrigerator van and a Diagram 1478 banana van, with a standard LNER banana van between them. This is on loan to the Southern (and lettered 'SR'). Some more details of these are given later in this chapter. *F. Foote*

Above:
Plate 260 Railway-owned containers were not the only load for this class of wagon. Carter-Paterson container No 203 is seen on conflat 'B' No 39230, one of those built to Diagram 1382 with 'power' brake gear, again at Southampton Docks in 1935. The container is clearly carrying a well-known brand of refreshment still going strong today! Carter-Paterson's livery is remembered as dark green with yellow lettering, shaded black on a red panel (just visible on the original print) and the firm later became part of British Road Services. Presumably the circles on the end are black, for chalking instructions *F. Foote*

Right:
Plate 261 Road vehicles were another common load, including these cars for disabled drivers, manufactured by AC Cars of Thames Ditton and loaded for many years at Surbiton station. The cars were mostly pale turquoise blue, but there may have been a few white or cream examples — possibly to special order only. No S39939 is a former conflat 'B', now BR code carfit 'S' and is a 10ft wheelbase example to Diagram 1399, dating from 1947. Note the odd wheelsets and axleboxes. The location is Feltham, in April 1968 and the wagon would last for just six more months before scrapping. *P. W. Bartlett*

The January 1961 audit lists all except five of the 905 SR container wagons still in traffic, however this would change rapidly within a decade and by the early 1970s both types were a comparatively rare sight; the short wagons especially so on the Southern Region as many were stencilled 'Empty to Morris Cowley WR' or 'Empty to Bathgate, Scottish Region' from 1963 onwards. Six Diagram 1383 wagons were retained in SR departmental use long after the rest and survived to the 1990s, at least three of which have now passed into preservation.

Above:

Plate 262 A posed view at Southampton (note that the containers are not roped down), showing Diagram 3002 containers 311 and 312 mounted on a Thornycroft six-ton platform lorry and trailer, dated 18 April 1931, one of several taken on that rather wet day. The publicity caption reads 'From ship to shop. Special Southern Railway insulated containers for fast road services from Southampton Docks to principal cities in Hampshire, Dorset, Wiltshire and Sussex'. Note that the containers are actually lettered 'Road Service Only', so perhaps the whole batch (Nos. 301-25) were so marked when new. Their livery is the usual stone with red writing. The lorry, No 2350M, to Diagram RV31, was also new in 1931, part of an order for 15 identical vehicles, numbered 2341-55M, however their registration numbers were not consecutive. The 'Harrow' trailer is number 2567M and both vehicles carry standard green livery with Chinese red wheels and gilt lettering — although that on the trailer is of a different style. *SR Official*

Left:

Plate 263 This interesting picture shows Diagram 3012 ventilated meat container M644 on conflat 'B' No 39010 at Waterloo, circa October 1932, when new. The interior lining and hooks for the hanging of carcasses can be seen. The container is painted silver with green lettering, but note that the classification letter appears to be black, so maybe this was added later. The wagon tare weight has also been amended — the chalked cwt and quarter figures may still be seen. The container wagon classification also includes the quotes — viz. Conflat 'B' — not always visible in photographs. *SR Official*

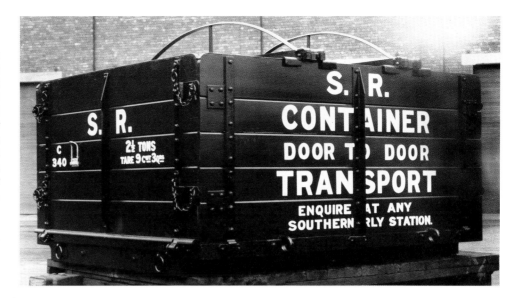

Right:

Plate 264 Open container C340 to Diagram 3006, the first of the type built by BRCW in April 1931 and photographed when new. The lettering is not the same as **Plate 188** and **Figure 62** in *Volume Four*, so for the purposes of advertising was probably different on each side, just like **Figure 65**. Whether this was a feature of all these open containers or varied during their lives is not known. *BRCW*

Right:

Plate 265 Insulated meat container FX554S (the S-suffix indicating ex-Southern Railway) at Eastleigh Carriage & Wagon Works in October 1949. This is now to Diagram 3015, but was built as Diagram 3002, one of 10 converted in 1933 with additional insulation, although the external alterations were minimal. This shows the early BR lettering style, although the colours remain stone with red writing, apart from the container number, which is black. One additional Diagram 3015 conversion (container No FX284S) was done post-1948, to replace one of the originals, withdrawn during 1949, leading to speculation that there was a particular traffic for these 10 conversions. *SR Official*

At this point it is worth briefly mentioning the baggage boxes used in conjunction with the boat train services via Dover and Folkestone. Although more associated with passenger rated traffic, these were, in effect, small containers and so might have been loaded onto container wagons or road vehicle trucks. There were three diagrams allocated, numbers 3651-3 and they were numbered in their own series, from 1-68. The older ones date from SECR ownership.

British Railways invested heavily in containers and construction of 302 more to former SR designs began in 1948/9, however these were numbered into the BR container series while by 1960 more than 30,000 had been completed, to no less than 90 different BR diagrams. By then SR containers were very much in the minority, the January 1961 audit giving the following statistics on those still in traffic:

SR Diagram	No.	SR Diagram	No.	SR Diagram	No.	SR Diagram	No.
3001	1	3010	2	3018	2	3025	48
3002	5	3012	1	3021	8	3026	83
3003	2	3013	27	3023	11	3027	77
3006	4	3016	1	3024	6	3028	25

Some containers were sold out of service and appeared mostly on farms in Southern England — a few still surviving to the 1990s in such use. The author recalls two green-liveried former SR ones at Chessington Zoo (now part of theme park Chessington World of

Adventure) in the 1960s, providing stabling for various species of antelope! As the subsequently applied paint finish deteriorated the former railway lettering could be seen, especially on the non-public side facing the perimeter fence.

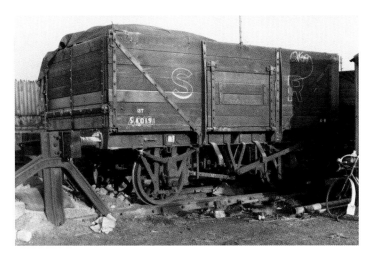

Mineral wagons

The Southern's new-build stock of these did not exceed 1,289 wagons — compare this with the average LMS production over the Grouping period of 1,568 wagons PER YEAR, so it is hardly surprising that apart from within the confines of East Kent they were a pretty rare breed. The single LNER order for 1,850 wagons in 1945 dwarfs the entire SR production at a stroke, while the 1946 follow-up order for 1,500 all-steel minerals to LNER Diagram 188 (LNER Nos 287689-289188) again puts the SR fleet in the shade. It does however illustrate that it was traffic demand, or rather lack of it, that limited production, certainly not the capacity of Ashford Works.

Above:
Plate 266 One of the RCH-type 16ft 6in wagons to Diagram 1384 — only the fourth picture known to the author — No S40191 at Oxford in September 1954, by now uprated to 13 tons capacity. The original 1933 lettering was still visible and was chalked around prior being photographed. There is no sign whatsoever of post-1936 lettering, so it must be presumed that the wagon did not get a full repaint during the 1936-48 period, if indeed at all since construction. Note also the complete absence of the full-length diagonal 'end-door' stripe, although there may be a trace of white paint on the left-hand diagonal strapping, the usual later method of indicating the end-door. General withdrawal of these wagons began in 1952 and no less than 160 of the 200 examples were withdrawn between then and 1958. Just six remained to be recorded by the 1961 census. *R. England, courtesy Pendon Museum*

Right:
Plate 267 The 20-ton eight plank wagons might be met with singly in any location — although almost all photographs seen by the author were taken on SR metals — a point perhaps not without significance. Diagram 1386 mineral No S40358 is seen at Sturry in February 1953, probably on its way back to Chislet Colliery sidings, a couple of miles to the east. The livery is grey/unpainted timber and the wagon has been uprated to 21 tons, typical 1950s condition. General withdrawal began in 1954 and 126 remained in service in January 1961. The LNER-style wagons to Diagram 1390, being rather newer, lasted better and 81 of the 100 SR examples were still in service at that date. *D. Cullum*

Covered goods wagons

The Southern managed to achieve remarkable standardisation in its covered goods vehicles and the 9,000+ wagons built for ordinary service (as opposed to some for meat/fruit/refrigerated traffic) could be instantly recognised on account of the Lynes roof profile — totally unlike GWR, LMS, LNER or, for that matter, the later BR vehicles. However, when it comes to detail there were many variations on the overall theme and at least 12 diagrams were allocated — not that these always reflected the changes in appearance caused by different bodywork or brake gear. Whilst highly relevant to the modeller, many of these would have been of no concern to the operators.

Right:
Plate 268 Typical even-planked bodywork style for vans built between 1929 and 1935, on a 9ft wheelbase underframe. No S46166 is actually a 10-ton van to diagram 1429, one of 600 completed using second-hand LSWR wheelsets and axleboxes in 1931/2. This was an unfitted example and is largely as built save for replacement 1947-type axleguards, yet it still retained LSWR parts when seen marked 'condemned' at Exmouth Junction in April 1963. The livery is grey with white lettering on black patches. Some 10-ton vans were reallocated to Diagram 1438 at some time, but the exact dates, numbers and the actual modifications are unknown. About 30 of the 10-ton unfitted vans received AVB in BR days, including Nos 44436/51/76, 44600/16, 45015/33, 46115/52, together with Morton brake gear, adding to the 150 that had been equipped from new. Drooping doors were also a common feature of SR vans! *A. E. West*

Right:

Plate 269 The equivalent 12-ton vans with even-planked bodywork on a 9ft underframe were to Diagrams 1428/1428A and 1276 of these were built, two-thirds being vacuum fitted. Departmental No DS487 was formerly unfitted van No 45995, part of the original order A129, dating from 1929 and was converted into a weighing machine van for Messrs H. Pooley & Sons in October 1948. This was one of nine such conversions (SR numbers 481S-489S, all ex-Diagrams 1428/9 during 1947/8), replacing the earlier LSWR Diagram 1410 and SECR Diagram 1422 vehicles. **Figure 45** is a reproduction of SR Diagram 1896 showing these conversions. When seen at Eastleigh on 1 August 1962, DS487 was painted black with white lettering and served until June 1966. Several diagram 1428 vans were reclassified as Diagram 1437 at some time, but like the Diagram 1438 vehicles noted above, no details are known. One 9ft wheelbase van to Diagram 1428, No 47323, is recorded as being rebuilt with a 'pent-house' roof in March 1943, presumably as the two vans to Diagram 1458, however no photographs are known. *A. E. West*

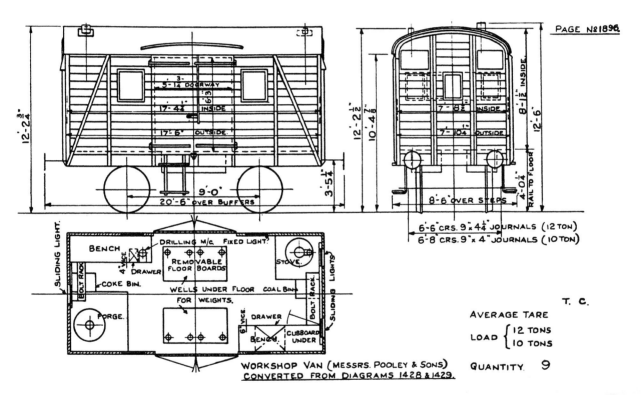

WORKSHOP VAN (MESSRS. POOLEY & SONS) CONVERTED FROM DIAGRAMS 1428 & 1429.

Right:

Plate 270 One of the ferry van conversions to diagram 1430, No 45953 at Salisbury in July 1935, during the 18-month period between conversion and the ferry service commencing. Chalked destinations include Nine Elms, Bournemouth and Salisbury, so probably the 'non-common-user' policy was observed and the wagons did not leave SR metals during this time — they might have been needed quickly once the ferry dock technical problems were overcome. Note a Diagram 1387 ferry open beyond (No 36888) and the ancient SER Diagram 1420 van No 44835 just visible to the right. *J. G. Griffiths*

Left:

Plate 271 A 10ft wheelbase van with uneven planking, to Diagram 1455. No 59123 was built against order A2506 in 1943, photographed *circa* 1970 and withdrawn in October 1971. It now has AVB, very different axleboxes and hydraulic buffers — all typical BR modifications applied to very many unfitted SR wagons between 1955 and 1963. All 2,833 Diagram 1455 wagons were originally unfitted owing to the prevailing wartime restrictions, including those built for the GWR and LMS (see **Plate 273**) and very few failed to receive vacuum brakes under British Railways. The equivalent fitted wagons were to diagram 1458 and a similar number of these were built between 1936 and 1941, with at least two different styles of body planking and several underframe variants. *D. Larkin*

Below:

Plate 272 Plywood construction became the standard body sheeting material in 1945 and was used for all subsequent Diagram 1452 vans until production ceased in December 1949 (but see the next two photographs). No S56628 from order A3218 is seen at Hoo Junction around 1968, now equipped with vacuum brakes by BR. Note the method of extending the buffer guides — with 2½in collars welded onto the original fittings. Also no tie bar is provided — unusual on a vacuum fitted wagon of this type. Most of the 1803 wagons to this diagram were built unfitted and almost all were subsequently vacuum-braked. Being the most modern SR vans, they could still be seen in reasonable numbers until the 1970s, this example being withdrawn in December 1970. The livery is bauxite, with white lettering, black roof and underframe. The ends have required much patching — the plywood panels being less easy to repair than planking. *D. Larkin*

Right:

Two minor mysteries, as neither of the vans in **Plates 273** and **274** are as expected. No M523357 in **Plate 273** should have 2+2 planking and be as Diagram 1455 — one of the second batch of vans built for the LMS in 1943. However, it is clearly a plywood van, so whether it has swapped identities with another or has been resheeted is uncertain, but in view of the lack of diagonal strapping the former may be more likely. Note also the end vent — again non-standard. By the time it was photographed (*circa* 1966) it had received the usual BR AVB modifications. The wagon code — helpfully 'van', is typical of the period. *D. Larkin*

Right:

No B752663 in **Plate 274** is just the reverse. This should be plywood sheeted and be to Diagram 1452 — part of order A3445 built in 1949 for BR. Instead it has a bit of everything; even-planked bodywork, 2+2 doors, diagonal strapping and the left-hand body stanchion cropped off at solebar level. It also has the 1947-pattern axleguards, together with flat-fronted axleboxes and AVB. Just what the explanation might be — who knows? The date is *circa* 1963.
D. P. Rowland

Some SR vans that failed to receive vacuum brake gear under BR are as follows:
Diagram 1452: Nos 49986, 54292, 56827/57.
Diagram 1455: Nos 44748, 44811, 45067/99, 45102/5/249, 54246, 65437, 65501/93, 66066.
As already stated, many of these vans lasted well and the January 1961 audit reveals the following situation:

9ft wheelbase vans		10ft wheelbase vans	
Diagram No	**Total in service**	**Diagram No**	**Total in service**
1428	1152	1452	1751
1429	583	1454	1
1430	98	1455	1774
		1458	2684
		1459	100
Percentage still in traffic = 97.7		Percentage still in traffic = 97.5	

Readers may be surprised to see that the survival rate of the older 9ft wheelbase vehicles just exceeds that for the later wagons, but it should be remembered that at least 76 to Diagram 1458 were taken for conversion to generator/workshop vans for both the War Department and the SR during the 1940s and so were removed from stock then. The survival rates for the 1,050 vans built for the GWR and LMS are not known, but examples of these could still be seen into the 1970s. It should also be noted that no new diagrams appear to have been issued for the 'pent-house roof' conversions.

Meat and fruit vans

No further illustrations of the six Diagram 1476 refrigerator vans have been found, however a few details of their workings have come to light. In March 1939, Nos 50494/5 were in use for butter traffic between Chard Junction and Nine Elms, being marked accordingly, while all six were withdrawn from traffic during 1963/4. Otherwise, they may have spent some of their time working out of Southampton Docks, although as specialised vehicles, all might have had specific duties allocated.

Right:

Plate 275 Photographs of the Diagram 1477 insulated vans in traffic are rare — this being the only one known to the author. Nos 50541/62 are seen, probably at Southampton in August 1936, looking extremely travel-stained and clearly still carrying their original 1931 paint finish. For a short time after Nationalisation these vans received white livery with black lettering — possibly the colours carried by the van illustrated in **Plate 90** of *Volume Four* — but later the more practical BR bauxite was applied. Van No 50573 was equipped with shelving for conveyance of milk in cartons in September 1932, on order E725, and appears to have been the only one so modified. No new diagram has been seen and it is not known for how long the shelving (or the duty — whatever it may have been) was retained. The January 1961 census records all except two still in traffic. *N. Parkhouse Collection*

Right:

Plate 276 Also at Southampton, but one month later we see 'B4' 0-4-0 tank No 96 *Normandy* (now preserved on the Bluebell Railway) shunting LNER banana vans. At the front is one of the former Great Eastern vehicles from the batch numbered 632822-921, while just visible beyond it is a standard LNER van, similar to that seen in the background of **Plate 259**. Each type came in fitted and unfitted versions, painted red oxide or grey respectively. Although lettered 'SR', they have the small initials 'NE' painted in the lower right-hand corner of each side. Examples of numbering of the LNER standard vans are:

Vac fitted: Nos 3473, 10653, 20257, 37788, 81079.
Unfitted: Nos 299, 3306, 7210, 11664, 20611, 40779, 61118, 78276, 96440, 101587.

An observer at Eastleigh noted the regular presence of these vans for repairs between July 1933 and September 1935. *H. F. Wheeller*

Right:

Plate 277 A diagram 1478 banana van, No S50704, in BR bauxite livery at Exmouth Junction in March 1961. Fyffe's had a depot in the yard at Exeter Central, so banana vans would have been a regular sight here — indeed two LMS vans may be seen left and right in the picture. There were many scheduled services upon which banana vans would be seen and complete trains were a common sight between Southampton Docks and Nine Elms, while smaller groups of vans could be seen in other goods trains and locations. The January 1961 audit shows that all except five remained in service while all bar Nos 50629/51/64/72/64/9/755 received the 'yellow spot' insulation in 1961-3. The last was withdrawn circa 1978, but by then few remained in banana traffic, most being used in their final years as 'fitted heads' for other freight trains in the early diesel era, mostly away from the Southern Region. For this purpose their numbers were prefixed 'DS' and the code name 'Tadpole' was applied. *A. E. West*

Above:

Plate 278 The later Diagram 1479 vans are represented by S50869, livery, date and location as **Plate 277**. These vans often had gummed paper labels added giving details of the consignment — a feature rarely modelled. The January 1961 audit records all bar four (Nos 50775/6/823/4) in traffic and all the others received the 'yellow spot' insulation by March 1963. Like Diagram 1478, some of these vans ended their days as 'Tadpole' fitted head wagons in the 1970s. An observer at Eastleigh noted that SR banana vans were rare visitors there after 1968, but were a daily sighting beforehand. *A. E. West*

Plate 279 The Lynes roof profile was used for SR-designed meat vans — and very distinctive these wagons were. Diagram 1486 van No S51245 is seen at Crewkerne in September 1961, in the usual BR bauxite livery. The very small lettering at high level records the next due overhaul date and works location responsible and was a feature on some 1950s/1960s covered goods vehicles. Sometimes the lettering appeared high up on the ends. In the early BR period some of these vans may have received crimson lake livery, with yellow lettering. This van dates from 1931, part of order A533. Those built against order A643 in 1934 were allocated Diagram 1486A, to signify the use of SECR axleboxes. The January 1961 census lists 80 still in traffic but by 1966 this total had reduced to just four. Some of these were by then reclassified as ordinary covered goods wagons and had all except the top end vent removed and replaced by planking. *A. E. West*

Livestock vehicles

By the 1950s much of the traditional cattle and sheep traffic had been lost, either to the roads or to refrigerated methods of transport, especially so for the short-haul traffic in South-east England. It is therefore possibly significant that most photographs of Southern Region livestock traffic are taken on the West of England main line and in Devon or Cornwall.

Below:
Plate 280 Maunsell Diagram 1529 cattle wagon No S53928, alongside the cattle dock at Axminster in July 1960, in company with a British Railways wagon. This was actually the last Maunsell cattle wagon, outshopped in March 1939 and is still as built, although the tare weight has reduced by 1 cwt since construction. The livery is bauxite with lettering low down on the wagon side — it was not BR policy to place the lettering on the ends after *circa* 1950. *A. E. West*

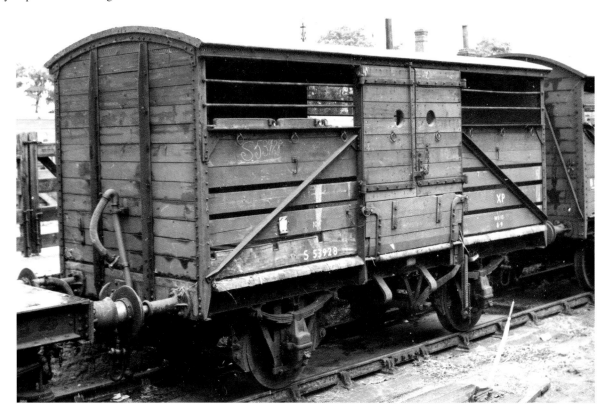

Above:
Plate 281 The Bulleid equivalent to Diagram 1530, No S52318 at Barnstaple Junction in August 1962, this example appearing to be vacuum piped only. In view of the imminent demise of the traffic it is perhaps surprising to find that 401 of these vehicles were completed between October 1947 and December 1949 and one might also ask why 401 were ordered. Was the odd vehicle to balance the fact that Maunsell vehicle 53845 had not been built? The last 150 wagons actually entered traffic with 'B' prefixed numbers (B891250-399), so it was not immediately obvious that they were of SR origin. The arrival of these new wagons allowed the withdrawal of most LSWR, LBSCR and the older SECR Diagram 1515 vehicles, but despite this, two of the SECR (albeit SR-built) wagons lasted until 1966. Just whether they did any work in their final years is, perhaps, another matter entirely. *A. E. West*

In March 1952 an order was issued to convert 40 of the Diagram 1530 cattle wagons for Dover ferry service — presumably by sealing the gaps in the planking and provision of urine tanks. However, 40 newer BR vehicles were actually substituted instead.

Later, in December 1954 another order was issued to convert 40 more (perhaps the same wagons) for beer traffic but no evidence of these has come to light.

The January 1961 census records the following numbers still in traffic:
Diagram 1529 — 106 wagons.   Diagram 1530 — 249 wagons.

Hardly surprisingly, cattle wagons seldom featured in departmental conversions, but Bulleid wagon DB891364 was rebuilt into a tunnel inspection truck about 1966, for which purpose it was given a flat roof as a working platform approximately 10ft 6in above rail level. It looked quite hideous!

Readers may wonder at the exclusion of any Southern Railway special cattle wagons, however these were always considered as passenger van stock post-1923, so although the pre-Grouping vehicles have been dealt with (because at various times they were classed as goods wagons), the one SR design was not and details may be found in *An Illustrated History of Southern Coaches*, published by OPC in 2003. For the same reason all horseboxes are excluded from the present work.

Goods brake vans

The Southern inherited an extremely varied collection of pre-Grouping goods brake vans, but only 16% of the 1923 stock of 1,252 vehicles exceeded 15 tons tare. There was an urgent need for more heavy brake vans and apart from one batch of 15-tonners, all later construction tared 20 tons or over. Initially, some from each pre-Grouping company were completed (most were on order at the Grouping), while one batch of ex-War Department LSWR-type vans was purchased in 1924.

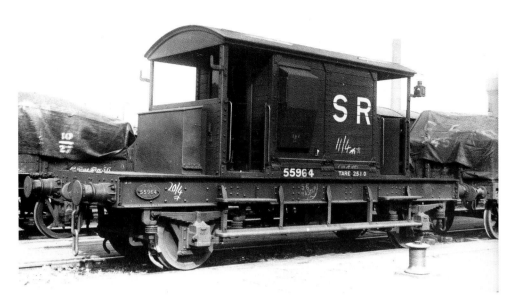

Left:
Plate 282 A semi-official view of Diagram 1578 brake van No 55964, taken at Bricklayers Arms in 1929. This was one of the original batch of left-hand ducket vehicles built at Lancing in 1928/9 under order L261, but was incorrectly recorded as Diagram 1579 in many of the registers, along with about half of the vans to order L344, built in 1929/30. The last left-hand ducket vans (Nos 55564/5) left the workshops week-ending 2 October 1929, while the first right-hand ducket van was No 55521, outshopped week-ending 9 October 1929. Full numbering details were given in Appendix One of *Volume Four*. *F. Moore*

Below:
Plate 283 Right-hand ducket van No S55583 correctly recorded as Diagram 1579, at Axminster in April 1959. This was built against order L473 in 1930 — the last lot with 'W' axleguards — all subsequent construction had plate-backed fittings. It has now lost its sandboxes but is one of 200 brake vans (of all types) equipped with vacuum pipes and a vacuum gauge in the brake compartment — hence the vertical pipe adjacent to the lookout, done during 1957/8. Note also the screw couplings and packings behind the buffers. The livery is recorded as bauxite — by no means all these vans were repainted and so it was possible to see piped ones in grey livery. At least 100 more vans were fully vacuum fitted around the same time, although the order for this does not specify which types of vehicle were involved. *A. E. West*

Right:

Plate 284 A 15-ton van to Diagram 1581, No S55703 at Seaton Junction in April 1963, being allocated to the Seaton branch since 1960. Sister-van 55702 was similarly allocated to the Lyme Regis branch at the same date, both previously having been used as 'local' vans in the Redhill area. Both are noted as being repainted grey for their new duties, yet the veranda ends remained dull SR Venetian red! This was not the only instance of this particular SR/BR colour combination being seen. Almost all of the 50 Diagram 1581 vans were allocated to specific duties after 1945 and every one was still in use in 1961 (although two were in departmental use with the weed-killing train). The two Diagram 1583 rebuilds for Whitstable Harbour were redeployed after the branch closed in 1952 — No 55675 being noted at Shepherdswell and finally Alton, however the later allocation of 55713 is not known. When two vans were required for Isle of Wight transfer in 1967, these were proposed, however only No 55675 could be traced, so two ordinary Diagram 1581's were sent over instead. *A. E. West*

Right:

Plate 285 Uneven body planking made its appearance on SR brake vans in 1940. This is one of the two ex-War Department vans taken back into BR stock in July 1949, No M360327. Originally built at Ashford in March 1942, as WD No 11029 (on SR order A1852), it received registration plate No 1020 in the Southern Railway private-owner wagon register. The van is seen leaving Feltham yard behind a 'Q1' 0-6-0 in the early 1960s. The sandboxes have now gone but the twin vacuum cylinders and through Westinghouse pipe remain, hence the two gauge pipes on the side of the body. This example lasted until the mid-1970s, however sister-van M360328 was withdrawn in 1966. Several were retained by the Army and some are now in the hands of preservation societies and have been outshopped in SR or BR (S) liveries and numbered between 56495 and 56500; numbers never allocated in Southern days. The January 1961 audit tells us that just three SR 25-ton 4-wheeled brake vans had been withdrawn by that date. Many were transferred away from the Southern Region from 1970 onwards and at least 100 remained in some form of BR stock in the 1990s. *Author's Collection*

Right:

Plate 286 The SR-allocated RCH brake van to Diagram 1570, No S56060 seen at Westerham in May 1956, probably still finished in SR brown. This van travelled about the Region considerably, as the author has photographs of it at Exeter, Feltham and Dover. By 1966 it was boarded 'Dover Town — Dover Priory Only' and was withdrawn a year later. SR modifications included gates to the verandas and standard lamp irons. A copy of the LMS diagram for the van may be found in *An Illustrated History of LMS Wagons* by R. J. Essery (OPC, 1984). Incidentally, the WR example was later allocated to 'Frome R.U.' (Restricted use) while the LNER van was used on the North Tyneside Quay branch. So much for common-user policies! *P. Coutanche*

Above:
Plate 287 Former LBSCR 'AC' motor luggage brake van rebuild No DS56281, one of the five Diagram 1580 vans reallocated to the Civil Engineer in 1957 — note the branding 'Es Redbridge Works Southampton'. Although transferred for use with long-welded rail trains, this was actually at the end of a line of ballast wagons, with one of the LBSCR Diagram 1760 ballast brake rebuilds on the rear. The livery may still be traffic department bauxite or, if repainted, black with yellow lettering. The other four transfers were Nos 56270/2/3/7 and some ran until 1964. Van No 56278 was lost to enemy action in August 1943, while general withdrawal commenced in 1955. No traffic department vans remained by January 1961. *Author's Collection*

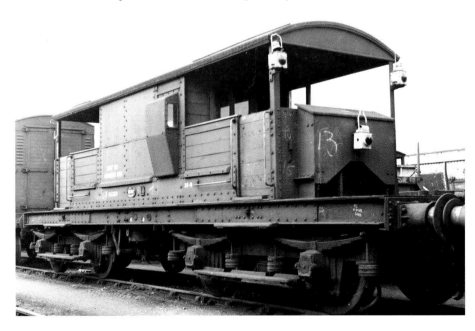

Left:
Plate 288 Diagram 1550 bogie brake No 56283 — one of those with partially steel-clad sides — at Exmouth Junction in April 1963, carrying the usual BR bauxite livery and 'Not in common use' instruction. This shows the other side to the illustrations in *Volume Four*, without the vacuum pipe running the length of the solebar. The six vans equipped with Westinghouse brakes in 1961 were Nos 56285/6/96/9/301/3. All 25 vans to the diagram were destined to give long service but until the 1970s were seldom seen away from ex-SR main lines. After that time it was a different story entirely and four were noted on the West Coast main line electrification between Carlisle and Glasgow in 1974, while others migrated to the Western and Eastern Regions. At least 16 were still in some form of BR service in the early 1990s. Some had received various bodywork modifications, including at least one that had the lookouts removed, plus some rather distinctive sector liveries. *A. E. West*

The earlier position regarding timber/steel cladding appears to be as follows:
Timber-planked — Nos 56282/8/9*/90/1*/2/4/5/7/9*/301/2/3*/4/6.
Partially steel-clad — Nos 56283/4/5/7**/96/8/300/5.
Not noted — Nos 56286/93.
* These later seen partially steel-clad.
**This van fully steel-clad by 1964 — the only one so noted.
By the 1990s the position may have been very different.

Bogie bolster wagons

Plate 289 A close-up of the end of Diagram 1598 bogie bolster No 64637 at Eastleigh P. Way yard in July 1950. This was built with traffic department number 57898 in January 1937, being renumbered in 1945. The load of flat-bottom rails is typical for an ED wagon of this type. The self-contained buffers with round heads and the diamond-frame bogies are usual for the wagons built in 1937. The livery was recorded as red oxide. *A. E. West*

Above:

Plate 290 One of the later Diagram 1599 wagons, traffic department No 58032, seen far from home at Sighthill, Glasgow, on 14 August 1947. It was then quite new, having been built against order A3221 in late 1946. The livery is presumably brown, and the letters 'ED' are absent. This has oval buffers and cast-steel 'AAR' bogies. One wonders how often these wagons were seen in Scotland? *A. G. Ellis*

The January 1961 census gives the following totals of SR bogie bolster wagons still running (of all types)

SR Diagram	Origin	No in service	SR Diagram	Origin	No in service
1597	LSWR	90	1794	SECR	1 ED
1598	SR	71 Traffic, 31 ED	1795/6	SECR	6 ED
1599	SR	49 Traffic, 9 ED	1802	LBSCR	1 ED
1787/1943	SR	11 ED	1803	LBSCR	2 ED
1789	LSWR	1 ED	1804	LSWR (reb)	Nil
1790	LSWR	1 ED			

Above:
Plate 291 For conveyance of long-welded rails some additional bogie bolster wagons were needed, for which purpose 10 former LSWR corridor coach underframes were converted in December 1949/January 1950, allocated SR Diagram 1804 and running numbers DS64755-64. Three more were done in December 1952 (Nos DS64765-7) utilising non-corridor coach frames, so these may have differed in detail. Each frame was stripped of bodywork and had a new floor with four bolsters spaced at 13ft centres added. Vacuum brakes were retained, with the addition of an external hand brake wheel. Small crescent-shaped extensions were welded on to the round buffer heads, in an attempt to avoid buffer locking on sharp curves. No DS64761 is seen at Yeovil Junction in August 1959, in black with minimal yellow lettering. Relatively little, if any modifications were made to the bogies so the rated capacity was limited to 8 tons and it was found that the wagons tended to derail while being unloaded. Six ex-LBSCR Hurst-Nelson bogie bolster wagons (to Diagram 1803, described in *Volume Two*) were also converted and it was found that by interleaving these with the LSWR conversions better success was achieved. When the later BR conversions (the 'Manta' and 'Marlin' wagons of 1970/1, ex-electric stock underframes) were done, either the bogie design was very much better or some modifications were made, as these performed very much more satisfactorily in the same role. *A. E. West*

Machinery, well and miscellaneous wagons

Below:
Plate 292 Not of the best technical quality, but an interesting official photograph of one of the first Diagram 1681 machinery wagons, outshopped in October 1923 in SR livery but with both SECR number (1796) and SR number (61050) visible. The lettering style is also unusual, but it is not known if this was applied to the whole batch of 12 vehicles, nor is it known if they entered service carrying the unique 9-digit numbers. Note that the wagon plate proclaims SECR No 1796. For the record, the SECR numbers were 1794-1805. The last of these in ordinary traffic were withdrawn in 1968 (Nos. 61152/62), however at that time several more were retained in the departmental fleet and would remain so until the mid-1990s. *SR Official*

Above and right:
Plates 293 and 294 Two detail views of the 40-ton bogie well wagon No S61099 to Diagram 1690, taken at Eastleigh on 1 June 1962, showing the bogie, brake wheel, well, removable baulks and cross-bars — useful for model-making. As was noted in *Volume Four*, few photographs seem to have been taken of these wagons in service and the only ones known to the author show No 61100 loaded with a large ships propeller at Portsmouth in 1930 and another SR publicity photograph of a sub-station generator being delivered on one of these wagons, instead of on special bogie well wagon No 387s, described on pages 176/7. Otherwise, an observer at Eastleigh noted the wagons on the following dates:

6 June 1928 – No 61099 in a goods from Basingstoke (tare 22-12-0, without timber baulks).
26 July 1933 — No 61100 in a goods from Bournemouth.
28 March 1934 — ditto.
24 October 1935 — Both passing through empty in a special goods to Southampton.
30 June 1950 — No 61100 dispatched in a special to Hamworthy Goods.
Additionally, one was seen at Devonport Dockyard on 2 April 1952.
When photographed, No 61099 was in works for departmental conversion and was recorded as being in dark grey livery. On transfer to internal use at Newhaven, wagon No 61100 was renumbered as 081602 and was withdrawn in 1964. The BR special wagon code was 'Weltrol SA.' *Both A. E. West*

Above:
Plate 295 The solitary bogie well wagon to Diagram 1850 (the first departmental series diagram number) remains absent from photographs, however this shows one of these wagons as built during World War One, complete with 12inch Howitzer gun. This was a Mark I gun trolley — there were Marks 2 and 3 and these differed in detail. **Figure 46** (right) is based on the SR diagram and a drawing from Sir W.G. Armstrong Whitworth & Co. Ltd., Elleswick Works, Newcastle-upon-Tyne. Even the drawing was marked 'confidential'. Any modifications made after purchase by the Southern Railway in February 1925 remain unknown, while the lettering style is also unconfirmed. The wagon was labelled 'Electrical ES' and was stationed at Peckham Rye, for conveyance of transformers to Gloucester Road, this lettering probably appearing on the side frame. The official withdrawal date is given as December 1948.
Imperial War Museum

Left:
Plate 296 Another detail view, this time showing the end of Bulleid Diagram 1682 'Flatrol' No 61108 at Eastleigh in July 1950. Several of these wagons had only a short life as traffic department vehicles, as Nos 61101/2/4/6/10 all entered departmental use in 1956/7, while the ED wagon (No. 64600) became internal user 080985 at Ashford Works in 1958 and DS61108 (already in departmental service by then) similarly became No 080996 at Lancing in January 1961. By comparison, Nos DS61103/7 were still in BR stock in 1992! *A. E. West*

SR (EX-WAR DEPARTMENT) 40 TON BOGIE WELL WAGON

S.R. DIAGRAM 1850. S.R. Nº 387s.

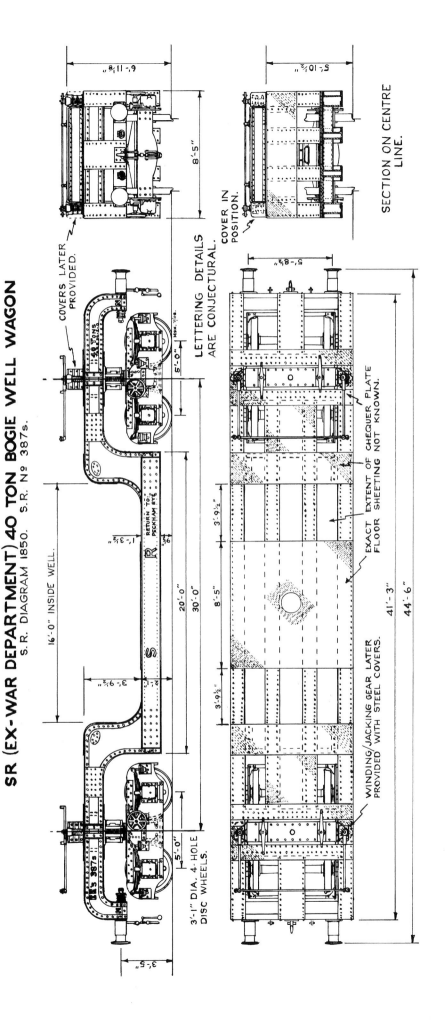

COVERS LATER PROVIDED.

LETTERING DETAILS ARE CONJECTURAL.

COVER IN POSITION.

SECTION ON CENTRE LINE.

9'-11⅜"

8'-5"

5'-10½"

5'-8¾"

16'-0" INSIDE WELL.

20'-0"

30'-0"

8'-5"

3'-9½"

3'-9½"

41'-3"

44'-6"

RETURN TO PECKHAM RYE.

1'-3½"

3'-9½"

2'-1"

5'-0"

3'-1" DIA. 4-HOLE DISC WHEELS.

3'-5"

WINDING/JACKING GEAR LATER PROVIDED WITH STEEL COVERS.

EXACT EXTENT OF CHEQUER PLATE FLOOR SHEETING NOT KNOWN.

40 TONS

S

387s

Left:
Plate 297 One of the two long-term BR survivors to Diagram 1682, DS 61103 at Strood in 1974, by now permanently converted as a cable wagon, to Diagram 1935. It had previously been adapted, *circa* 1959, to carry a contractor's hydraulic lift. The livery was now olive green and the wagon was by then based at Horsham. *D. Larkin*

Centre left:
Plate 298 Bournemouth West shunting truck No 61326 alongside the carriage shed at its home depot on 29 August 1961. The number and company initials are just visible on the timber side rail at the left-hand end of the vehicle. The livery was recorded as black overall with faded white lettering and it seems unlikely that either wagon received a complete repaint following Nationalisation. SR Diagram 1715 was allocated and the two wagons were withdrawn in November 1975 and April 1969 respectively — long after the closure of Bournemouth West station. *A. E. West*

Figure 47 A drawing of both types of shunting truck converted from former locomotive tenders, to SR Diagrams 1712 and 1715.

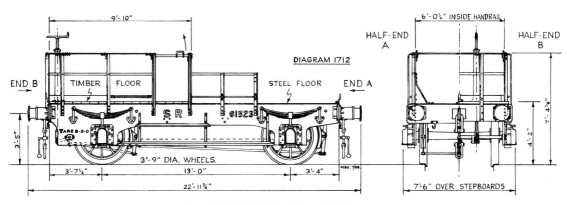

S R SHUNTING TRUCKS

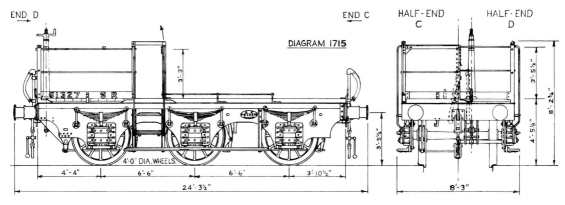

Ballast wagons and brake vans

This section may be considered in three subject areas — brake vans, the traditional dropside ballast wagons and the bogie ballast hoppers.

Above:
Plate 299 Following the Sevenoaks accident of August 1927, some more ballast brake vans were urgently needed. Four former LCDR carriages were quickly converted in October 1927, on order E267 (they were already on order before the accident). This is No 62527, formerly a five-compartment third of 1878 vintage, seen towards the end of its life at Norwood Junction on 11 May 1946. Despite being the oldest, it was the last survivor of the four and was not withdrawn until August 1950. Its dimensions were 25ft long x 8ft 6in wide. Similar vehicle 62525 (seen in **Plate 165** in *Volume Four*) was actually a newer coach and was only 8ft wide, withdrawn in 1945. Note that only No 62527 had vertical mouldings below the waistline. *R. E. Tustin*

Right:
Plate 300 Former three-compartment brake No 62526 is seen at Sevenoaks (Tubs Hill) on 4 March 1934, engaged on cable laying works and painted red oxide with Venetian red ends. This van and No 62524 were both 26ft long and 8ft wide. The lookouts have been removed and most of the lower bodyside has also been steel-sheeted. Both were withdrawn in 1946. *R. W. Kidner*

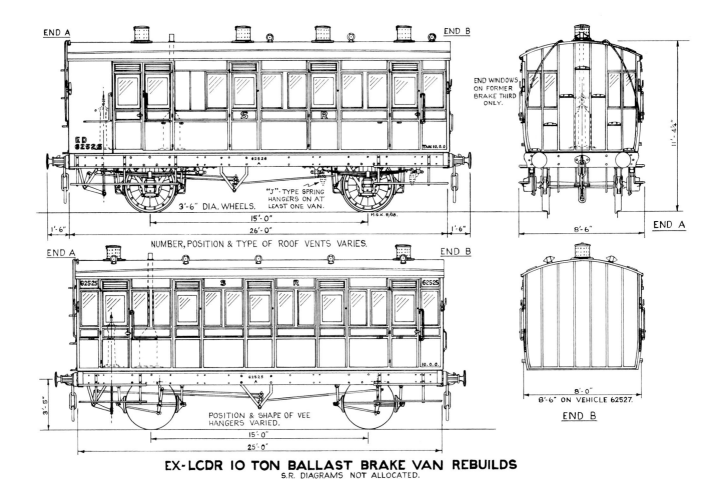

END A · END B · END WINDOWS ON FORMER BRAKE THIRD ONLY. · END A

S R · ED 62526 · TARE 10.0.0. · "J"-TYPE SPRING HANGERS ON AT LEAST ONE VAN. · 3'-6" DIA. WHEELS. · M.S.K. 8/68. · 1'-6" · 15'-0" · 26'-0" · 1'-6" · 11'-4½" · 8'-6"

NUMBER, POSITION & TYPE OF ROOF VENTS VARIES.

END A · END B · 62525 · 3 · R · 62525 · 62525 · 10.0.0. · 3'-5" · POSITION & SHAPE OF VEE HANGERS VARIED. · 15'-0" · 25'-0" · 8'-0" · 8'-6" ON VEHICLE 62527. · END B

EX-LCDR 10 TON BALLAST BRAKE VAN REBUILDS
S.R. DIAGRAMS NOT ALLOCATED.

Figure 48 The ex-LCDR ballast brake van conversions of 1927. No SR diagram numbers appear to have been issued. These were the last ex-London, Chatham and Dover Railway 'wagons' in SR service.

Left:
Plate 301 The first of three Diagram 1748 ballast plough brake vans, No 62030, as completed by Charles Roberts & Co in 1932, specifically to run with the new ballast hopper wagons and photographed by the builders. There were eventually 12 such vans, the original SECR 1914 example and another eight that did not appear until after Nationalisation. The latter were allocated SR Diagram 1749, but they differed in only minor details. All survived to the 1980s, No 62030 being condemned at Doncaster in 1985. *C. Roberts & Co*

Left:
Plate 302 An interior view of one of these vans, probably No 62030 again, showing the various control wheels and locking mechanisms for the ploughs. The paint finish of purple brown lower walls, stone coloured upper panels and white ceiling does little to relieve the overall gloom. Although not apparent from the photograph, there should be a 1½inch black line between the two wall colours. The writing on the upper right-hand wall reads: 'Notice — All persons are requested to ride in the vans and not on the wagons and not to leave or enter the vans in motion' — a reminder to stay seated while the train was moving. With all that rather lethal-looking equipment to fall against, this was a wise precaution. The vacuum cylinder was housed inside the seat at the far right-hand corner. *C. Roberts & Co.*

Right:
Plate 303 A close-up of the veranda of plough brake No 62032, in olive green livery at Meldon Quarry in May 1965, showing the brake wheel and vacuum release valve. The code name 'Shark' was applied to all BR plough brake vans. *A. E. West*

Above:

Plate 304 One of the 60 BRCW-built five plank dropside wagons delivered in 1928, to Diagram 1771, No S61962 at Eastleigh in August 1962, wearing black livery with yellow lettering. Most of these have led very long lives — all except one (a war loss) being listed in the January 1961 audit and no less than 40 were still allocated to the Western Region in the early 1990s, although how many saw any use by then is debateable. Some, including No 61953, were still in store at Swindon in 2005. The BR ballast wagon code was 'Tunny'. Several are now in preservation. *A. E. West*

Above:

Plate 305 The 50 similar four plank wagons to Diagram 1773 were built in 1937 and are represented by DS63025 at Dorchester South in June 1964, again in black with yellow lettering and stencilled 'Return to Concrete Works, Exmouth Junc.' All 50 survived to more recent times but perhaps because they were unfitted, general withdrawal took place during the 1980s. The BR ballast wagon code was 'Ling', although at least one five plank wagon has been noted so lettered. Again, several are now preserved. *A. E. West*

Above:
Plate 306 The prototype 'Lamprey', No DB991000, with modern insignia on its olive green livery, but still with the original lift-link brake gear, is seen at Wadhurst in February 1977, flanked by two BR 'Grampus' wagons. This was the final Bulleid development of the traditional SR dropside ballast wagons, completed in 1951/2. Had it received its originally allocated SR number, it would have been S63051. Only the fitted wagons were coded 'Lamprey' (Nos DB991000-20 and 991301-20), the rest (DB991141-300) were unfitted and were coded 'Grampus'. Most of these received AVB and clasp brakes later, while many have been reconstructed since the 1970s, losing the rather distinctive strengthening boxing along the tops of the sides and making them look superficially similar to the BR-designed 'Grampus' wagons. This caused them to bow outwards under load so at least one (No DB991317) was rebuilt as a fixed-sided wagon in 1983 — BR wagon code 'Crab'. *E. R. Kemp*

Below:
Plate 307 40-ton ballast hopper DS62011, one of the 1928/9 batch built by Metropolitan, to SR Diagram 1772. It is seen at Meldon Quarry in May 1965, in a livery described by the photographer as 'dirty brown', with the lettering on rather more recently painted bauxite patches. The BR wagon code 'Walrus' is carried. Evidence of repairs both to the hopper sides and to the solebars may be seen, nevertheless for a wagon still on front-line duty after more than 35 years the appearance is still creditworthy. Note the plough brake to the right, freshly repainted in olive green (No. 62032, seen in **Plate 303**). *A. E. West*

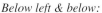

Left:
Plate 308 A close-up of the non-working platform end of similar hopper No 62006, showing the vacuum cylinder and additional solebar plating, at Exmouth Junction in August 1963. The livery was recorded this time as 'rusty brown'. *A. E. West*

Below left & below:
Plates 309 and 310 Two detail views of 1947-built hopper No S62065 at Seaton Junction in April 1963, this time finished in 'red' livery. Diagram 1775 applies. The cast-steel AAR bogie and hopper control wheels may be seen. Compare the different profile of the hopper end with **Plates 307** and **308**. It will come as no surprise to the reader to learn that every one of the 67 SR-ordered hopper wagons was still in traffic in 1961 and it is probably fair to state that the design was the most far-reaching of all SR wagons, whose influence has spread, quite literally, way beyond the Southern Railway/Region. *A. E. West*

Goods department travelling cranes

Above:
Plate 311 The four-wheeled Booth Bros cranes ordered in 1943 could not be illustrated in *Volume Four*, but this is No DS1746 in grey livery at Tenterden Town in November 1953 — possibly there to assist in recovery of equipment prior to closure of the KESR to passenger traffic, set for 2 January 1954. The match truck, by now renumbered as DS3124, was purpose-built on a standard underframe to run with the crane. *D. Cullum*

Right:
Plate 312 A useful top-view of one of the Cowans & Sheldon 10-ton cranes, No ADS1854, at Tonbridge in March 1976. The 'A' prefix was part of the TOPS coding system introduced in 1973 and signified that the vehicle was the property of the CM & EE Department. Engineer's Department wagons retained their plain DS numbers, while vehicles allocated to BREL received a 'C' prefix, 'K' was for the S & T Department and 'T' was for traffic. The original match truck has been replaced by ex-LMS one plank open ADM460338. Both have recently been repainted in light grey livery. Similar crane DS1855 has been preserved on the Swanage Railway. *E. R. Kemp*

Appendix
Southern Railway Goods Rolling Stock Orders

Note: All orders for new construction are listed, however some for rebuilding and conversion works have not been traced.

HOO No	Date Authorised*	Details	Diagram	Running Nos	Completed By*
E1	25/5/22 (reissued 1/1/24)	6 x 10-ton refrigerator vans	1476	50494-9	9/28
E2	25/5/22	1 machinery truck	Not allocated	Possibly included on E109	Cancelled
E3	25/5/22	100 x 10-ton covered goods LSWR pattern	1408	44326-425	9/24
L8	3/5/23	250 x 10-ton open goods LBSCR pattern (partial renewals)	1369	27462-711	4/25
E9	3/5/23	100 x 12-ton open goods LSWR pattern	1316	9141-240	1/25
A15	3/5/23 (revised 20/5/24)	150 x 10-ton open goods SECR pattern (rebuilds)	1347	19079-228	11/25
A25	27/5/24	100 x 10-ton cattle wagons SECR pattern	1515	52819-81, 53391-427	7/25
A26	17/3/24	100 x 12-ton (later 10T) covered goods SECR pattern	1426	47101-200	1/26
L27	17/3/24	350 x 10-ton open goods LBSCR pattern (partial renewals)	1369	18729-19078	7/26
A28	17/3/24 (revised 7/10/25)	800 x 12-ton open goods (500 x SECR pattern, 300 x RCH)	1355 / 1379	28501-29000 / 29001-300	6/26 / 1/27
A29	27/5/24	20 x 25-ton goods brake vans SECR pattern	1560	Not allocated, see E44	Cancelled
E30	17/3/24	100 x 12-ton open goods LSWR pattern	1316	Not allocated, see E77	Cancelled
E44	9/7/24	Make ready 20 x 20-ton goods brake vans purchased from G. Cohen	1549	55100-19 Ex-War Department	1/25
A55	29/7/24	Convert 3 x SE Section covered goods to Messrs Pooley's weighing vans	1422	221s-223s	2/25
E77	26/1/25	100 x 12-ton open goods LSWR pattern on timber underframe (was originally E30)	1316A	9241-340	12/25
E79	12/2/25	Convert 30 road vans to meat containers (may have been revised and reissued later)	Possibly 3003 (later)	Not allocated (possibly reissued for DM1-50)	Cancelled 14/1/28
G. Cohen	2/25	Purchase one bogie well wagon, ex-WD	1850	387s	1925
E86	23/4/25	Refit 90 covered goods with fruit shelves	1401	Between 42001 and 42175	6/25
C. Roberts	6/4/25	2 x 40-ton bogie well wagons (see also E213)	1690	61099-100	11/27
J. & F. Howard	6/4/25	4 x 8-ton bogie open goods for L & BR & 4 x 8-ton bogie covered goods for L & BR	1396 / 1456	28316-9 / 47042-5	8/27 / 8/27
G. Cohen	6/4/25	Purchase 3 cranes for L&BR (see L227)	Not allocated	441s, 441sm, 442s	1926
E105	11/5/25	2 x 15-ton stone trucks to LSWR design	1317	61029-30	11/26
A106	11/5/25	100 x 10-ton cattle wagons SECR pattern	1515	53428-527	6/27
E107	6/4/25	25 x 8-ton meat vans to LSWR design	1482	51171-95	11/26
E108	11/5/25	30 x 40-ton bogie timber trucks LSWR pattern	1597	57853-82	9/26
E109	11/5/25	13 x 20-ton machinery trucks	1681	61086-98	5/28
L110	11/5/25	20 x 25-ton goods brake vans SECR pattern	1560	55496-515	3/27
A128	6/8/25	800 x 12-ton RCH open goods	1379	29801-30600	10/27
A129	6/8/25	100 x 12-ton covered goods	1428	45908-46007	6/29
Mid RCW	7/10/25	250 x 12-ton RCH open goods	1379	29301-550	3/26
GRCW	7/10/25	250 x 12-ton RCH open goods	1379	29551-800	3/26
HOO131 (ODM Dept)	10/8/25	Fit 562 (later 538) SW goods brake vans with four outside lamp irons in place of side lamps	1541-9 / 1736/7	Between 54501 & 55122 / Between 61912 & 61944	8/28
HOO133 (ODM Dept)	10/8/25	Fit 303 (later 251) SEC & LBSC goods brake vans with additional lamp irons	1552-59 / 1564-77	Between 55187 & 55495 / Between 55586 & 55942	8/28
L139	27/10/25	Supply 56 Central section 10T open goods for IOW. Round ends to be made square	1369	18980-19017/33/4/60-75	6/26

Note: Some IOW transfers were sent over requiring no work other than repainting or renumbering and did not have any HOO number allocated. These included the first Diagram 1369 and 1352 transfers (Nos. 26119-23/31-45 and 62885-902), in 1924 and Diagram 1751 ballasts in 1927/8.

HOO No	Date Authorised*	Details	Diagram	Running Nos	Completed By*
E140	27/10/25	Recondition 3 x 10-ton goods brake vans for IOW	PDSWJ & 1541	56042-4 (56042/3 not sent)	11/25
HOO146	10/12/25	Fit up two SECR vans as vacuum cleaning units (done at Longhedge)	1424	230s, 231s	4/26
L148	15/1/26	Brake fitting of Central section stock. Fit 34 cattle trucks & 1 refrigerator van with through vac pipes, strip Westinghouse gear from 4 poultry vans. (Amended 1/9/26, omit refrigerator van, add 1 cattle)	1433/71 & 1527	46311/70/81/9 & 50595 Between 52897 & 53269	3/27 6/28

HOO No	Date Authorised*	Details	Diagram	Running Nos	Completed By*
E153	8/4/26	Fit either-side brakes on Western section wagons below 25 years of age at 7/11/31, if in good condition. Amended 20/3/29 - 30 years old at 7/11/31 if again being returned to traffic	All	422 to be done originally. Total 2586 done by 4/1939	4/39
A164	8/7/26	400 x RCH 12-ton open goods	1379	31601-32000	3/28
A165	8/7/26	100 x 10-ton cattle wagons to SECR pattern	1515	53528-627	5/28
E174	4/6/26	Equip 3 SW section pass cattle vans with steam htg	1041/3	3670 (ex-SDJR)/6/7	2/28
A175	4/6/26	Equip 12 Eastern section cattle vans (with stockman's compartment) with full steam htg and fit 21 (later 19) without stockman's compartment with steam pipes	1052 1049-51	3758-69 3731/5/8-40/2-4/6-57/70 (3731/44 not done)	2/30 1/31
B178	16/7/26	Make bearing springs & brake blocks for RCH opens	1373	Between 27237 & 27461	8/26
E209	23/9/26	Prepare 2 x 10-ton goods brake vans for IOW	1541	56045-6	1/27
E212	24/9/26	Convert 2 x 10-ton plough brakes & 2 (later 3) ballast brake vans to 15-tons	1736/7	61913/4/32/8/40	2/28
E213	30/9/26	Prepare & fit bolsters & loading baulks to 2 x 40-ton crocodile wagons built by Chas. Roberts	1690	61099-100	11/27
L224	6/12/26	Fit either-side brakes on Central section wagons below 25 years of age at 7/11/31, if in good condition. Amended 29/5/28 - fit 24 Central section cattle wagons Amended 20/3/29 - below 30 years old at 7/11/31.	All	1089 done against original order Total 2873 done by 11/1939	11/39
L227	12/12/26	Convert one crane carriage to match truck for L & BR	Not allocated	441SM	9/27
E245	19/2/27	Prepare 4 x 10-ton road van trucks for IOW	1641	60561-4	8/27
L246	19/2/27	Prepare 68 Central section 10-ton open goods for IOW Round ends to be made square as for Order L139	1369	28321-88	4/27
L247	19/2/27	Prepare 12 x 10-ton Central section covered goods for IOW	1436	46963-8 WB 46969-74 WP	8/27
L248	19/2/27	Prepare 3 x 10-ton Central section cattle wagons for IOW	1527 (Some to 1528)	53374-6	5/27
BRCW	17/3/27	250 x 12-ton RCH open goods	1379	30601-725, 31101-225	1927
Mid RCW	17/3/27	250 x 12-ton RCH open goods	1379	30726-850, 31226-350	1927
Met RCW	17/3/27	250 x 12-ton RCH open goods	1379	30851-975, 31351-475	1927
GRCW	17/3/27	250 x 12-ton RCH open goods	1379	30976-1000, 31476-600	1927
A255	7/4/27	1250 x 12-ton RCH open goods	1379	32001-33250	1/29
L261	7/6/27	50 x 25-ton goods brake vans	1578	55943-92	6/29
A262	20/6/27	100 x 12-ton covered goods	1428	46008-107	6/29
L263 (part)	20/6/27	Alter vac pipe to full vacuum brake on 23 Central section passenger cattle vans	1059/60	3820-42	5/28
E267	22/7/27	Convert 4 old LCDR 4w coaches to ballast brake vans	Not allocated	62524-7	10/27
L278 (part)	18/8/27	Fit either-side handbrake to 23 passenger cattle vans	1059/60	3820-42	6/28
E281	14/10/27	Convert 3 x 15-ton Western section goods brake vans for service on Whitstable Harbour branch	1550	54940/1/4	3/28
BRCW	25/1/28	60 x 20-ton dropside ballast wagons (see A299 & A380)	1771	61945-62004	10/28
A298	16/2/28	Alter 4 ballast brake vans as drawing W715	Not allocated	Presumed to be 62524-7	7/28
Met RCW	23/3/28	25 x 40-ton bogie ballast hoppers (see A347)	1772	62005-29	2/29
A299	15/2/28	Recondition 30 x 18in vac brake cylinders for 20-ton ballast wagons on order from BRCW	For 1771	61945-74	10/28
L309	14/3/28	Recondition 9 x single bolster wagons to Diagram 1617 for IOW Engineer's dept	1616/7	59033-41 (59037-41 to Diagram 1616)	5/28
E310	27/3/28	Construct 50 insulated meat containers	3001	BN151-200	10/28
A311	29/3/28	Convert 15-ton open goods to crane test weight truck	ex-1360	253s (ex-18717)	8/28
HOO312	4/4/28	Convert 30 road meat vans to meat containers	3003	DM51-80	3/29
A318	20/4/28	Secure binding chains to 12 B-type well wagons	1681	61048-59	11/28
Mid RCW	24/4/28	Construct 50 insulated meat containers	3001	BN101-50	7/28
L323	10/5/28	Prepare 70 x 10-ton Central section open goods for IOW. Round ends to be made square as for L246	1369	28389-458	8/28
L324	25/5/28	Prepare 13 x 10-ton Central section covered goods for IOW	1436	46950-6 WP 46957-62 WB	11/28 10/29
L325	25/5/28	Prepare 3 x 10-ton Central section cattle wagons for IOW	1527 (all to 1528?)	53371 WP 53372-3 WB	12/28
E326	10/5/28	Prepare 12 x 10-ton Central section road van trucks for IOW	1661	60565-76	7/28
E327	10/5/28	Prepare 1 x 10-ton goods brake van for IOW	1541	56047	8/28
L331	17/5/28 (revised 30/5/29)	20 (later 18) Eastern section passenger cattle vans at present fitted with WB and VP, to be equipped with vacuum brake complete, retaining Westinghouse pipes	1049-51	3738-40/2-4/6-57	Not stated
L332	17/5/28	Prepare 6 x 10-ton Central section single bolster wagons to Diagram 1616 for IOW	1616/7	59042-7 (59046 to Diagram 1617)	6/28
A337	4/6/28	Fit either-side brakes to 85 Eastern section wagons (list attached) provided that condition warrants this course. Amended later to include any SE section wagon not over 30 years old at 7/11/31, if returned to traffic	As listed	507 done by 11/1939	11/39
L341	5/6/28	Convert 5 x 20-ton Central section goods brake vans to vacuum-fitted ballast brake vans	1760	62840-4	1/29
A342	6/6/28	750 x 12-ton RCH open goods	1379	33251-34000	11/29
A343	6/6/28	100 x 10-ton cattle wagons	1529	53629-728	4/30
L344	23/3/28	50 x 25-ton goods brake vans	1578/9	55516-65	3/30
A345	8/6/28	100 x 12-ton covered goods	1428	47201-300	12/29

187

HOO No	Date Authorised*	Details	Diagram	Running Nos	Completed By*
A347	15/6/28	Recondition 50 x 18in vac brake cylinders for 40-ton ballast hoppers on order from Met RCW	For 1772	62005-29	2/29
E379	31/8/28	Prepare 1 x 10-ton goods brake van for IOW	1541	56048	10/28
A380	4/9/28	Recondition 30 x 18in vac brake cylinders for 20-ton ballast wagons on order from BRCW	For 1771	61975-62004	10/28
L382	24/9/28	Convert 2 x 20-ton Central section goods brake vans to vacuum-fitted ballast brake vans	1760	62845-6	1/29
L388	15/10/28	Convert 6 Central section cattle vans from gas to oil lighting	1061	3843-8	11/30
L402	24/11/28	Prepare 75 Central section 10-ton open goods for IOW. Round ends to be made square as for L323	1369	28253-300/459-85	5/29
L403	24/11/28	Prepare 10 x 8/10-ton Central section covered goods for IOW	1433/6	46940-4 WB 46945-9 WP	5/30
E404	24/11/28	Prepare 1 x 10-ton goods brake van for IOW	1541	56049	12/28
E405	12/12/28	Prepare 4 x 10-ton Central section road van trucks for IOW	1661	60577-80	7/29
HOO421	30/1/29	Fit 67 open meat containers with bar stretchers	3003	DM1-67	2/32
E430	15/2/29	Construct 50 insulated meat containers	3002	F201-50	7/29
HOO432	25/2/29	Alterations to bottoms of 80 open meat containers	3003	DM1-80	1/32
A/E437 (?)	4/3/29	Construct 2 x 18-ton double-ended snowploughs	1691	S1-S2	12/29
E451	19/4/29	Ironwork for alterations to 100 existing meat containers	3001	BN101-200	6/30
HOO453	19/4/29	Alter bottom and end door fastenings on above containers	3001	BN101-200	10/31
A466	17/5/29	1150 x 12-ton RCH open goods	1379	34001-35150	10/30
A469	17/5/29	300 x 10-ton open goods (rebuild type 1)	1380	9341-640	6/30
A470	17/5/29	100 x 12-ton covered goods with AVB	1428	47301-400	9/30
A471	17/5/29	100 x 10-ton cattle wagons	1529	53729-828	6/30
E472	17/5/29	25 x 10-ton refrigerator vans	1477	50500-24	3/31
L473	17/5/29	50 x 25-ton goods brake vans	1579	55566-85, 55993-56022	1/31
A507	2/8/29	Convert 2 x 15-ton open goods to crane test weight trucks	ex-1360	264s, 265s	11/29
A508	2/8/29	Repair underframes for above	1360	ex-18700 & 18676	11/29
E514	27/8/29	Alter end lights of 17 (later 13) x 15-ton goods brake vans	1541	54925-39/42/3	2/33
A533	29/1/30	75 x 10-ton ventilated meat vans with AVB	1486	51196-220/41-90	4/31
A534	2/12/29	Construct 2 match trucks for travelling cranes	Not stated	118SM, 119SM	3/30
A538	19/12/29	Prepare 75 Central section 10-ton open goods for IOW	1369	27721-95	7/30
A539	19/12/29	Prepare 10 (later 13) x 8-ton Central section covered goods for IOW	1434	46927-31/6/7/9 WB 46932-5/8 WP	1/31
A540	19/12/29	Prepare 5 x 10-ton Central section single bolster wagons for IOW	1616	59048-52	1/30
A541	19/12/29	Prepare 3 x 10-ton Central section road van trucks for IOW	1661	60581-3	1/30
E542	19/12/29	Prepare 1 x 10-ton goods brake van for IOW	1541	56050	4/30
A543	19/12/29	Prepare 3 x 10-ton Central section cattle wagons for IOW	1527	Not allocated	Cancelled
E548	3/1/30	Construct 50 BD-type containers	3004	B251-300	7/30
A575	16/5/30	1200 x 12-ton RCH open goods	1379	35151-36350	4/31
A576	16/5/30	600 (later 550) x 10-ton open goods (rebuild type 1)	1380	9641-10205 with gaps	7/31
A577	16/5/30	50 x 10-ton open goods (rebuild type 1) constructed with whole dropsides suitable for conveyance of containers. Amended to be as A576, 19/3/1931	1380	10206/7/9-56	7/31
A578	16/5/30	300 x 12-ton covered goods (150 with AVB)	1428	47401-550, 47551-700 AVB	10/31
A579	16/5/30	50 (actually 49) x 10-ton cattle wagons	1529	53829-78 (53845 not built)	11/31
E580	16/5/30	50 x 10-ton refrigerator vans	1477	50525-74	3/31
L581	16/5/30	100 x 25-ton goods brake vans (70 @ Lcg, 30 @ Afd)	1579	56061-160	4/32
A592	30/7/30	10 steel baggage boxes at £6-15-0d each	3653	49-58	5/31
E593	12/8/30	Construct 25 insulated containers	Not allocated	See later BRCW order	Cancelled
A608	17/11/30	Prepare 86 x 10-ton Central section open goods for IOW	1369	27796-881	10/31
E610	19/11/30	Conversion of 2 old A-12 class tenders to shunting trucks	1712	61322-3	6/31
BRCW	17/12/30	Construct 25 insulated containers	3002	BN301-25	4/31
Butterley Co.	2/1/31	Construct 2 large insulated containers (experimental)	3008	BN326-7	2/31
BRCW	2/1/31	Construct 10 small A-type containers	3005	A328-37	5/31
BRCW	2/1/31	Construct 2 small A-type pressed steel containers	3007	A338-9	5/31
BRCW	2/1/31	Construct 40 C-type small open containers	3006	C340-79	4/31
Butterley Co.	2/1/31	Construct 10 C-type small pressed steel containers	3009	C380-9	4/31
Metro-Camm	7/1/31	Construct 100 C-type small open containers	3010	C390-489	10/31
A637	14/4/31	1000 (amended to 600, 7/7/31) x 12-ton RCH open goods	1379	36351-950	5/33
A638	14/4/31	200 x 10-ton open goods (rebuild type 3). See A668. Bodies to be of standard capacity as RCH 12-ton opens	1381A	10258-471 with gaps	10/34
A639	14/4/31	200 x 12-ton end-door minerals (RCH pattern)	1384	40001-200	10/33
A640	14/4/31	450 x 10-ton covered goods (rebuilds)	1429	44427-718 with gaps, 44994-45041/562-91, 46108-90	2/32
A641	14/4/31	150 x 10-ton covered goods with AVB (rebuilds)	1429	46774-923	4/32
A642	14/4/31	50 x 10-ton cattle wagons (reissued as A763)	1529	Not allocated	Cancelled
A643	14/4/31	25 x 10-ton ventilated meat vans with AVB	1486A	51291-315	6/34
L644	14/4/31	21 x 40-ton bogie timber trucks ex-AC vehicle u/f's	Not allocated	Not allocated	Cancelled
L645	14/4/31 (revised 9/31)	100 x 25-ton goods brake vans (12 originally to have AVB, cancelled 9/31)	1579	56161-260	9/33
E646	14/4/31	15 x 15-ton stone trucks to LSWR design	1317	61121-35	8/33
E651	13/5/31	Prepare 2 x 10-ton Western section dropside wagons for IOW. Transferred to Ashford 18/5/31, to Diagram 1352	1352	62903-4	7/31

HOO No	Date Authorised*	Details	Diagram	Running Nos	Completed By*
E652	13/5/31	Prepare 2 x 10-ton goods brake vans for IOW	1541	56051-2	7/31
E655	18/5/31	Construct 100 insulated containers	3002	BN490-589	11/31
C. Roberts	8/31	Construct 3 x 20-ton ballast plough brake vans	1748	62030-2	1932
A668	18/7/31	400 x 10-ton open goods (rebuild type 3). See A638	1381	10472-911 with gaps	6/32
A678	4/9/31	100 x 20-ton loco coal wagons on RCH underframes	1386	40201-300	2/34
BA679	8/9/31	Fit 100 containers with removable wooden floors	3002	BN490-589	1/32
A681	24/10/31	150 wagons for conveyance of containers (75 with AVB)	1383	39501-650 (conflats C & D)	5/33
A682	24/10/31	50 wagons for conveyance of containers (25 with AVB)	1382	39001-50 (conflats A & B)	7/32
A685	11/11/31	10 steel baggage boxes	3653	59-68	9/32
E688	26/11/31	Supply parts and alter 100 insulated meat containers	3001	F101-200	Not stated
E696	2/2/32	One crane testing truck for Engineer's Dept.	Not allocated	610s	4/32
GRCW	27/1/32	Construct 50 large covered containers	3011	K590-639	7/32
E716	5/5/32	Complete painting of 50 K-class containers ex-GRCW	3011	K590-639	7/32
E717	13/5/32	Prepare 3 x 10-ton goods brake vans for IOW	1541	56053-5	5/32
E724	4/7/32	Construct 25 (later 20) fresh meat containers	3012	BM640-59	1/33
E725	16/8/32	Fit one insulated van with shelves to carry milk in cartons	1477	50573	9/32
A727	29/8/32	200 x 10-ton (later 12T) container trucks with AVB	1382	39051-250	7/33
A737	7/10/32	500 x 10-ton open goods (rebuilds types 2 & 3) (100 to have sheet supports - later cancelled)	1381A 1381B	26200-307 with gaps 26308-718 with gaps	10/34 10/35
A738	7/10/32	225 x 10-ton (later 12T) covered goods with AVB	1428	47701-925	4/34
A745	21/12/32	25 x 40-ton bogie bolster wagons	Not allocated	Not allocated	Cancelled
A746	21/12/32	50 x 15-ton goods brake vans	1581	55675-724	10/34
E752	4/2/33	Construct 25 insulated containers for Southampton fish traffic (one to have drikold bunkers fitted)	3013/6	F660-84 (F684 to Diagram 3016)	6/33
?	2/33	Fit 3 small containers with additional insulation for ice cream traffic	3014	AF337-9	1933
?	2/33	Fit 10 large containers with additional insulation for refrigerated traffic (one more in 1949)	3015	FX510/20/4/8/48/51/4/63/8/9 FX248 as later replacement	1933 1949
A759	21/4/33	100 x 12-ton RCH open goods with sheet supports & AVB	1385	36951-37050	11/33
A763	9/6/33	51 x 12-ton covered goods with AVB	1428	47926-76	4/34
E772	11/7/33	Convert one ex-AC motor brake to bogie brake van	1580	10108 to 56263	9/33
A786	25/10/33	200 x 20-ton open goods (later mineral wagons)	1386	41001-200	4/35
E787	7/11/33	Construct 100 insulated containers (timber by Met-Camm)	3013	F685-784	6/34
E788	7/11/33	Construct 1 experimental container for strawberry traffic	Not allocated	Not allocated, see E795	Cancelled
E790	24/11/35	Convert 20 ex-AC motor brakes to goods brake vans	1580	56261/2/4-81	1/35
E795	17/1/34	Construct 6 containers for strawberry traffic	3017	BS785-90	5/34
A810	27/3/34	700 (later 680) x 20-ton mineral wagons (see A826)	1386	40301-980	4/35
?	?	Convert 2 x 10-ton Central section opens to minerals	1374	18780, 27545	1934
A811	27/3/34	300 x 12-ton covered goods (rebuilds) with AVB	1428A	47977-48276	7/35
A812	27/3/34	200 x 10-ton banana vans with s/htg and AVB	1478	50575-774	12/35
A818	29/3/34	100 x 12-ton container trucks (rebuilds) with AVB	1382A	39251-350	11/35
E823	3/8/34	Fit 100 standard 12-ton covered goods and 30 standard 12-ton open goods with equipment for train ferry service	1387 & 1430	Between 36352 & 36941 and between 45918 & 47414	5/35
A826	13/8/34	20 x 20-ton (mineral) open goods for train ferry service	1388	40981-41000	4/36
E827	5/9/34	2 shunting trucks for Dover ferry service, on s/h u/frames	1714	61324-5	7/35
E857	16/4/35	Construct 23 furniture containers & 2 to carry bicycles	3018/9	BC791-2, BK793-815	5/36
E858	16/4/35	Construct 25 B-type containers	3021	B816-40	6/36
E859	16/4/35	Construct 15 A-type containers	3020	A841-55	4/36
A864	30/4/35	250 x 12-ton open goods with sheet supports & AVB	1398	37051-300	1/36
A865	30/4/35	650 x 10-ton open goods (rebuild type 4)	1400	26719-27417 with gaps	1/37
A866	30/4/35	500 x 12-ton covered goods with AVB, 12 with partitions	1458/9	48277-776	9/36
A867	30/4/35	25 x 25-ton bogie goods brake vans with AVB	1550	56282-306	8/36
A872	24/5/35	50 x 15-ton dropside ballast wagons	1773	63001-50	4/37
L873	24/5/35	25 x 40-ton bogie flat wagons (built at Ashford)	1598	57883-907 (later 64622-46)	1/37
A876	14/6/35	Alter 20 x 12-ton open goods as approved by Messrs Pledge & Sons Ltd, for grain traffic (LSWR vehicles)	1320	Between 8042 & 9237	8/35
A884	14/9/35	Fit existing container wagons with AVB complete	1382 & 1383	39026-50 & 39576-650	1937
Met-Cammell	21/11/35	22 x 40-ton bogie ballast hoppers	1774	62033-54	1/37
A914	3/4/36	750 x 10-ton open goods (rebuild type 4)	1400	10912-11801 with gaps	11/37
A915	3/4/36	100 x 12-ton open goods with sheet supports & AVB	1398	37301-400	7/37
A916	3/4/36	450 x 12-ton covered goods with AVB (see A959)	1458	48777-49226	1/38
A917	3/4/36	50 x 12-ton container trucks with AVB	1399	39351-400	9/38
A918	18/4/36	Construct 10 A-type containers	3020	A856-65	9/37
A919	18/4/36	Construct 25 B-type containers	3021	BD866-90	6/37
A920	18/4/36	Construct 25 D-type open containers to RCH drawing	3023	D891-915	8/37
A921	18/4/36	Construct 50 F-type containers	3013	F916-65	3/37
A922	18/4/36	Construct 25 furniture containers	3018	BK966-90	7/37
?	c4/36	Convert 12 (later 60) RCH open goods for cable laying	1378	Between 29079 & 36897	4/37
A937	3/7/36 (revised 3/8/37)	Construct 6 (later 9) additional 20-ton mineral wagons utilising u/frames recovered from 4w milk tanks	1386	41201-9	12/39
A941	24/9/36	Convert 10 x 20-ton Central section goods brake vans to vacuum-fitted ballast brake vans	1760	62847-56	12/37
A955	17/12/36	4 wagons for conveying crane test weights	Not allocated	1085-8s	1937
A959	1/2/37	Fit 38 vans to A916 for Huntley & Palmers biscuit traffic	1459	Between 48777 & 48843	3/37
?	c11/37	Convert 4 vans ex-D1458 for Express Dairy egg traffic	1460	48323/59/980, 49168	6/38
A968	6/5/37	500 x 12-ton open goods	1377	37401-900	10/39
A969	6/5/37	450 (later 325) x 12-ton coverd goods with AVB	1458	49227-551	10/39

HOO No	Date Authorised*	Details	Diagram	Running Nos	Completed By*
A970	6/5/37	50 x 10-ton cattle wagons	1529	53879-928	3/39
A971	6/5/37	25 (later 20) x 25-ton goods brake vans	1579	56307-26	3/40
A985	21/5/37	Construct 10 meat containers	3012	M991-1000	1/39
A997	29/9/37	Convert 3 tenders to 15-ton brakes for Folkestone Harbour	1561	55180-2	10/38
A998	29/9/37	Convert 2 tenders to shunting trucks for Bournemouth W	1715	61326-7	1/39
A1009	22/12/37	125 x 10-ton banana vans with AVB (originally on A969)	1479	50775-899	7/38
E1014	13/1/38	Prepare 2 x 15-ton goods brake vans for IOW	1541	56056-7	5/38
		Note: This is the last mention of any Isle of Wight wagon transfers, however wagons continued to be sent right through until 1949.			
A1015	21/1/38	Fit 50 more covered goods with partitions similar to A959	1458	Between 49039 & 49193	3/38
A1033A	14/6/38	500 (later 488 and finally 250) x 12-ton open goods	1377	37901-38150	12/39
A1033B	6/2/39	238 x 12 (later 13)-ton open goods with small bodies	1375	38151-388	9/42
A1034	14/6/38	500 x 12-ton covered goods with AVB (200 bodies at Elh)	1458	47001-100, 49552-951	12/40
A1035	14/6/38	50 x 12-ton container trucks with AVB (see A1193/1733)	1399	39401-25/7-49, 39658/9	9/42
L1036	14/6/38	25 x 25-ton goods brake vans	1579	56327-51	10/40
E1037	15/6/38	Construct 50 F-type meat containers	3013	F1001-50	8/39
A1063	18/1/39	12 x 12-ton open goods with shock absorbing device	1376	38389-400	7/40
A1096	16/5/39	2 x 20-ton well wagons (altered to 22, 6/1940)	1681	61151-72	8/42
E1097	18/10/39	Construct 10 M-type meat containers	3012	M1051-60	4/41
E1098	18/10/39	Construct 20 D-type open containers to modified design	3024	D1061-80	7/40
A1111	6/7/39	Adapt & fit 8 x 12-ton covered goods with generator sets	ex-1458	1458-66s	12/39
A1127(part)	13/7/39	Fit up as necessary fuel tanks and mount in standard 12-ton open goods wagons with AVB	ex-1385 & 1398 & loco tenders	1483-92s	12/39
A1160	11/39	Construct 1 match truck for travelling crane	Not allocated	712sm	4/40
		From this point onwards many HO orders were issued for war work, often of a non-railway nature.			
L1167	9/1/40	Recondition 20 rectank wagons for Longmoor Military Rly	Not stated	Not stated	4/40
A1172	19/2/40	18 x 13-ton wagons for carriage of coal containers for SS. Invicta	Not stated	Not stated	1940
A1175	27/2/40	750 x 12-ton covered goods with AVB	1458	59251-60000	11/41
A1181	28/3/40	Convert 2 mobile workshops from existing vehicles for WD	ex-1458/3103	ex-49880/1/3/4/950/1 & Van 'U's	12/40
A1182	1/5/40	360 x 12-ton covered goods with AVB (REC order)	1458	64921-65280	1/41
A1183	1/5/40	890 x 12-ton LMS covered goods (REC order)	LMS 2039 & 2070	LMS 514325-515214	1941
A1184	1/5/40	750 x 12-ton LNER covered goods with AVB REC order.(150 later allocated to Eastleigh)	LNE 116	LNER 245913-246662	1941
A1185	1/5/40	50 x 25-ton goods brake vans	1579	56352-401	9/43
A1186	19/4/40	Convert 2 mobile workshops from existing vehicles for WD	ex-1458/3103	47057-60 & Van 'U's	4/40
A1192	1/5/40	350 x 13-ton open goods	1375	38401-750	2/43
A1193	1/5/40	50 x 13-ton container trucks with AVB (see A1035/1733)	1399	39426/651-7/60-76/8-702	9/42
L1194	1/5/40	40 x 25-ton goods brake vans	1579	56402-41	6/43
E1195	1/5/40	Construct 25 D-type open containers	3023	D1081-1105	8/42
E1196	2/5/40	Construct 10 M-type meat containers	3012	BM1106-15	11/43
A1203	2/5/40	50 (later 75) ramp wagons for WD	Not allocated	1-75	5/41
A1204	9/5/40	Convert 4 x 12-ton coverd goods as welding units for WD	ex-1458	ex-49948/9/50/1	2/41
L1240	16/7/40	100 petrol tank wagons for Air Ministry	Not allocated	301-400	1/41
L1282	8/8/41	30 x 40-ton bogie bolster wagons (originally for Ashford)	1598	57908-37	12/43
HOO1367	14/12/40	Convert 2 mobile workshops from existing vehicles for WD	ex-1458/3103	Two ex-A1204,47063/79/768/75 & Van 'U's	8/41
L1409	21/1/41	225 x iron ore hoppers - cancelled 18/3/41	Not allocated	Not allocated	Cancelled
A1471	14/3/41	Convert 2 mobile workshops from existing vehicles for WD	ex-1458/3103	47036/45/85, 49667/917/42 & Van 'U's	12/41
E1489	31/3/41	Conversion of 50 open wagons to carry propellers (REC)	1362	5071-120	8/41
E1544	5/5/41	Conversion of open goods wagons for fire-fighting duties	ex-1369	1659-82s	10/41
L1656	16/7/41	20 x 25-ton goods brake vans with AVB & WP for MOS	1579	WD11002-21	10/41
A1720	11/9/41	1000 x 13-ton open goods for MOS (Persia)	1375/LMS 2151	1-1000 (some to LMS in 1949)	11/41
A1731	1/10/41	322 x 13-ton open goods	1375	6801-7122	6/43
A1732	1/10/41	534 x 12-ton covered goods (some at Eastleigh/Lancing)	1455	44719-45321 with gaps	9/42
A1733	1/10/41	103 x 13-ton container trucks with AVB (see A1035/1193)	1399	39450/677/703-803	11/42
A1813	19/11/41	Convert 2 mobile workshops from existing vehicles for WD	ex-1458/3103	Between 47053 & 49943 & Van 'U's	3/43
E1820	27/11/41	Construct 27 BK-type containers	3018	BK1116-42	5/43
E1828	27/11/41	Construct 25 B-type containers	3021	B1143-67	12/42
A1831	10/12/41	600 x 13-ton open goods with West. pipe for MOS	1375/LMS 2151	1-600 (some to LMS in 1949)	1/42
A1843	16/12/41	53 x 25-ton goods brake vans	1579	56442-94	7/42
A1852	23/12/41	20 x 25-ton goods brake vans with AVB & WP for MOS	1579	WD11022-41	3/42
A1886	22/1/42	Convert 3 mobile workshops from existing vehicles for WD	ex-1458/3103	Between 49572 & 49934 & Van 'U's	4/43
L1887	23/1/42	11 x 20-ton well wagons (design to be agreed)	1682	61101-10, 64600 (ED)	6/45
A1939	9/3/42	1000 x 12-ton covered goods (650 for SR, rest for GWR and LMS)	1455, GW V35, LMS 2078	65281-480, GWR 144269-918, LMS 521140-289	1/43
HOO1958	24/3/42	Construct 1 match truck for travelling crane	Not stated	1748sm	1/43
A2047	20/5/42	Construct 4 match trucks for travelling cranes	Not stated	1746/7/9/50sm	1/43
A2249	28/9/42	Convert 10 mobile workshops from existing vehicles for WD	ex-1458/3103	Between 47016 & 49930 & Van 'U's (inc 1xSECR pattern)	3/44
A2300	20/11/42	500 x 12-ton covered goods (some at Eastleigh/Lancing)	1454/5	65481-980 (65980 to D1454)	11/43
A2301	9/11/42	500 x 13-ton open goods (REC order)	1375	5601-6100	1/44
A2451	5/3/43	Adapt 6 x 13-ton open goods for AA defences	1389	7116-20, 38432	5/43
E2484	3/4/43	Supply 2 axleboxes for WD brake van	1579	WD11034	Not stated

HOO No	Date Authorised*	Details	Diagram	Running Nos	Completed By*
A2503	13/4/43	50 x 40-ton bogie bolster wagons	1598	57938-87	3/45
E2504	14/4/43	Construct 50 BK-type containers to RCH design	3025	BK1168-1217	4/44
A2505	13/4/43	350 x 13-ton open goods	1375	6101-450	5/45
A2506	14/4/43	300 x 12-ton covered goods (some comp. at Lancing)	1455	59101-250, 65981-66130	3/44
A2516	15/4/43	400 x 13-ton open goods for LNER	1375 (LNE 178)	LNER 262449-848	7/44
A2517	15/4/43	250 x 12-ton covered goods for LMS (as D1455 vans)	LMS 2078	LMS 523290-539	4/44
A2518	16/4/43	250 x 12-ton covered goods	1455	54001-250	12/43
A2519	16/4/43	100 (later 102) x 13-ton container trucks with AVB	1399	39804-905	10/44
L2530	24/5/43	25 x 40-ton well wagons for WD (see order L3545)	Later 1903	1-25, later WD14176-200	7/44
A2533	4/5/43	465 x 13-ton open goods for LMS (materials by LMS)	LMS 2094	LMS 417610-8074	8/44
A2534	4/5/43	375 x 13-ton open goods for LNER (materials by LNER)	LNE 184	LNER 262849-3223	10/44
E2613	28/7/43	Construct 50 BD-type containers for LMS	LMS 64	LMS B2238-87	11/44
E2749	23/12/43	Convert 1x12-ton covered goods into mobile welding unit	1852	1971s (ex-59773)	10/44
A2766	8/1/44	Convert 4 double bolster wagons to match trucks	ex-1618	1854-7SM	4/44
A2843	6/4/44	100 x 13-ton end-door mineral wagons	1390	41210-309	4/45
A2853	19/4/44	543 x 12-ton covered goods (inc 93 war losses)	1452	49952-94, 50901-100, 51351-500, 54251-500	12/45
A2854	19/4/44	502 (later 501) x 13-ton open goods (inc 52 war losses)	1375	5400-572, 6452-779	4/45
E2865	18/4/44	Construct 50 BD-type containers (36 for LMS)	3026 (LMS 65)	BD1218-31, LMS B2941-76	6/45
LMS order	1944	Supply 3 A-type containers for SR	3027 (LMS 18)	A1232-4	2/44
E2889	18/5/44	Construct 17 BD-type containers	3026	BD1235-51	3/45
E3014	29/8/44	Supply spares for SR 25-ton bogie goods brake vans on loan to WD	1550/80	56275 & 56306	Not stated
A3083	7/11/44	1850 x 13-ton end-door mineral wagons for LNER	1390 (LNE 192)	LNER 267100-8949	2/46
L3094	15/11/44	1 x 14-ton experimental open goods on triangulated u/f	1391	6780	9/45
A3097	1/2/45	Convert 4 double bolster wagons to match trucks	ex-1618	1582-5SM	4/45
A3114	13/12/44	Convert 50 airscrew wagons back to open goods	ex-1362	ex-5071-120	5/46
A3124	20/2/45	Convert 13-ton AA protection wagons back to open goods	1389	7116-20, 38432	2/45
E/L3155	23/2/45	Remove vac brake and repair 27 warflats for MOS	Not stated	Not stated	Not stated
A3217	4/5/45	753 (later 600) x 13-ton open goods (see A3305)	1375	12001-600	4/46
A3218	4/5/45	510 x 12-ton covered goods	1452	56501-57010	7/46
A3219	4/5/45	101 x 10-ton cattle wagons	1530	52418-518	11/47
A3220	4/5/45	50 x 13-ton container trucks with AVB	1399	39906-55	7/47
A3221	4/5/45	52 x 40-ton bogie bolster wagons	1599	57988-58039	11/46
A3222	4/5/45	54 x 25-ton goods brake vans	1582	55621-74	11/48
L3223	4/5/45	Construct 75 A-type containers	3027	A1339-1413	10/46
E3224	4/5/45	Construct 62 BD-type containers	3026	BD1252-1313	11/46
E3225	4/5/45	Construct 25 BK-type containers	3028	BK1314-38	11/47
A3301	10/8/45	8 x 20-ton ballast plough brake vans	1749	62857-64	4/49
A3302	10/8/45	11 x 40-ton bogie rail wagons for Robel cranes	1599/1787	64738-48	8/46
A3303	10/8/45	41 (later 21) x 15-ton (later 20-ton) ballast wagons	BR1/570	DB991000-20	12/51
L3303	20/11/46	20 x 20-ton ballast wagons (amended order)	BR1/570	DB991301-20	12/51
Butterley Co	1951	160 x 20-ton ballast wagons to SR design	BR1/570	DB991141-300	1952
A3305	21/8/45	153 x 13-ton open goods (originally ordered on A3217)	1375	11848-12000	3/48
A3311	31/8/45	1500 x 16-ton all-steel mineral wagons for LNER	LNE 188	LNER 287689-9188	11/47
A3327	21/11/45	20 x 40-ton bogie ballast hoppers	1775	62055-74	12/47
A3352	15/4/46	900 x 13-ton open goods	1375	12601-13080/2-494/6-13502	5/48
A3353	15/4/46	400 (later 240) x 12-ton covered goods (160 with AVB)	1452	B752350-589/790-949 (AVB)	11/49
A3354	15/4/46	150 x 10-ton cattle wagons	1530	52268-417	12/47
A3355	15/4/46	50 x 25-ton goods brake vans	1582	55121-70	11/48
A3356	15/4/46	6 x 40-ton bogie rail wagons	1599	64749-54	2/48
E3357	16/4/46	Construct 50 D-type open containers	3024	D21000-49B	6/49
L3358	16/4/46	Construct 250 (later 252, 17/11/48) F-type containers	3029	F12000-251B	12/49
RCH	4/46	I x 20-ton goods brake van from LMS (LMS lot 1352)	1570	56060	4/46
E3395 (part)	14/1/47	Convert 2 LSWR tenders to tar tanks for IOW	1716	61384-5	5/47
HOO3409	22/4/47	Fit 19 x 20-ton & 30 x 13-ton ferry opens with sheet rails (20-ton wagon 40990 done on return to UK in 7/50)	1387/88	40981-41000 & between 36352 & 36941	5/49
HOO3409?	4/47	Replacement u/frames for Dover ferry shunting trucks (ex- Maunsell coaches 1145 & 4077)	1717	61328-9	11/47
?	1947	Convert 60 open goods wagons for cable laying	1378A/1899	Between DS1657 & 1713 & others in Diagram 1379 series	7/49
E3422	5/6/47	Construct 50 A-type containers	3027	A61-110B	Cancelled
E3423	5/6/47	Construct 25 BD-type containers	3026	BD4340-64B	Cancelled
E3438	17/7/47	Work in connection with construction of steel superstructure for wagon (see E3492)	Not allocated	Possibly 1428-9s	12/47
A3442	31/7/47	Supply spares for 13-ton high-sided open wagons	Not stated	Not stated	Not stated
A3443 (part)	1/8/47	762 x 13-ton open goods	1375	5153-395, 13503-672/84-14032	9/48
A3443 (part)	1/8/47	38 x 12-ton open goods with shock absorbing device	1392	14033-70	3/49
A3444	1/8/47	100 x 13-ton medium dropside goods wagons	BR1/33	B457000-99 (later B483650-749)	12/49
A3445	1/8/47	200 x 12-ton covered goods	1452	B752590-789	12/49
A3446	1/8/47	150 x 12-ton (some were 10-ton) cattle wagons	1530	B891250-399	12/49
A3447	1/8/47	100 x 21-ton mineral wagons-revised to 13-ton low opens	BR1/16	B457100-99	12/49
A3448	1/8/47	150 x 12-ton covered goods with AVB	1452	B752950-3099	12/49
A3475	14/1/48	3250 (later 2730, then 2230) x 13-ton open goods for ER (very similar to diagram 1375)	LNE 210	E310891-313120	7/49
?	?	Convert 2 x 15-ton goods brake vans for Whitstable Hbr	1583	55675, 55713	7/48
E3492	7/5/48	Work in connection with construction of experimental steel wagon superstructures (see E3438)	Not allocated	Possibly 1428-9s	9/48

HOO No	Date Authorised*	Details	Diagram	Running Nos	Completed By*
A3500	27/8/48	Convert 7 ex-WD warflats to bogie bolster wagons	LMS diagram	Not stated	12/48
A3501	26/8/48	2 x 18-ton double-ended snowploughs	1691	S3-S4	12/48
A3520	17/11/48	Convert 50 (later 58, 5/5/49) WD ramp wagons to twin bolster wagons (ex order A1203)	Gen arrt dwg E.41374 amd 3	Between 1 & 75	6/50
HOO3521	23/11/48	500 x 13-ton open goods on triangulated underframes	For ER/NER	Cancelled 14/2/51	Cancelled
A3532	24/2/49	Conversion of 13 old carriage u/frames to carry l/w rails	1804	64755-67	12/52
A3533	24/2/49	Repairs to 19 LSW & LBSC underframes for Order A3532	1803/4	64728/31-3/6/7/55-67	12/52
A3542	21/4/49	Repairs to ex-WD goods brake vans 11029/37	1579	M360327-8	7/49
L3545	7/6/49	Convert 6 x 50-ton warwells to carry locomotive boilers	1903	DS3146-51 (see order L2530)	2/50
A3568	9/9/49	600 x 13-ton open goods to SR design	BR 1/34	B477050-649	4/50
A3585	9/9/49	500 x 12-ton shock-absorbing open goods with AVB to SR design	BR 1/35	B720425-924	5/50
A3588	13/9/49	400 x 12-ton shock-absorbing open goods with AVB to SR design (100 with sheet supports)	BR 1/35 / BR 1/36	B720925-1224 / B721225-324	7/50 / 7/50

Beyond this point there are many orders for BR wagons and containers, which have not been listed.

HOO No	Date Authorised*	Details	Diagram	Running Nos	Completed By*
A/E/L3686	25/7/50	5000 standard wagons with light-type RCH underframes to be fitted with angle tiebars as they pass through shops	All	7923 done up to 1/1/56	1/56
A3797	22/5/51	Convert 10 x 25-ton brake vans to ballast brake vans	1761	55476/82/6/9/92-4/9, 55502/8	11/53
A3842	12/2/52	Fit 50 SR shock-absorbing wagons with guard plates	1376/92	14033-70, 38389-400	1/60
A3859	5/3/52	Convert 1 (later 40) cattle wagons for ferry service (see order A4148)	1530	BR diagram 1/352 & 353 done instead, alloc BR diagram 1/354	11/52
E3891	1/7/52	Modify fasteners on A, B, BD and BK containers	All	522 done by 6/59	6/59
E3924	11/9/52	Adapt 2 flatrol wagons for conveyance of cable drums	1682	61103/7	11/52
L4029	13/8/53	Fit 3 SR flatrols with wooden floors	1682	Between 61101-10	12/53
A4070	28/1/54	Adapt 12 wagons for cable laying	1899	Between 10489 & 33712	3/54
		Note: Previous orders for these conversions in 1936 and 1948 have not been recorded.			
E4088	10/3/54	Convert underframes of former ferry shunting trucks to service vehicles	ex-1717	61328/9 to DS88-9	11/54
E/A4125	11/8/54	Modify 200 (later 352) x 20-ton ballast wagons	BR1/570	Between DB991000 & 991320	10/64
A4148	16/12/54	Alter 40 cattle wagons for beer traffic (see order A3859)	1530	Not stated	3/55
E/A4342	27/9/56	Equip 2400 (later 9200) covered goods with AVB	All	8739 done by 10/63	10/63
A4343	27/9/56	Equip 100 goods brake vans with AVB	All	Not stated	5/58
E/A4387	8/2/57	Replace stoves in 631 SR goods brake vans & fit guards around stove pipe	All	Between 55121 & 56494 (564 done by 6/65)	6/65

Beyond this point many individual departmental and other conversions are listed. Only the most significant are noted.

HOO No	Date Authorised*	Details	Diagram	Running Nos	Completed By*
E4448	20/8/57	Prepare 2 x 10-ton goods brakes for W/loo & City line	1541	54892/4	9/57
A4465	1/10/57	Fit 200 goods brake vans with thro' pipe & guards gauge	All	Not stated	2/59
E/A4595/6	16/3/59	Fit 3596 open wagons with AVB & s/contained buffers	All	Work transferred to Order 4342	Cancelled
A4598	16/3/59	Equip 134 goods brake vans with through pipes	All	Work transferred to Order 4343	Cancelled
HOO4742	10/2/60	Repair & convert 1 goods brake van for departmental use	1576	55907	4/60
E4766	8/4/60	Repair & convert 13 SR GBV's to non-plough ballast brake vans	1559/60	55456-9/66/8/70/2/4//81/8/91, 55504	11/60
IOW4777	12/5/60	Reletter 15 bolster wagons & 10 road van trucks for IOW service use	1616/7 & 1641/61	59038-52, 60562/6-8/71/2/9-82	10/60
E4806	4/7/60	Apply additional insulation to 195 SR banana vans	1478	Between 50575 & 50774	3/63
E4807	4/7/60	Apply additional insulation to 121 SR banana vans	1479	Between 50777 & 50899	11/62
L5003	17/5/61	Equip 6 x 25-ton bogie brake vans with WB	1550	56285/6/96/9, 56301/3	12/61
ODM 5065	20/10/61	Convert 36 cable drum wagons to open service wagons	ex-1899	Between DS1657 & 1713, & between 29223 & 34933	5/62
E5114	28/3/62	Adapt 13 SR bogie bolster wagons for Bertram Mills circus traffic	1597	Not stated, but probably al least 25 done	12/62
E5156	2/7/62	Repair & convert 1 x 40-ton well wagon to match truck	1690	61099	8/62
ODM5258	30/5/63	Convert 1 x 13-ton open goods to test weight wagon	Not allocated	13443	8/63
A5360	1/7/64	Equip 4 (later 6) x 25-ton goods brake vans with WB for ferry service workings Dover-Hither Green	1550?	Not stated But see order L5003?	6/66
ODM5436	8/3/65	Repair & convert 25 open goods to cable wagons for Electrical Engineer	1379	Various	6/66
ODM5476	8/7/65	Repair & modify 18 SR bogie bolster wagons for CCE flats (ex-Bertram Mills). See order E5114	1597	Between 57815 & 57882 plus 1 BR wagon	6/66
ODM5510 & 5511	26/10/65	Repair & convert 4 x 8-plank open goods to 5-plank for use as refuse/material wagons	ex-1379	DS1660/71/6/80	6/66
ODM5524	15/12/65	Repair & convert 5 x 8-plank open goods to 5-plank for use of Electrical Engineer	ex-1379	DS1658, DS1891/5, 34949, 36993	4/66
ODM5526	20/12/65	Convert 9 x 8-plank cable wagons to 5-plank for C Sig & Tel Engineer	ex-1355/79/81A	26261/8717/9030,30385, 33972, 34527/600/5929/6454	4/66
ODM5543 & 5544	2/66	Repair & convert 2 x 8-plank open goods to 5-plank for S & T Engineer	ex-1379	35561, 36690	6/66
ODM5568	29/4/66	Repair & modify 7 SR bogie bolster wagons for CCE flats (ex-Bertram Mills). See order E5114	1597	Not stated	10/66
ODM5594	5/9/66	Convert 1 flatrol as a cable laying vehicle	1682	61103	9/66
ODM5691	7/4/67	Repair/convert 2 x 15-ton goods brake vans for IOW	1581	55710/24	5/67
IOW5695	7/4/67	Repair/convert 6 x 10-ton open goods for CCE use	1369/1352	27730/44/66/78/99, 28345	12/67
IOW5701	18/4/67	Repair/convert 2 x 10-ton open goods to ballast wagons	1369/1352	27725/96 (some records state 27775, 28360)	12/67

* Dates authorised and dates completed can vary somewhat depending on source.
Order numbers checked as far as HOO 5778, dated 29/5/1968.